Bears' Guide to College Degrees by Mail & Internet

9TH EDITION

Bears' Guide to College Degrees by Mail & Internet

9TH EDITION

100 Accredited Schools That Offer Bachelor's, Master's,
Doctorates, and Law Degrees by Distance Learning

John Bear, Ph.D.
Mariah Bear, M.A.

TEN SPEED PRESS
Berkeley / Toronto

Ten Speed Press
Box 7123
Berkeley, California 94707
www.tenspeed.com

Distributed in Australia by Simon & Schuster Australia, in Canada by Ten Speed Press Canada, in New Zealand by Southern Publishers Group, in South Africa by Real Books, and in the United Kingdom and Europe by Airlift Book Company.

Cover design by Cale Burr
Book design by Jeff Brandenburg/image-comp.com

Library of Congress Control Number 2001206931
International Standard Serial Number 1534-0570

Printed in the United States
First printing this edition, 2003

1 2 3 4 5 6 7 8 9 10 – 07 06 05 04 03

Dedication

To our respective spouses, Marina and Joe, who have given us a total of more than fifty years of love and support.

Table of Contents

Introduction

Four Essential Assumptions

This book is built upon four basic assumptions. You already know the first, you probably know the second, you probably don't know the third, and the fourth should be your reason for buying this book.

1. There is often no connection whatsoever between ability and degree.

2. There are extremely talented and capable people who never went to college for a single day. And, as everyone knows, some of the most incompetent boobs on our planet have degrees from prestigious universities.

3. A degree is often more useful than a good education or valuable skills in your field.

4. You may be the best business manager, teacher, or pilot in three counties, but if you don't have a piece of imitation parchment that certifies you as an associate, bachelor, master, or doctor, you are somehow perceived as less worthy and are often denied the better jobs and higher salaries that go to degree holders, regardless of their competence.

It is easier than it ever has been to earn a degree.

Since the mid-1970s, there has been a virtual explosion in what is now called "alternative" or "nontraditional" or "external" or "off-campus" education—ways and means of getting an education or a degree (or both, if you wish) without sitting in a classroom day after day, year after year.

But it is not always easy to find the right school.

Many good schools never advertise or promote themselves, either because they don't know how or because they think that doing so would be tacky. And most of the bad schools—the illegal or barely legal diploma mills—advertise all of the time in national newspapers and magazines. Let this book be your starting point, your guide, and your road map. You will need to put in some effort to end up with the degree you want, of course. Still, we think it is safe to say that if you cannot find what you are looking for or hoping for in this book, it probably doesn't exist.

College Degrees by Distance Learning

The Two Ideas That Make It All Possible

There are two very clever ideas that make it possible to earn good, usable college degrees by distance learning. Surprisingly, both have been around for a long time, although many people in the degree-granting business are just beginning to pay attention to them.

Idea Number One

If you've already done it, you don't have to do it again.

When Aristotle arrived to train Alexander T. Great, it was clear to the old boy that his student already had learned a great deal that did not have to be taught again, and so they could get on with studying the arts of war and diplomacy. Compare that with many of today's students, who "learn" about the exports of Brazil and the parts of speech every year for eight consecutive years. As John's mentor, Dr. Elizabeth Drews, wrote, "It is immoral to teach someone something he or she already knows."

Fortunately, more and more colleges and universities are giving credit for the things one already knows. If you can speak a second language—it doesn't matter whether you learned it from your grandmother or out of a book or by living in another country—you'll get credit for it. If you learned journalism by working on a newspaper, you'll get credit for it. If you learned meteorology while studying for your pilot's license, you'll get credit for it. That sort of thing. (How do you get that credit? Read on. That's what much of this book is about.)

Idea Number Two

Meaningful learning can take place outside the classroom.

Abraham Lincoln studied law at night, by the fire, in his home. We have always known that learning can take place anywhere, anytime, although for years most universities have pretended that the only worthwhile learning, the only degree-worthy learning, takes place in classrooms and lecture halls. Now, more and more schools are not only acknowledging the learning that you may have done before enrolling, but making their own courses available in a multitude of ways, including

- courses by correspondence, or home study
- courses over cable television or by videotape
- courses through guided independent study at your own pace
- courses over home computers linked to a university computer, most often via the Internet
- courses offered in your neighborhood by schools that are actually located in another state or country

Important Issues

College Degrees

What Are They?

A *degree* is a title conferred by a school to show that a certain course of study has been successfully completed. A *diploma* is the actual document or certificate given to the student as evidence of the awarding of a degree. U.S. colleges and universities award the following six kinds of degrees.

The associate's degree

The associate's degree is a relatively recent development, reflecting the tremendous growth of two-year community colleges (the new and presumably more respectable name for what used to be known as junior colleges).

Because many students attend community colleges for two years but do not continue on to another school for the bachelor's degree, both students and schools felt a need to award a degree at the end of these two years of full-time study (or their equivalent by nontraditional means). More than two thousand two-year schools now award associate's degrees, and a small but growing number of four-year schools also award them to students who leave after two years.

The two most common associate's degrees are the A.A. (Associate of Arts) and the A.S. (Associate of Science). But more than one hundred other titles have been devised, ranging from the A.M.E. (Associate of Mechanical Engineering) to the A.D.T. (Associate of Dance Therapy).

An associate's degree typically requires sixty to sixty-four semester hours of credit, normally taking two academic years (four semesters, or six quarters) to complete in a traditional program.

The bachelor's degree

In most places in the world, the bachelor's is the first university degree earned. (The associate's is little used outside the United States.) Most people believe that the traditional bachelor's degree in the United States requires four years of full-time study (120 to 128 semester units). A rather alarming report recently revealed, however, that because more students are attending on a part-time basis, and because of difficulties getting into overcrowded classes, the average time to earn this degree is actually closer to six years! Through nontraditional approaches, some people with a good deal of prior learning have earned bachelor's degrees in as short a time as two or three months.

More than three hundred different bachelor's degree titles have been used in the last hundred years, but the great majority of the million-plus bachelor's degrees awarded in the United States each year are either the B.A. (Bachelor of Arts) or the B.S. (Bachelor of Science), sometimes with additional letters to indicate the field (e.g., B.S.E.E. for electrical engineering, B.A.B.A. for business administration, and so on). Other common bachelor's degree titles include the B.B.A. (another Bachelor of Business Administration), B.Mus. (music), B.Ed. (education), and B.Eng. (engineering). Some nontraditional schools or programs award their own degrees: B.G.S. (general studies), B.I.S. (independent studies), B.L.S. (liberal studies), and so on. (Incidentally, in the late nineteenth century, educators felt that the title of "bachelor" was inappropriate for young ladies, so some schools awarded female graduates titles such as Mistress of Arts or Maid of Science.)

The master's degree

The traditional master's degree requires one to two years of on-campus work after completion of the bachelor's degree. Some nontraditional master's degrees may be earned entirely through nonresidential study, whereas others require anywhere from a few days to a few weeks on campus.

There are several philosophical approaches to the master's degree. Some schools regard it as a sort of advanced bachelor's, requiring only the completion of one to two years of advanced-level studies and courses. Other schools see it as a junior doctorate, requiring creative, original research and culminating in the writing of a thesis, or an original research paper. Some programs give the option of either approach: students may choose to earn a master's degree either by taking ten courses and writing a thesis, for example, or by taking thirteen courses and not writing a thesis.

Master's degree titles tend to follow closely the titles of bachelor's degrees. The M.A. (Master of Arts) and M.S. (Master of Science) are by far the most common, along with the standby of American business, the M.B.A. (Master of Business Administration). Other common master's degrees include the M.Ed. (education), M.Eng. (engineering), M.F.A. (fine arts), M.L.S. (library science), and M.J. (either journalism or jurisprudence).

The doctorate

The academic title of "Doctor" (as distinguished from the professional and honorary titles, to be discussed shortly) is awarded for completion of an advanced course of study that culminates in a piece of original research in the field of study, known as the doctoral thesis, or dissertation.

The total elapsed time for earning a doctorate can be anywhere from three to twelve years. The trend has been for doctorates to take longer and longer. A typical doctorate degree now takes six or seven years, not all of that time necessarily spent in residence on campus.

Some doctorate programs permit the use of work already done (books written, symphonies composed, business plans created, etc.) as partial (or, in a few cases, full) satisfaction of the dissertation requirement. But many schools insist on all, or almost all, new work.

The most common doctorate is the Doctor of Philosophy (Ph.D. in North America, D.Phil. in many other countries), which need not have anything to do with philosophy. It is awarded for studies in dozens of fields, ranging from chemistry to communications to agriculture. More than five hundred other doctorate titles exist in the English language alone. After the Ph.D., the most common include the Ed.D. (education), D.B.A. (business administration), D.P.A. (public administration), D.A. (art or administration), Eng.D. (engineering), and Psy.D. (psychology).

Finally, several American schools, concerned with what one called the "doctoral glut," are reported to be seriously considering instituting a new degree, higher than the doctorate, presumably requiring more years of study and a more extensive dissertation. The name *chancellorate* has been bandied about. Indeed, the prestigious *Chronicle of Higher Education* devoted a major article to this possibility in 1990. It may well be that holders of a chancellorate (Ph.C.?) would not appreciably affect the job market, with most on Social Security by the time they completed this degree.

The professional degree

Professional degrees are earned by people who intend to enter what are often called "the professions"—medicine, dentistry, law, the ministry, and so forth. In the United States, these degrees are almost always earned after completion of a bachelor's degree, and they almost always carry the title of "doctor" (e.g., Doctor of Medicine, Doctor of Divinity). In many other countries, professional school follows directly after high school, with the first degree earned being a bachelor's. (Holders of the British Bachelor of Medicine, for instance, are invariably called "Doctor" unless they have earned the advanced degree of Doctor of Medicine. Then they insist on being called "Mister." No one ever said the British were easy to understand!)

The honorary degree

The honorary degree is the stepchild of the academic world—and a most curious one at that. It has no more relationship or connection with academia than bandleader Doc Severinson has with the world of medicine. It is, purely and simply, a title that some institutions (and some scoundrels) have chosen to bestow from time to time, and for a wide variety of reasons, upon certain people. These reasons often have to do with the donation of money or with efforts to attract celebrities to a commencement ceremony.

The honorary doctorate has no academic standing whatsoever; yet because it carries with it the same title ("Doctor") as used for the earned degree, it has become an extremely desirable commodity for those who covet titles and the prestige they bring. For respectable universities to award the title of "Doctor" via an honorary doctorate is as peculiar as if the army were to award civilians the honorary title of "General"—a title the honorees could then use in their everyday lives.

More than a thousand traditional colleges and universities award honorary doctorates (anywhere from one to fifty per year each), and a great many Bible schools, spurious schools, and degree mills hand them out with wild abandon to almost anyone willing to pay the price. And that is why we have Doctor Michael Jackson, Doctor Ed McMahon, Doctor Frank Sinatra, Doctor Ella Fitzgerald, Doctor Mister Rogers, Doctor Captain Kangaroo, Doctor Dr. Seuss, Doctor Jane Pauley, Doctor Bob Hope, Doctor Robert Redford, Doctor Stevie Wonder, Doctor Dan Rather, and thousands of other "doctors."

Checking Out Schools

Two Problems, Two Questions to Ask

Completing a degree program is, for many people, one of the most expensive and time-consuming things they will do in their lives. Yet some people spend more time and energy to choose a refrigerator or a television set than to select a school. For such people, one of two major problems may later set in.

Problem One: The school turns out to be less than wonderful

Some people enroll in a questionable school and then, when they see their alma mater exposed on *Sixty Minutes* or *Inside Edition*, wail, "But I didn't know; they had such a lovely catalog." If you apply to one of the schools listed in this book, you won't have that problem. All of these schools have proper accreditation, whether regional, national, or international (see "Accreditation," later in this section, for an explanation of these terms). Even so, in our experience, some people buy a book such as this, note all of the accredited schools, and still end up studying at a less-than-wonderful institution. Why? Maybe the other school was less expensive or seemed easier, or maybe it swore that it was just as good as the schools in this book.

In addition, good, accredited programs will almost certainly debut after this book does (with distance learning being such an active, growing field). You may well be faced with advertisements or Websites for interesting-looking degree programs that aren't listed here and need to know how to evaluate them.

Problem Two: There are unpleasant surprises down the road

Some people enroll in good, legitimate schools but then discover that the program just doesn't suit their needs. For instance, although most M.B.A. programs have an analytic or mathematical bent, some are more focused on people management or leadership. The program you have your heart set on may not be exactly what you need; perhaps another program would serve the same purpose as well or better. Or maybe the school's sales reps said the program could be finished in two years, but a closer reading of the catalog shows that only a full-time, nonworking student could accomplish this.

Thus you have two kinds of "checking out" to do: Is the school legitimate? And will the school meet my needs?

Question One: Is the school legitimate?

If you have any doubts, concerns, worries, or hunches about any school, whether in this book or not, you have every right to check it out. It's a buyers' market.

You can ask any questions you want about accreditation, number of students, credentials of the people in charge, campus facilities (some schools with very impressive-looking catalogs are operated from mail-forwarding services), and so on. Of course, the school has the right not to answer, whereupon you have the right not to enroll.

You may also want to confirm what a school tells you about its accreditation or legal status. Recognized accrediting agencies are more than happy to tell you what schools they accredit; we list contact information under "Accreditation" later in this section. To check whether a school is operating legally or not, inquire with the appropriate state or government agency; you'll find a list of these higher-education agencies in appendix E.

The information in this book is as complete and current as we could make it. But things change: schools change their policies, bad schools get better, good schools get worse, new schools appear, old schools disappear. For ways and means of getting more information, see appendices B and C.

Question Two: Will the school meet my needs?

You would think people would know this before spending thousands of dollars and years of their lives. But we have received hundreds of letters from people who have had very unpleasant surprises after enrolling—from some even after they have graduated. It is essential that you satisfy yourself that a given school will meet your needs before you spend any money. Make sure you know exactly what costs you will have (e.g., that there are no hidden "graduation fees"), whether your employer will accept (and perhaps pay for) your degree, whether any relevant licensing agencies will accept the work, and so on.

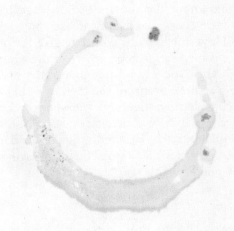

Applying to Schools

How Many Schools Should You Apply To?

No single answer to this question is right for everyone. Each person determines his or her own best answer. The decision should be based on the following four factors.

1. Likelihood of admission

Some schools are extremely competitive or popular and admit fewer than 10 percent of qualified applicants. Some have an "open admission" policy and admit literally everyone who applies. Most are somewhere in-between.

If your goal is to be admitted to one of the highly competitive schools (for instance, Harvard, Yale, Princeton, or Stanford), where your chances of being accepted are not high, then it is wise to apply to at least four or five schools that would be among your top choices and to at least one "safety valve" (easier school), in case all else fail.

If you are interested in one of the good (but not world-famous) nonresident programs, your chances for acceptance are probably better than nine in ten, so you might decide to apply to only one or two.

2. Cost

Possible costs for any given degree range tremendously. A respectable Ph.D. could cost around $5,000 at a good nonresidential school, for instance, or more than $80,000 at a prestigious university—not even taking into account the salary you would lose by taking the time to complete such a degree in residence.

3. What is offered

Shopping for a school is a little like shopping for a new car. Many schools either have money problems or operate as profit-making businesses. In either case, they are most eager to enroll new students. Thus it is reasonable to ask the schools what they can do for you. Let them know that you are a knowledgeable "shopper" and that you have this book. Do they have courses or faculty advisers in your specific field? If not, will they get them for you? How much credit will they give for prior life-experience learning? How long will it take you to earn the degree? Are there any scholarships or tuition-reduction plans available? Must you pay tuition all at once, or can you spread it out over time? If factors like these are important to you, then it could pay to shop around for the best deal.

You might consider investigating at least two schools that appear somewhat similar, because surely they will have differences.

Caution: Remember that academic quality and reputation are probably the most important factors—so don't let a small financial savings be a reason to switch from a good school to a less-good school.

4. Your own time

Applying to a school can be a time-consuming process. But applying to schools also costs money. Because many schools have application fees, ranging from $25 to $100, you may want to apply to only one or two schools at a time. If you do this and the school turns you down, however, or if you experience long delays, it can take a month or two to go through the admission process again elsewhere. Some people get so carried away with the process of applying to school after school that they never get around to earning their degree!

One factor to consider, then, is how much of a hurry you are in. If you apply to several schools at once, chances are good that at least one will admit you, and you can begin work promptly. Once you have prepared a good and detailed resumé, curriculum vitae, or life-experience portfolio, you can, of course, use it to apply to more than one school.

How to Speed Up the Admission Process

The admission process at most traditional schools is very slow; most people apply nearly a year in advance and do not learn whether their application has been accepted for four to six months. The schools in this book vary immensely in their policies in this regard. Some grant conditional acceptance within a few weeks after receiving an application. (*Conditional* means that they must later verify the prior learning experiences you claim.) Others take just as long as traditional programs.

The following three factors can result in a much faster admission process.

1. Select schools by admission policy

A school should state its admission policy in its catalog. You will find a range among schools of a few weeks to six months for a decision. The simple solution to speeding the process is to ask about and then apply to schools with a fast procedure.

2. Ask for speedy decisions

Some schools have formal procedures for you to request an early decision on acceptance. Others have informal procedures for speeding things up if you ask.

In effect, a request for a speedy decision puts you at the top of the pile in the admissions office, so you will have a decision in perhaps half the usual time. Other schools use what they call a "rolling admissions" procedure, considering each application soon after it is received rather than holding it for several months to be considered with a large batch of others.

3. Apply pressure

Many schools are eager to have new students. If you make it clear to a school that you are in a hurry and may consider going elsewhere if you don't get a response promptly, it will usually speed up the process. It is not unreasonable to specify a time frame. If, for instance, you mail in your application on September 1, you might enclose a note saying that you would like to have a decision mailed or phoned to you by October 1. (Some schools routinely telephone acceptances, others do so if asked, some do so only by collect call, and others do not call, no matter what.)

How to Apply to a School

The basic procedure is essentially the same at all schools, traditional or nontraditional:

1. Write (or telephone) for the school's catalog, bulletin, or other literature and an admission form.

2. Complete the admission form and return it to the school with the application fee, if any.

3. Complete any other requirements the school may have (exams, transcripts, letters of recommendation, etc.).

4. Wait for the school to notify you of its decision.

Step 3 can vary tremendously from school to school. Some schools require only the admission application. Others require various entrance examinations to test your aptitude or knowledge level, transcripts, three or more letters of reference, a statement of financial condition, and possibly a personal interview, either on the campus or with a local representative in your area.

The majority of schools in this book have relatively simple entrance requirements. All schools should tell you exactly what they expect you to do to apply. If the procedure is not clear, ask. If the school does not supply prompt, helpful answers, you probably don't want to deal with it anyway. Remember, it's a buyers' market.

It is advisable, in general, not to send a whole bunch of stuff to a school the first time you write to it. A short note asking for a catalog should suffice. You may wish to indicate your field and degree goal ("I am interested in a master's and possibly a doctorate in psychology") in case the school has different sets of literature for different programs. It probably can do no harm to mention that you are a reader of this book; you might get slightly prompter or more personal responses. (On the other hand, we have gotten more than a few grouchy letters from readers who have said, "I told them I was a personal friend of yours, and it still took six months for an answer." Oh, dear. Well, if they hadn't said that, it might have been even longer. Or perhaps shorter. Who knows?)

The Matter of Entrance Examinations

Many nonresident degree programs, even at the master's and doctorate levels, do not require entrance examinations. On the other hand, the majority of residential programs do require such exams. This discrepancy appears to be primarily because nontraditional schools do not have to worry about overcrowding on campus, so they can admit more students. Nontraditional schools also tend to deal with more mature students, who have the ability to decide which program is best for them.

There are, needless to say, exceptions to both reasons. If you have particular feelings about examinations—positive or negative—you will be able to find schools that meet your requirements. Do not hesitate to ask any school about its exam requirements if they are not clear from the catalog.

Bachelor's Admission Examinations

Most residential universities require applicants to take the Scholastic Aptitude Test (SAT), run by a private agency, the College Entrance Examination Board (45 Columbus Avenue, New York, NY 10023-6992; [212] 713-8000; Website www.collegboard.org). The general SAT measures verbal and mathematical abilities. Subject exams test knowledge levels in specific areas, such as biology, U.S. history, Spanish, and so forth. These examinations are given at centers all over North America several times each year for modest fees and by special arrangement in many foreign locations.

A competing private organization, American College Testing program, or ACT (2201 North Dodge Street, Post Office Box 168, Iowa City, IA 52243-0168; [319] 337-1000; Website www.act.org), offers a similar range of entrance examinations.

The important point is that few schools have their own exams; virtually all rely on either the SAT or the ACT.

Graduate Degrees

Again, many nonresidential schools do not require entrance examinations. Many, but by no means all, residential master's and doctorate programs ask their applicants to take the Graduate Record Examination (GRE), administered by the Educational Testing Service (Post Office Box 6000, Princeton, NJ 08541; [609] 771-7670; Website www.gre.org). The basic GRE consists of a three-and-a-half-hour aptitude test (of verbal, quantitative, and analytic abilities). Some schools also require GRE subject-area exams, which are available in a variety of specific fields (chemistry, computer science, psychology, etc.).

Professional Schools

Most law, business, and medical schools also require a standard examination, rather than having one of their own. The Medical College Admission Test (MCAT) and Law School Admission Test (LSAT) are given several times each year by ACT; the Graduate Management Admissions Test (GMAT) is given by Educational Testing Service (ETS).

Exam Preparation

Many excellent books are available at most libraries and larger bookstores on how to prepare for these various exams, complete with sample questions and answers. Some are listed in the bibliography of this book. The testing agencies themselves also sell literature on their tests as well as copies of examinations from previous years.

Testing agencies used to deny vigorously that either cramming or coaching could affect test scores. In the face of overwhelming evidence to the contrary, however, they no longer make those claims. Some coaching services have documented score increases of 25 to 30 percent. Check the Yellow Pages or the bulletin boards on high school or college campuses for test-preparation workshops in your area.

Accreditation

Accreditation is one of the most complex and confusing issues in higher education. It is also one of the most misused concepts—both intentionally and unintentionally. Let us try to make some sense out of the situation.

What Is Accreditation?

Quite simply, accreditation is validation—a statement by a group of persons who are (theoretically) impartial experts in higher education that a given school or department within a school has been thoroughly investigated and found to be worthy of approval. It is important to know these things about accreditation:

- It is voluntary. No school is required to be accredited.

- It is not a government process. Accrediting agencies are private, independent organizations. (The U.S. government does have a role in recognizing accreditors, however.)

- It is a peculiarly American concept. In every other country in the world, the government either operates the colleges and universities or directly gives them the right to grant degrees, so an independent agency does not need to say that a given school is okay.

- Hundreds of accrediting agencies exist. Some are generally recognized as legitimate; others are not. (The rest of this section explains how to tell the difference.)

- A small number of acceptable schools (or departments within schools) are not accredited, either by their own choice (because accreditation is a voluntary and often expensive procedure) or because they are too new (all schools were unaccredited at one time) or too experimental (some would say too innovative) for the generally conservative accreditors.

- A few less-than-wonderful schools (in our opinion, of course) are legitimately accredited, but not many.

- Many very bad schools claim to be accredited—but such accreditation is always by unrecognized, sometimes nonexistent, accrediting associations, often of their own creation.

- Accreditation is a controversial topic in higher education. The last two U.S. secretaries of education stated in no uncertain terms that the accrediting agencies are not doing their jobs, especially with respect to nontraditional schools such as some of the distance-learning institutions described in this book.

- Having accreditation is not the same thing as being licensed, chartered, approved, authorized, or recognized.

How Important Is Accreditation?

The answer to this question depends on what you intend to use your degree for. If you want only personal knowledge and edification—not career advancement, a listing on your resumé, or pursuit of a higher degree—then accreditation is really not that important.

Most of us, however, invest time and money into a degree not merely for the knowledge it bestows but also for the doors it opens as we move onward and upward in our lives. And in the United States, particularly in the realms of business and academia, doors generally open only to those with degrees that are legitimately accredited.

So if you want your degree to be useful (for job hunting, for pursuing graduate studies, etc.), then you should pay attention to accreditation—and not simply to whether a school has got it, but to whether that accreditation is generally accepted.

Generally Accepted Accreditation Principles

In the world of accounting is the concept of GAAP: Generally Accepted Accounting Principles. These principles are *generally* accepted: not absolutely, not always, not universally, but generally. The same concept makes just as much sense in the world of accreditation: GAAP—Generally Accepted Accreditation Principles.

We first heard the term used, informally, at the national convention of the American Association of Collegiate Registrars and Admissions Officers (AACRAO) in Reno a few years ago. It made good sense to us, and we have adopted it.

In the United States, the relevant key decision makers—especially university registrars, admissions officers, corporate human resource officers, and government agencies—are in near-unanimous agreement. Not everyone calls the concept GAAP, but the idea is the same: if a school meets certain criteria, its credits or degrees will probably be accepted; if not, they probably won't be.

What are the criteria for GAAP?

- For schools based in the United States: accreditation by an accrediting agency recognized by the U.S. Department of Education and/or the Council for Higher Education Accreditation (CHEA).

- For schools in Great Britain and the British Commonwealth: membership in the Association of Commonwealth Universities and a listing in the *Commonwealth Universities Yearbook*.

- For schools in Australia: recognition by the Australian Qualifications Framework.

- For schools in other countries: a description in the World Education Series (published by Projects in International Education Research [PIER], a joint venture of AACRAO and NAFSA [the Association of International Educators], with the participation of the College Board); or a listing in the Countries Series, published by the Australian National Office for Overseas Skills Recognition (NOOSR).

All of the schools profiled in this book meet the standards of GAAP.

Recognized Accrediting Agencies

There are six regional accrediting associations (each covering a particular region of the United States and its territories), several national accrediting agencies, and about eighty professional associations (which accredit specific departments or programs within a school). What makes these agencies "recognized"? They have been evaluated and approved by either the U.S. Department of Education (www.ed.gov) or the CHEA (www.chea.org).

If an accredited degree is important to you, the first question to ask is, "Has the school been accredited by the relevant national accreditor or by one of the six regional accreditors?" The next question is, "Has the department in which I am interested been accredited by its relevant professional association?"

It may be the case, for instance, that the North Central Association of Colleges and Schools (one of the six regional accreditors) has accredited Bennett University. This would mean that the entire school is accredited, and all of its degrees would be called accredited degrees or, more accurately, degrees from an accredited institution.

Or it may be that just the art department of Bennett University has been accredited by the relevant professional association—in this case, the National Association of Schools of Art. Then only the art majors at Bennett University could claim to have accredited degrees.

For some jobs (psychology and nursing, for example), professional accreditation may be more important than regional accreditation. In other words, even if a school is accredited by its regional association, its degree will be most useful for psychology majors only if its psychology department is also accredited by the American Psychological Association (APA). (One of the persistent legends about accreditation—the belief that Harvard University is not accredited—has arisen because of this distinction. Harvard is duly accredited by its regional agency, but many of its departments, including psychology, have chosen, for various reasons—prescribed curriculum is a common one—not to pursue accreditation by the relevant professional agencies.)

Approved accreditors will gladly supply lists of all of the schools (or departments within schools) that they have accredited and of those that are candidates for accreditation. They will also answer questions pertaining to any school's status (or lack of status) with them.

The six regional accrediting agencies

The most important accreditors are the six regional agencies, each responsible for dealing with all schools in the states over which it has jurisdiction. Following are contact information and jurisdictions for each of these accreditors.

Middle States Association of Colleges and Schools
Commission on Higher Education
3624 Market Street
Philadelphia, PA 19104
(215) 662-5606 • Fax: (215) 662-5501 • Website: www.msache.org
Delaware, District of Columbia, Maryland, New Jersey, New York, Pennsylvania, Puerto Rico, Virgin Islands

New England Association of Schools and Colleges
209 Burlington Road
Bedford, MA 01730
(781) 271-0022 • Fax: (781) 271-0950 • Website: www.neasc.org
Connecticut, Maine, Massachusetts, New Hampshire, Rhode Island, Vermont

North Central Association of Colleges and Schools
30 North La Salle Street, Suite 2400
Chicago, IL 60602
(800) 621-7440 • Fax: (312) 263-7462 • Website: www.ncacihe.org
Arizona, Arkansas, Colorado, Illinois, Indiana, Iowa, Kansas, Michigan, Minnesota, Missouri, Nebraska, New Mexico, North Dakota, Ohio, Oklahoma, South Dakota, West Virginia, Wisconsin, Wyoming

Northwest Association of Schools and Colleges
11300 Northeast Thirty-Third Place, Suite 120
Bellevue, WA 98004
(425) 827-2005 • Fax: (425) 827-3395 • Website: www.cocnasc.org
Alaska, Idaho, Montana, Nevada, Oregon, Utah, Washington

Southern Association of Colleges and Schools
1866 Southern Lane
Decatur, GA 30033
(404) 679-4500 • Fax: (404) 679-4558 • Website: www.sacs.org
Alabama, Florida, Georgia, Kentucky, Louisiana, Mississippi, North Carolina, South Carolina, Tennessee, Texas, Virginia

Western Association of Schools and Colleges
985 Atlantic Avenue, Suite 100
Alameda, CA 94501
(510) 748-9001 • Fax: (510) 748-9797 • Website: www.wascweb.org
California, Guam, Hawaii, Trust Territory of the Pacific

The relevant national accrediting agency

The only recognized agency with responsibility for distance-learning schools everywhere in the United States is the Distance Education and Training Council (DETC). Although many of the schools it accredits are vocational (truck driving, small-engine repair, real estate, etc.), the council is empowered to accredit distance-learning academic schools offering associate's, bachelor's, and master's degrees; it cannot deal with schools offering doctorates.

Distance Education and Training Council
1601 Eighteenth Street NW
Washington, DC 20009
(202) 234-5100 • Fax: (202) 332-1386 • Website: www.detc.org

Professional accrediting agencies

More than eighty specialized agencies are responsible for accrediting programs in architecture, art, Bible education, business, chiropractic, and scores of other fields. Lists of these agencies can be found in many standard reference books (including our own *Bears' Guide to Earning Degrees by Distance Learning,* described in appendix C) or by contacting either the U.S. Department of Education or CHEA.

Unrecognized Accrediting Agencies

A great many accrediting agencies are not approved or recognized by either CHEA or the Department of Education. A small number are clearly sincere and legitimate, but most are not, and none will meet the needs of a person who requires an accredited degree. Here are some of the more prominent unrecognized accreditors. Bear in mind that more than a hundred others are not listed here and that new ones are established almost every week, nearly all ranging somewhere between bad and very, very bad.

Accrediting Commission for Specialized Colleges (ACSC)

The accrediting procedures of ACSC, according to its literature, seem superficial at best. Its only requirement for becoming a candidate for accreditation is to mail in a check for $110.

Accrediting Commission International for Schools, Colleges and Theological Seminaries (ACI)

After authorities fined and closed down the International Accrediting Commission (IAC) for Schools, Colleges and Theological Seminaries in Missouri in 1989 (see listing in this section), the director of that agency retired and turned his work over to a colleague, who juggled the words in the name and opened up one state over, in Arkansas. All IAC schools were offered automatic accreditation by the ACI; we are not aware of any that turned down the offer. Accrediting Commission International refuses to make public a list of schools it has accredited. We have noted more than 150 schools that claim ACI accreditation, most of them apparently evangelical Bible schools, but more than a few nonreligious schools are included as well.

Alternative Institution Accrediting Association

Allegedly in Washington, DC, this association is the accreditor of several phony schools.

American Council of Private Colleges and Universities (ACPCU)

Hamilton University, the Wyoming-based diploma mill, set up this fake accrediting agency.

APIX Institute

This institute is claimed by the probably-phony Horizons University, whose campus is either a driving school or a hairdresser in Paris.

Arizona Commission of Non-Traditional Private Postsecondary Education

This commission was established in the late 1970s by the proprietors of Southland University, which claimed to be a candidate for its accreditation. The name was changed after a complaint by the real state agency, the Arizona Commission on Postsecondary Education.

Association for Online Academic Excellence

Trinity College and University (in the United States) claims this unrecognized accrediting agency.

Association Internationale des Educateurs pour la Paix Mondiale

Many schools claim a "diploma of recognition" from this organization, supposedly affiliated with the United Nations Educational, Scientific, and Cultural Organization (UNESCO). It's not hard to get one. In fact, if you are "interested in the promotion of international understanding and world peace through education, the protection of the environment from man-made pollution, and/or the safeguard of human rights everywhere," you too can have one!

Association of Accredited Private Schools

This unrecognized agency wrote to many schools in 1997, inviting them to send a $1,000 application fee.

Association of Career Training Schools

A slick booklet sent to schools says, "Have your school accredited with the Association. Why? The Association Seal . . . could be worth many $ $ $ to you! It lowers sales resistance, sales costs, [and] improves image." Nuff said.

Association of Private Colleges and Universities (APCU)

Before a school can buy the APCU "seal of approval," it must provide three student email addresses and show that it delivers the student's diploma within thirty days of graduation. The APCU says it is "not an accreditation agency, and makes no claims to be so"; considering such "tough" standards for gaining approval, we're glad it makes no such claims.

Association of World Universities and Colleges

The University of Asia has claimed this unrecognized accreditor, allegedly from Switzerland. The Website happens to be registered to the president of the University of Asia. This association is not to be confused (although perhaps that was intended) with the also-unrecognized World Association of Universities and Colleges (WAUC).

Correspondence Accreditation Association

This association was created by and is the accreditor for the dreadful Trinity College and University (the British version).

Council for National Academic Accreditation

In 1998, the council wrote to schools from Cheyenne, Wyoming, offering the opportunity to be accredited on payment of a fee of up to $1,850.

Council for the Accreditation of Correspondence Colleges

Several curious schools have claimed accreditation by this agency, supposed to be in Louisiana.

Council on Postsecondary Alternative Accreditation

Western States University claims this accreditor in its literature. Western States never responded to requests for the address of the accreditor.

Distance Education Council of America

Quite reminiscent in name and literature to the recognized Distance Education and Training Council, this agency arose in Delaware in 1998, offering schools the opportunity to pay $200 or more for accreditation and $150 more for an "Excellence" rating.

Distance Graduation Accrediting Association (DGAA)

The dreadful Capitol University and Concordia College and University claim this unrecognized agency.

European Committee for Home and Online Education

Strassford University and a few other worthless institutions created this apparently nonexistent agency in 2002.

Integra Accreditation Association

We somehow intercepted an email from this agency, sent June 2000, offering its accrediting services to a who's who list of nonwonderful schools.

International Accreditation and Recognition Council
This unrecognized accreditor is based in Australia.

International Accreditation Association of Nontraditional Colleges and Universities
This unrecognized accreditor is allegedly located in the British West Indies. Its Website (www.iaancu.nu) does not list its accredited members.

International Accrediting Association
The address in Modesto, California, is the same as that of the Universal Life Church, an organization that awards doctorates of all kinds, including the Ph.D., to anyone making a "donation" of $5 to $100.

International Accrediting Commission for Schools, Colleges and Theological Seminaries (IAC)
This organization accredited more than 150 schools. In 1989, the attorney general of Missouri conducted a clever sting operation, in which he created a fictitious school, the East Missouri Business College, which rented a one-room office in Saint Louis and issued a typewritten catalog with such school executives as Peelsburi Doughboy and Wonarmmd Mann. The Three Stooges were all on the faculty. The school's marine biology text was *The Little Golden Book of Fishes*. Its motto, translated from Latin, was "education is for the birds." Nonetheless, Dr. George Reuter, director of the IAC, visited the school, accepted its money, and duly accredited it. Soon after, the IAC was enjoined from operating and slapped with a substantial fine, and the good Dr. Reuter decided to retire. (But the almost-identical Accrediting Commission International [see previous listing in this section] immediately arose in Arkansas, offering instant accreditation to all IAC members.)

International Association of Non-Traditional Schools
This claimed accreditor of several British degree mills and one now-defunct nonwonderful Mexican school is allegedly located in England.

International Association of Schools, Colleges, and Universities (IASCU)
This association, located in Antwerp, Belgium, is the accreditor for Newport University International, which happens to own IASCU's email domain name. Other schools claiming accreditation from IASCU include Westbrook University, American Pacific University, and e Online University.

International University Accreditation Foundation
The Web domain name for this accreditor is owned by Saint George University International. Guess who is the accreditor for Saint George University International?

International University Accrediting Association (IUAA)
This is one of two unrecognized accrediting agencies (the other is the Virtual University Accrediting Association) founded and operated by Dr. Chief Swift Eagle of the Cherokee Western Federation Church and Tribe. The only accredited member we know of is International Theological University, also founded by Dr. Chief Swift Eagle.

Life Experience Accreditation Association (LEAF)
Earlscroft University claims this unrecognized agency. We never found an address or URL.

Middle States Accrediting Board
Thomas University and other degree mills made up this nonexistent accreditor for the purpose of self-accreditation. The name was chosen, of course, to be confused with the Middle States Association of Colleges and Schools, in Philadelphia, one of the six regional associations.

National Accreditation Association (NAA)
In a mailing to presidents of unaccredited schools, the NAA offered full accreditation by mail, with no on-site inspection required.

National Association of Private, Nontraditional Schools and Colleges (NAPNSC)
Formerly the National Association for Schools and Colleges, this was a serious effort to establish an accrediting agency specifically concerned with alternative schools and programs. It was established in Grand Junction, Colorado, in the 1970s by a group of educators associated with Western Colorado University, a nontraditional school that has since gone out of business. Although NAPNSC's standards for accreditation have grown more rigorous over the years, its application for recognition has been turned down many times by the U.S. Department of Education—but it plans to keep trying.

United Congress of Colleges
This is another unrecognized agency claimed by Earlscroft University. We never found an address or URL.

West European Accrediting Society
Proprietors of a chain of diploma mills such as Loyola, Roosevelt, Lafayette, Southern California, and Cromwell Universities established this society from a mail-forwarding service in Liederbach, Germany, for the purpose of accrediting themselves.

Western Association of Schools and Colleges
This is the name of the legitimate regional accreditor for the West Coast. However, it is also the name of a fake accreditor with a Los Angeles address set up by the proprietors of such diploma mills as Loyola, Roosevelt, Lafayette, Southern California, and Cromwell Universities.

Western Council on Non-Traditional Private Post Secondary Education
The founders of Southland University started this accrediting agency, presumably for the purpose of accrediting themselves and others.

World Association of Universities and Colleges (WAUC)
Dr. Maxine Asher established this association, run from a secretarial service in Nevada, in 1992. The WAUC accredits a long list of nonwonderful institutions, including, not surprisingly, American World University, also operated by Dr. Asher. In February 1995, the national investigative publication *Spy Magazine* ran a most unflattering article on WAUC. Dr. Asher also operates the Ancient Mediterranean Research Association, which has produced a film that "clearly demonstrates the existence of Atlantis off the coast of Spain."

World Council of Excellence in Higher Education
The council shares all of its addresses—mail, email, and URL—with Intercultural Open University (based in the Netherlands), the only school we know of that claims this accreditor.

World Council of Global Education

As part of the World Natural Health Organization, this council issues accreditation to institutions that provide an education in the natural health care field.

World Organization of Institutes, Colleges, and Universities

Omega University "enjoys" the international accreditation of this organization, but a fairly thorough Internet search suggests that it must be the only school doing so.

Worldwide Accrediting Commission

This commission, operated from a mail-forwarding service in Cannes, France, is for the purpose of accrediting various American-run degree mills.

Ways to Earn Credit

Correspondence Courses

More than a hundred major universities and teaching institutions in the United States and dozens in other countries offer academic correspondence (or email) courses—more than thirteen thousand courses in hundreds of subjects, from accounting to zoology. Virtually all of these courses can be counted toward a degree at almost any college or university.

Most schools have a limit on the amount of correspondence credit they will apply to a degree. This limit is typically around 50 percent, but the range is from 0 to 100 percent. Through schools such as Excelsior College, Thomas Edison State College, and Western Illinois University, it is possible to earn an accredited bachelor's degree entirely through correspondence study.

Every school publishes or offers online a catalog or bulletin listing its available correspondence courses. Some schools offer just a few courses; others have hundreds. All of the schools accept students living anywhere in the United States, although some charge more for out-of-state students. Most accept foreign students.

Correspondence courses offer from one to six semester hours of credit and can cost anywhere from less than $60 to more than $300 per semester hour. The average is just over $100, so a typical three-unit course would cost about $300. Because of the wide range in costs, it pays to shop around.

A typical correspondence course consists of five to twenty lessons, each requiring a short written paper, answers to questions, or an unsupervised test graded by the instructor. There is almost always a supervised final examination, which can usually be taken anywhere in the world as long as a suitable proctor (usually a high school or college teacher) is found.

People who cannot go to a testing center because, for instance, they are disabled, live too far away, or are in prison can usually arrange to have a test supervisor come to them. Schools can be extremely flexible. One correspondence program administrator told us he had two students—a husband and wife—working as missionaries on a remote island where they were the only people who could read and write. He allowed them to supervise each other.

Many schools set limits on how quickly and slowly you can complete a correspondence course. The shortest time is generally three to six weeks, whereas the upper limit ranges from three months to two years. Some schools limit the number of courses you can take at one time, but most do not. Even those with limits are concerned only with courses taken from their own institution. There is no cross-checking, so, in theory, you could take simultaneous courses from all 100+ institutions.

Where to Find Them

Peterson Publishing used to publish an excellent compendium of all 13,000+ correspondence courses in a book called *The Independent Study Catalog*. Sadly, no new edition has been published for several years.

What has risen in place of that catalog are a group of Websites—so-called higher-education portals—that have put vast databases of correspondence courses online. Search engines allow you to browse these databases by subject, whether for introductory astronomy, management information systems, or home ice cream making (the legendary course taken from Penn State University by Ben and Jerry for a cost of five bucks).

Here are some of the leading portals at the time we went to press—with the warning, perhaps needless to give, that dot-com companies come and go with the morning dew.

www.embark.com

www.mindedge.com

www.cyberu.com

www.petersons.com/distancelearning

www.dlcoursefinder.com

Some Schools That Offer Lots of Correspondence Courses

We don't have enough space to list all of the hundreds of schools that offer correspondence courses, but we will prime the pump for you by identifying a couple of dozen with a wide range of available courses, undergraduate and graduate.

UNITED STATES

Brigham Young University
Independent Study
206 Harman Building,
Post Office Box 21514
Provo, UT 84602
(801) 378-2868 • (800) 914-8931
www.ce.byu.edu/is

Charter Oak State College
55 Paul J. Manafort Drive
New Britain, CT 06053-2142
(860) 832-3800
www.cosc.edu

Colorado State University
Division of Educational Outreach
Spruce Hall
Fort Collins, CO 80523-1040
(970) 491-5288 • (877) 491-4336
www.csu2learn.colostate.edu

Indiana University
School of Continuing Studies
Owen Hall 002
Bloomington, IN 47405
(812) 855-2292 • (800) 334-1011
www.scs.indiana.edu

Louisiana State University
Office of Independent Study
E106 Pleasant Hall
Baton Rouge, LA 70803
(225) 388-3171 • (800) 234-5046
www.is.lsu.edu

Ohio University
Office of Independent Study
302 Tupper Hall
Athens, OH 45701
(740) 593-2910 • (800) 444-2910
www.cats.ohiou.edu/independent

Pennsylvania State University
Department of Distance Education
207 Mitchell Building
University Park, PA 16802
(814) 865-5403 • (800) 252-3592
www.cde.psu.edu/de

Stephens College
School of Graduate and Continuing Education
Campus Box 2083
Columbia, MO 65215
(573) 876-7125 • (800) 388-7579
www.stephens.edu

University of California—Berkeley
UC Extension Online
2000 Center Street, Suite 400
Berkeley, CA 94704
(510) 642-4124
www.learn.berkeley.edu

University of Iowa
Guided Correspondence Study
116 International Center
Iowa City, IA 52242
(319) 353-2575 • (800) 272-6430
www.uiowa.edu/~ccp

University of Minnesota
Independent and Distance Learning
150 Wesbrook Hall
77 Pleasant Street SE
Minneapolis, MN 55455
(612) 624-4000 • (800) 234-6564
www.uc.umn.edu/idl

University of Missouri
Center for Distance and Independent
Study
136 Clark Hall
Columbia, MO 65211-4200
(572) 882-6431 • (800) 609-3727
www.cdis.missouri.edu

University of Wisconsin
Independent Learning
505 South Rosa Road, Suite 200
Madison, WI 53719-1257
(800) 442-6460
www.learn.wisconsin.edu/il

**U.S. Department of Agriculture
Graduate School**
Correspondence and Online Program
Room 1112, South Building
1400 Independence Avenue SW
Washington, DC 20250-9911
(202) 314-3670
www.grad.usda.gov

Some Non-U.S. Schools with English-Language Correspondence Courses

AUSTRALIA
Curtin University of Technology
GPO Box U 1987
Perth, Western Australia 6845
www.curtin.edu.au

Deakin University
221 Burwood Highway
Burwood, Victoria 3125
www.deakin.edu.au

Edith Cowan University
Pearson Street, Churchlands, Western
Australia 6018
www.cowan.edu.au

James Cook University
Townsville, Queensland 4811
www.jcu.edu.au

University of South Australia
Underdale Campus, External Studies
Holbrooks Road
Underdale, South Australia 5032
www.unisa.edu.au

CANADA
Acadia University
Division of Continuing and Distance
Education
Wolfville, Nova Scotia B0P 1X0
www.acadiau.ca

Athabasca University
1 University Drive
Athabasca, Alberta T95 3A3
www.athabascau.ca

McGill University
Centre for Continuing Education
688 Sherbrooke Street West
Montreal, Quebec H3A 3R1
www.mcgill.ca

University of Manitoba
Distance Education Program
188 Continuing Education Complex
Winnipeg, Manitoba R3T 2N2
www.umanitoba.ca/coned

University of New Brunswick
Post Office Box 4400
Fredericton, New Brunswick E3B 5A3
www.unb.ca/coned

University of Toronto
School of Continuing Studies
158 Saint George Street
Toronto, Ontario M5S 2V8
www.learn.utoronto.ca/uoft/

University of Waterloo
Continuing Education
Waterloo, Ontario N2L 3G1
www.dce.uwaterloo.ca

South Africa

University of Cape Town
Rondebosch 7701, South Africa
www.uct.ac.za

University of South Africa
Post Office Box 392
Unisa 0003, South Africa
www.unisa.ac.za

United Kingdom

Open University
Walton Hall, Milton Keynes MK7 6AA
www.open.ac.uk

Equivalency Examinations

Most of the schools in this book would agree that if you have knowledge of an academic field, you should get credit for that knowledge, regardless of how or where you acquired the knowledge. The simplest and fairest way (but by no means the only way) to assess that knowledge is through an examination.

About three thousand colleges and universities in the United States and Canada, many of which would deny vigorously that there is anything nontraditional about them, award students credit toward their bachelor's degrees (and, in a few cases, master's and doctorate degrees) solely on the basis of passing examinations.

Many of the exams are designed to be equivalent to the final exam in a typical college class. The assumption is that if you score high enough, you get the same amount of credit you would have gotten by taking the class—or, in some cases, a good deal more.

There are many sources of equivalency exams (with, in fact, a trend toward schools developing their own), but two national testing agencies are dominant in this field: the College-Level Examination Program (CLEP) and Excelsior College Examinations. Together, these agencies administer more than seventy equivalency exams given at hundreds of testing centers all over North America. By special arrangement, many of these exams can be administered almost anywhere in the world.

CLEP Tests

CLEP is offered by the College Entrance Examination Board, known as the College Board (45 Columbus Avenue, New York, NY 10023-6992; [212] 713-8000; email clep@info.collegeboard.org; Website www.collegeboard.org/clep). Military personnel who want to take CLEP exams should see their education officer or contact the Defense Activity for Non-Traditional Education Support (DANTES), DANTES/CLEP, at Post Office Box 6604, Princeton, NJ 08541-6604; (609) 720-6740. Be sure to indicate on your request that you are a member of the armed forces.

CLEP tests are given at more than fourteen hundred centers, most of them on college or university campuses. Each center sets its own schedule for frequency of testing, so it may pay to shop around for convenient dates.

The exams are designed to correspond to typical one-semester or full-year introductory-level courses offered at a university, and they are titled accordingly. Test takers are given ninety minutes to answer multiple-choice questions at a computer terminal. The composition and literature exams have an optional essay section (required by some colleges). The cost of a test in any of the following fields is about $50.

BUSINESS

Information Systems and Computer Applications

Introductory Business Law

Principles of Accounting

Principles of Management

Principles of Marketing

COMPOSITION AND LITERATURE

American Literature

Analyzing and Interpreting Literature

English Composition

English Literature

Freshman College Composition

Humanities

HISTORY AND SOCIAL SCIENCES

American Government

History of the United States. I: Early Colonizations to 1877

History of the United States. II: 1865 to the Present

Human Growth and Development

Introduction to Educational Psychology

Introductory Psychology

Introductory Sociology

Principles of Macroeconomics

Principles of Microeconomics

Social Sciences and History

Western Civilization I: Ancient Near East to 1648

Western Civilization II: 1648 to the Present

LANGUAGES OTHER THAN ENGLISH

College-Level French

College-Level German

College-Level Spanish

SCIENCE AND MATHEMATICS

Biology

Calculus

Chemistry

College Algebra

College Algebra—Trigonometry

College Mathematics

Natural Sciences

Trigonometry

Please note: Before 2001, CLEP made a distinction between "general" exams and "subject" exams. These days, that distinction has been eliminated, and what were the five general exams—English Composition, Humanities, Social Sciences and History, College Mathematics, and Natural Sciences—have been integrated into the subject exam categories of the preceding list.

Excelsior College Examinations

Excelsior College Examinations are developed by Excelsior College (Test Administration Office, 7 Columbia Circle, Albany, NY 12203-5159; (888) 723-9267; Website www.excelsiorcollege.edu).

Note: Excelsior College was formerly known as Regents College, and the exam program was known as Regents College Examinations. Prior to that, these exams were part of what was called the Proficiency Examination Program, or PEP—just in case you see these terms and names and wonder how they all relate.

Excelsior College Examinations are administered at Prometric Testing Centers (formerly Sylvan Technology Centers) at more than two hundred locations throughout the United States and Canada (see www.educate.com for locations). Persons living more than 250 miles from a test center may make special arrangements for the test to be given nearer their home.

Whereas CLEP tests generally correspond to introductory-level college courses, Excelsior College Examinations are geared more toward the intermediate to advanced college level. Most tests are three hours long, but a few are four hours. They range in price from $70 to $370 per exam and are offered in the following fields.

ART AND SCIENCE

Abnormal Psychology

American Dream

Anatomy and Physiology

English Composition

Ethics: Theory and Practice

Foundations of Gerontology

History of Nazi Germany

Life Span Developmental Psychology

Microbiology

Pathophysiology

Psychology of Adulthood and Aging

Religions of the World

Research Methods in Psychology

Statistics

World Population

BUSINESS

Business Policy and Strategy

Ethics: Theory and Practice

Human Resource Management

Labor Relations

Organizational Behavior

Production/Operations Management

EDUCATION

Reading Instruction in the Elementary School

NURSING

Twenty specialized exams, ranging from professional strategies in nursing to maternity nursing

How Exams Are Scored and Credited

Each college or university sets its own standards for passing grades and also decides how much credit to give for each exam. Both of these factors can vary substantially from school to school. For example, hundreds of schools give credit for passing the Excelsior exam in Anatomy and Physiology, a three-hour multiple-choice test. The amount of credit given and the score required to pass is different for almost every school, however:

- Central Virginia Community College requires a score of 45 (out of 80) and awards nine credit hours for passing.

- Edinboro University in Pennsylvania requires a score of 50 to pass and awards six credit hours for the same exam.

- Concordia College in New York requires a score of 47 but awards only three credit hours.

Similar situations prevail for most of the exams. There is no predictability or consistency, even within a given school. At the University of South Florida, for instance, a three-hour multiple-choice test in maternal nursing is worth eighteen units, whereas a three-hour multiple-choice test in psychiatric nursing is worth only nine.

So with dozens of standard exams available, and with about three thousand schools offering credit, it pays to shop around a little and select both the school and the exams that will give you the most credit.

How Hard Are These Exams?

This is, of course, an extremely subjective question. We have heard from a great many readers who have attempted CLEP and Excelsior exams, however, and the most common feedback is "Gee, that was a lot easier than I had expected." This is especially true with more mature students. The tests are designed for eighteen- to twenty-year-olds, and people appear to acquire a certain amount of factual knowledge, as well as experience in dealing with testing situations, through ordinary life situations as they grow older.

No stigma is attached to poor performance on these tests. In fact, if you wish, you may have the scores reported only to you, so that no one but you and the computer know how you did. Then, if your scores are high enough, you can have them sent on to the schools of your choice. CLEP allows exams to be taken every six months; you can take the same Excelsior College exam twice in any twelve-month period.

Preparing (and Cramming) for Exams

Both testing agencies issue detailed syllabi describing each test and the specific content area it covers. Both sell an "official study guide" that gives sample questions and answers from each examination. On its Website, CLEP also offers practice tests with sample questions.

The testing agencies create their exam questions from college textbooks, so they recommend that you go to the source for studying. At the bookstore of a local college, browse the textbook selection for the course that corresponds to the test you'll be taking. At least four educational publishers have produced series of books on how to prepare for such exams, often with full-length sample tests. These can be found in the education or reference section of any good bookstore or library.

For years, testing agencies vigorously fought the idea of letting test takers take copies of a test home with them. But consumer legislation in New York has made at least some of the tests available, and it's a good thing, too. Every so often, someone discovers an incorrect answer or a poorly phrased question that can have more than one correct answer, necessitating a recalculation and reissuance of scores to all the thousands of people who have taken that test.

In recent years, there has been much controversy over the value of cramming for examinations. Many counseling clients report having been able to pass four or five CLEP exams in a row by spending an intensive few days (or weeks) cramming for them. Although various testing agencies used to deny that cramming can be of any value, some extremely persuasive research studies in the last few years have demonstrated the short-term effectiveness of intensive studying.

These data have vindicated the claims made by people and agencies that assist students in preparing for examinations. Such services are offered in a great many places, usually in the vicinity of college campuses, by graduate students and moonlighting faculty. The best place to find them is through the classified ads in campus newspapers, on bulletin boards around campus, and through on-campus extension programs. Prices vary widely, so shop around.

But buyer beware: test prep services are an unregulated industry, and quality varies widely. Some make promises that they simply cannot keep. We have heard reports of a growing number of fraudulent test prep services; many seem to be targeting members of the military and their families. Watch out for demands of large payments up front, strange-looking credit agreements, outdated preparation materials, book lists that include dictionaries or encyclopedias, or claims to be representing one of the testing agencies such as CLEP. The people who make the tests don't make sales calls.

Often the best strategy is to take a self-scoring test from one of the guidebooks. If you do well, you may wish to take the real exam right away. If you do badly, you may conclude that credit by examination is not your cup of hemlock. If you score in-between, consider studying (or cramming) on your own or with the help of a paid tutor or tutoring service.

Other Examinations

Here are some other examinations that can be used to earn substantial credit toward many nontraditional degree programs.

Graduate Record Examination (GRE)

The GRE is administered by the Educational Testing Service (Post Office Box 6000, Princeton, NJ 08541; (609) 771-7670; email gre-info@ets.org; Website www.gre.org). A general test—more of an aptitude test— is now given on demand at more than six hundred computer centers throughout North America. On completing this exam by computer, the student is given the choice of either erasing the exam entirely and walking out (no harm, no foul) or pressing another button and being given an instantaneous (but still unofficial) score.

The GRE subject tests are still given in written form, although this may change in the near future. Each is a three-hour multiple-choice test designed to test knowledge that would ordinarily be gained by a bachelor's degree holder in that given field. The exams are available in the fields of

Biochemistry, cell and molecular biology

Biology

Chemistry

Computer science

Literature in English

Mathematics

Physics

Psychology

This menu changes often, so check the GRE Website for the latest list.

Few schools give credit for the general GRE. Schools vary widely in how much credit they give for each subject-area GRE; some schools even base amount of credit on your score. The range is from none at all to thirty semester units (in the case of Excelsior College).

A National Guard sergeant we know of crammed for, took, and passed three GRE exams in a row, thereby earning ninety semester units in ten-and-a-half hours of testing. Then he took five CLEP exams in two days and earned thirty more units, which was enough for him to earn an accredited bachelor's degree (from what is now Excelsior College), start to finish, in eighteen hours, starting absolutely from scratch, with no college credit. This is not typical—maybe not even advisable—but it is doable!

DANTES

The Defense Activity for Non-Traditional Education Support offers its own tests, the DANTES Subject Standardized Tests (DSSTs). The ETS developed these tests for the U.S. Department of Defense, but they are available to civilians as well. Hundreds of colleges and universities offer the tests nationwide. Although there is some overlap with CLEP and Excelsior exams, many unique subjects are also tested. DANTES information is available from the DANTES Program, Post Office Box 6604, Princeton, NJ 08541-6604; (609) 720-6740; Website http://voled.doded.mil/dantes/exam.

Tests are in the general areas of business, humanities, math, sciences, social sciences, and education, and include

BUSINESS

Business, Introduction to

Business Law II

Finance, Principles of

Financial Accounting, Principles of

Human Resource Management

Introduction to Computing

Management Information Systems

Money and Banking

Organizational Behavior

Personal Finance

Supervision, Principles of

EDUCATION

Education, Foundations of

HUMANITIES

Art of the Western World

Modern Middle East, A

World Religions, Introduction to

MATHEMATICS

Business Mathematics

College Algebra, Fundamentals of

Statistics, Principles of

SCIENCES

Astronomy

Environment and Humanity: The Race to Save the Planet Earth

Physical Geology

Principles of Physical Science I

SOCIAL SCIENCES

Anthropology, General

Civil War and Reconstruction

Contemporary Western Europe

Counseling, Fundamentals of

Criminal Justice

Drug and Alcohol Abuse

Ethics in America

Geography, Human Cultural

Here's to Your Health

A History of the Vietnam War

Law Enforcement, Introduction to

Lifespan Developmental Psychology

Public Speaking, Principles of

Rise and Fall of the Soviet Union

Technical Writing

University End-of-Course Exams

Several schools offer the opportunity to earn credit for a correspondence course solely by taking and passing the final exam for that course. One need not be enrolled as a student in the school to do this. Two schools with especially large programs of this kind are Ohio University (Independent Study, 302 Tupper Hall, Athens, OH 45701; Website www.cats.ohiou.edu/independent/ccewords.htm) and the University of North Carolina (UNC Division of Continuing Education, CB #1020 The Friday Center, Chapel Hill, NC 27599-1020; Website www.fridaycenter.unc.edu).

Advanced Placement (AP) Examinations

The College Board (45 Columbus Avenue, New York, NY 10023-6992; [212] 713-8066; email ap@collegeboard.org) offers subject-specific exams for students who wish to earn college credit while still in high school. For a list of available subjects, go to Website www.collegeboard.org/ap/students.

Special Assessments

For people whose knowledge is both extensive and in an obscure field (or at least a field for which no exams have been developed), some schools are willing to develop special exams for a single student. Each school has its own policy in this regard, so once again, it can pay to shop around.

What If You Hate Exams or Don't Do Well on Them?

Don't despair. There are two other less-threatening ways to get credit for life-experience learning: special assessments and presentation of a life-experience portfolio. These are discussed in the following section.

Credit for Life-Experience Learning

The philosophy behind credit for life-experience learning can be expressed very simply: academic credit is given for what you know, without regard for how, when, or where you acquire the knowledge.

Consider a simple example. Quite a few colleges and universities offer credit for courses in typewriting. For instance, at Western Illinois University, Business Education 261 is a basic typing class. Anyone who takes and passes that class is given three units of credit.

An advocate of credit for life-experience learning would say, "If you know how to type, regardless of how and where you learned, even if you taught yourself at the age of nine, you should still get those same three units of credit, once you demonstrate that you have the same skill level as a person who passes Business Education 261."

Of course, not all learning can be converted into college credit. But many people are surprised to discover how much of what they already know is, in fact, credit worthy. With thousands of colleges offering hundreds of thousands of courses, it is a rare subject indeed that someone hasn't determined to be worthy of some credit. There is no guarantee that a given school will honor a given learning experience, or even accept another school's assessment for transfer purposes. Yale might not accept typing credit. But then again, the course title often sounds much more academic than the learning experience itself, as in "Business Education" for typing, "Cross-Cultural Communication" for a trip to China, or "Fundamentals of Applied Kinesiology" for golf lessons.

The following eight major types of life experience may be worth college credit, especially in nontraditional degree-granting programs.

1. Work. Many of the skills acquired in paid employment are also skills that are taught in colleges and universities. These include, for instance, typing, filing, shorthand, accounting, inventory control, financial management, map reading, military strategy, welding, computer programming or operating, editing, planning, sales, real estate appraisal, and literally thousands of other things.

2. Homemaking. Skills include home maintenance, household planning and budgeting, child rearing, child psychology, education, interpersonal communication, meal planning and nutrition, gourmet cooking, and much more.

3. Volunteer work. Imporant skills come from community activities, political campaigns, church activities, service organizations, volunteer work in social service agencies or hospitals, and so forth.

4. Noncredit learning in formal settings. Such settings include company training courses, in-service teacher training, workshops, clinics, conferences and conventions, lectures, courses on radio or television, noncredit correspondence courses, and so forth.

5. Travel. Study tours (organized or informal), significant vacation and business trips, periods of living in other countries or cultures, and participation in activities related to other cultures or subcultures all provide life experiences.

6. Recreational activities and hobbies. Musical skills, aviation training and skills, acting or other work in a community theater, sports, arts and crafts, fiction and nonfiction writing, public speaking, gardening, museum visits, clothing design

and creation, attendance at plays and concerts, and many other leisure-time activities are also valuable skills.

7. Reading, viewing, and listening. This category may cover any field in which a person has done extensive or intensive reading and studying and for which college credit has not been granted. It has, for instance, included viewing various series on public television.

8. Discussions with experts. A great deal of learning can come from talking to, listening to, and working with experts, whether in ancient history, carpentry, or theology. Significant, extensive, or intensive meetings with such people may also be worth credit.

The Most Common Error Most People Make

The most common error most people make when thinking about getting credit for life experience is confusing time spent with learning. Being a regular churchgoer for thirty years is not worth any college credit in and of itself. But the regular churchgoer who can document that he or she has prepared for and taught Sunday school classes, worked with youth groups, participated in leadership programs, organized fund-raising drives, studied Latin or Greek, taken tours to the Holy Land, or even engaged in lengthy philosophical discussions with the clergy, is likely to get credit for those experiences. Selling insurance for twenty years is worth no credit—unless you describe and document the learning that took place in areas of marketing, banking, risk management, entrepreneurial studies, and so forth.

It is crucial that the experiences can be documented to a school's satisfaction. Two people could work side by side in the same laboratory for five years. One might do little more than follow instructions—running routine experiments, setting up and dismantling apparatus, and then heading home. The other, with the same job title, might do extensive reading in the background of the work being done, get into discussions with supervisors, make plans and recommendations for other ways of doing the work, propose or design new kinds of apparatus, and/or develop hypotheses on why the results turned out the way they did.

It is not enough just to say what you did or to submit a short resumé. You must document the details and specifics. The two most common ways to do this are by preparing a life-experience portfolio (essentially a long, well-documented, annotated resumé) or by taking an equivalency examination to demonstrate knowledge gained.

Presenting Your Learning

Most schools that give credit for life-experience learning require that the student make a formal presentation, usually in the form of a life-experience portfolio. Each school has its own standards for the form and content of such a portfolio; many, in fact, offer either guidelines or courses (some for credit, some not) to help the nontraditional student prepare a portfolio.

Several books on this subject have been published by the Council for Adult and Experiential Learning. For a list of current publications, contact the CAEL at 55 East Monroe Street, Suite 1930, Chicago, IL 60603; (312) 499-2600; Website www.cael.org. CAEL offers for sale a few books designed to help people prepare life-experience portfolios. Sadly, CAEL no longer offers sample portfolios for sale; that excellent service has been discontinued.

Following is a sampling of some twenty-four other means by which people have documented life-experience learning, sometimes as part of a portfolio, sometimes not. These should help get you thinking about the possibilities.

- Official commendations
- Audiotapes
- Slides
- Course outlines
- Bills of sale
- Records or photographs of exhibitions
- Programs of recitals and performances
- Videotapes
- Awards and honors
- Mementos
- Copies of speeches made
- Licenses (pilot, real estate, etc.)
- Certificates
- Testimonials and endorsements
- Interviews with others
- Newspaper articles
- Official job descriptions
- Copies of exams taken
- Military records
- Samples of arts or crafts made
- Samples of writing
- Designs and blueprints
- Works of art
- Films and photographs

How Life-Experience Learning Is Turned into Academic Credit

It isn't easy. In a perfect world, there would be universally accepted standards, and it would be as easy to measure the credit value in a seminar on refrigeration engineering as it is to measure the temperature inside a refrigerator. Some schools and national organizations are striving to create extensive "menus" of nontraditional experiences, to ensure that anyone doing the same thing would get the same credit.

Progress in this direction continues. Many schools have come to agree, for instance, on aviation experience: a private pilot's license is worth four semester units, an instrument rating is worth six additional units, and so forth.

The American Council on Education (ACE), a private organization, regularly publishes a massive multivolume set of books in two series: *The National Guide to Educational Credit for Training Programs* and *Guide to the Evaluation of Educational Experiences in the Armed Forces*, which many schools use to assign credit directly; others use these publications as guidelines in doing their own evaluations. A few examples demonstrate the sort of thing done.

- A nine-day Red Cross training course called The Art of Helping is evaluated as worth two semester hours of social work.

- The John Hancock Mutual Life Insurance Company's internal course in technical skills for managers is worth three semester hours of business administration.

- Portland Cement Company's five-day training program in kiln optimization, whatever that may be, is worth one semester hour.

- The Professional Insurance Agents' three-week course in basic insurance is worth six semester units: three in principles of insurance and three in property and liability contract analysis.

- The U.S. Army's twenty-seven-week course in ground surveillance radar repair is worth fifteen semester hours: ten in electronics and five in electrical laboratory.

- The U.S. Army's legal-clerk training course can be worth twenty-four semester hours, including three in English, three in business law, three in management, and so forth.

Hundreds of additional business and military courses have been evaluated already, and thousands more will be worth credit for those who have taken them, whether or not they appear in these ACE volumes.

Some Inspiration

There are always some people who say, "Oh, I haven't ever done anything worthy of college credit." We have yet to meet anyone with an IQ higher than room temperature who has not done at least some credit-worthy things. Often it's just a matter of presenting the experience properly, in a portfolio. Here, for instance, is a list of one hundred things that could be worth credit for life-experience learning. This list could easily be ten or a hundred times as long. Please note the "could." Some reviewers in the past have made fun of this list, suggesting that we were saying you could earn a degree for buying Persian rugs. Not so. We do suggest, however, that a person who has made a high-level study of Persian art and culture preparatory to buying carpets—and who could document the reading, consultations, time spent, sources, and so forth—could probably earn some portfolio credit for this out-of-classroom endeavor. Here, then, is the list.

- Playing tennis
- Preparing for natural childbirth
- Leading a church group
- Taking a bodybuilding class
- Speaking French
- Selling real estate

- Studying gourmet cooking
- Reading *War and Peace*
- Building model airplanes
- Traveling through Belgium
- Learning shorthand
- Starting a small business
- Navigating a small boat
- Writing a book
- Buying a Persian carpet
- Watching public television
- Decorating a home or office
- Attending a convention
- Being a summer camp counselor
- Studying Spanish
- Bicycling across Greece
- Interviewing senior citizens
- Living in another culture
- Writing advertisements
- Throwing a pot
- Repairing a car
- Performing magic
- Attending art films
- Welding and soldering
- Designing and weaving a rug
- Negotiating a contract
- Editing a manuscript
- Planning a trip
- Steering a ship
- Appraising an antique
- Writing a speech
- Studying first aid or cardiopulmonary resuscitation (CPR)
- Organizing a Canadian union
- Researching international laws
- Listening to Shakespeare's plays on tape
- Designing a playground
- Planning a garden
- Devising a marketing strategy
- Reading the newspaper
- Designing a home
- Attending a seminar
- Playing the piano
- Studying a new religion
- Reading about the Civil War
- Taking ballet lessons
- Helping a dyslexic child
- Riding a horse
- Pressing flowers
- Keeping tropical fish
- Writing press releases
- Writing for the local newspaper
- Running a Parent-Teacher Association (PTA)
- Acting in a little theater
- Flying an airplane
- Designing a quilt
- Taking photographs
- Building a table
- Developing an inventory system
- Programming a home computer
- Helping in a political campaign
- Playing a musical instrument
- Painting a picture
- Playing political board games
- Serving on a jury
- Volunteering at a hospital
- Visiting a museum
- Attending a "great books" group

- Designing and sewing clothes
- Playing golf
- Talking intensively with a doctor
- Teaching the banjo
- Reading the Bible
- Leading a platoon
- Learning Braille
- Operating a printing press
- Eating in an exotic restaurant
- Running a store
- Planning a balanced diet
- Reading *All and Everything*
- Learning sign language
- Teaching Sunday school
- Training an apprentice
- Being an apprentice
- Weaving a rug
- Learning yoga
- Laying bricks
- Making a speech
- Being Dungeonmaster
- Negotiating a merger
- Developing film
- Learning calligraphy
- Applying statistics to gambling
- Doing circle dancing
- Taking care of sick animals
- Reading this book

Foreign Academic Experience

Many thousands of universities, colleges, technical schools, institutes, and vocational schools all over the world offer courses that are at least the equivalent of work at American universities. In principle, most universities are willing to give credit for work done at schools in other countries.

But can you imagine the task of an admissions officer faced with the student who presents an Advanced Diploma from the Wyzsza Szkola Inzynierska in Poland, or the degree of Mishigas from the Khazerai Institute in Israel? Are these equivalent to a high school diploma, a doctorate, or something in-between?

Until 1974, the U.S. Office of Education helped by evaluating educational credentials earned outside the United States and translating them into approximately comparable levels of U.S. achievement. This service is no longer available. There have arisen, to fill this gap, quite a few private independent credential and transcript evaluation services. Some deal exclusively with credentials and transcripts earned outside the United States and/or Canada, whereas others also consider experiential learning wherever it took place (such as military courses, aviation credentials, company training programs, and the like).

It is important to note that the U.S. government neither endorses, licenses, nor recommends these organizations, and nor are they regulated. The various organizations would appear to have very different ways of going about their work, often yielding quite different results. Sometimes it actually pays to shop around and get a report from more than one agency.

Some of these organizations are used mostly by the schools themselves, to evaluate applicants from abroad or with foreign credentials, but individuals may deal with them directly at relatively low cost. Many schools accept the recommendations of these services, but others do not. Some schools do their own foreign evaluations, whereas others have a short list of credential evaluators they accept. We have heard of at least two cases of really dreadful schools allying with really dreadful evaluators. (These dreadful folks are not listed here, but as always, if anything seems shady, get a second opinion.) It may be wise, therefore, to determine whether a school or schools in which you have interest will accept the recommendations of such services before you invest in them. We have also noted that schools that appear to require the evaluation from a certain agency or group of agencies are still, sometimes, willing to accept the evaluation from an agency not on their list.

Depending on the complexity of the evaluation, the cost runs from $50 to $200, or occasionally even more. One agency, which we have deleted from our list, provided our experimental subject with a one-sentence response to his initial paid $50 application and said that the full report would cost $800. Some of the services are willing to deal with non-school-based experiential learning as well. The services operate quickly. Less than two weeks for an evaluation is not unusual.

Typical evaluation reports give the exact U.S. equivalents for non-U.S. work, in terms of both semester units earned and any degrees or certificates earned. For instance, we would expect all of these services to report that the Japanese degree of Gakushi is almost exactly equivalent to the U.S. bachelor's degree.

Given the significant differences in the opinions of these services, if one report seems inappropriate or incorrect, it might be wise to seek a second (and even a third) opinion.

Here is a list of some of the organizations that perform these services, in alphabetical order, first in the United States and then in Canada. Listed first are those that are members of the industry's trade association, the National Association of Credential

Evaluation Services (NACES): (414) 289-3412; email margit@ece.org; Website www.naces.org.

The state of California's Commission on Teacher Credentialing (Website www.ctc.ca.gov) has approved those with an asterisk.

One special case worth noting is the AACRAO (American Association of Collegiate Registrars and Admissions Officers). This invaluable organization once offered its service only directly to member schools, but it has now made this service available to students as well. Contact it at

AACRAO
Foreign Education Evaluation Service
One Dupont Circle NW, Suite 520
Washington, DC 20036-1135
Phone: (202) 293-9161
Fax: (202) 872-8857
Email: info@aacrao.org
Website: www.aacrao.org/credential/individual.htm

UNITED STATES
Members of NACES (the industry trade association):
Center for Applied Research, Evaluation and Education
Post Office Box 20348
Long Beach, CA 90801-3348
Phone: (562) 430-1105
Fax: (562) 430-8215
Email: evalcaree@earthlink.net

Educational Credential Evaluators, Inc.*
Post Office Box 514070
Milwaukee, WI 53203-3470
Phone: (414) 289-3400
Fax: (414) 289-3411
Email: eval@ece.org
Website: www.ece.org

Educational Evaluators International, Inc.
Post Office Box 5397
Los Alamitos, CA 90720-5397
Phone: (562) 431-2187
Fax: (562) 493-5021
Email: gary@educei.com

Educational International, Inc.
24 Denton Road
Wellesley, MA 02482
Phone: (781) 235-7425
Fax: (781) 235-6831
Email: edint@gis.net
Website: www.educationinternational.org

Educational Records Evaluation Service*
777 Campus Commons Road, #200
Sacramento, CA 95825
Phone: (916) 565-7475
Fax: (916) 565-7476
Email: edu@eres.com
Website: www.eres.com

Evaluation Service, Inc.
Post Office Box 85
Hopewell Junction, NY 12533
Phone: (845) 223-6455
Fax: (845) 223-6454
Email: esi@capital.net
Website: www.evaluationservice.net

Foreign Academic Credential Service, Inc.
Post Office Box 400
Glen Carbon, IL 62034
Phone: (618) 288-1661
Fax: (618) 288-1691
Email: facs@aol.com
Website: www.facsusa.com

Foreign Educational Document Service
Post Office Box 4091
Stockton, CA 95204
Phone: (209) 948-6589
Fax: (209) 937-0717

Foundation for International Services, Inc.
19015 North Creek Parkway, #103
Bothell, WA 98011
Phone: (425) 487-2245
Fax: (425) 487-1989
Email: info@fis-web.com
Website: www.fis-web.com

Global Services Associates
2554 Lincoln Boulevard, #445
Marina del Rey, CA 90291
Phone: (310) 828-5709
Fax: (310) 828-5709
Email: info@globaleval.org
Website: www.globaleval.org

International Consultants of Delaware, Inc.
109 Barksdale Professional Center
Newark, DE 19711
Phone: (302) 737-8715
Fax: (302) 737-8756
Email: icd@icdel.com
Website:
www.cgfns.org/cgfns/icd/index.html

International Education Research Foundation*
Post Office Box 3665
Culver City, CA 90231-3655
Phone: (310) 390-6276
Fax: (310) 397-7686
Email: info@ierf.org
Website: www.ierf.org

Josef Silny and Associates, Inc.
Post Office Box 248233
Coral Gables, FL 33124
Phone: (305) 666-0233
Fax: (305) 666-4133
Email: info@jsilny.com
Website: www.jsilny.com

SpanTran Educational Services, Inc.
7211 Regency Square Boulevard, #205
Houston, TX 77036
Phone: (713) 266-8805
Fax: (713) 789-6022
Email: info@ spantran-edu.com
Website: www.spantran-edu.com

World Education Services*
Post Office Box 745
Old Chelsea Station
New York, NY 10013
Phone: (212) 966-6311 • (800) 937-3895
Fax: (212) 966-6395
Email: info@wes.org
Website: www.wes.org

Not Members of NACES:

Academic Credentials Evaluation Institute*
Post Office Box 6908
Beverly Hills, CA 90212
Phone: (310) 275-3530 • (800) 234-1597
Fax: (310) 275-3528
Email: acei@acei1.com
Website: www.acei1.com

Academic and Professional International Evaluations, Inc.*
Post Office Box 5787
Los Alamitos, CA 90721
Phone: (562) 594-6498
Email: apie@email.msn.com
Website: www.apie.org

American Education Research Corporation*
Post Office Box 996
West Covina, CA 91793-0996
Phone: (626) 339-4404
Fax: (626) 339-9081
Email: aerc@cyberg8t.com
Website: www.aerc-eval.com

Global Credential Evaluators, Inc.
Post Office Box 9203
College Station, TX 77842
Phone: (979) 690-8912
Fax: (979) 690-6342
Email: jringer@mail.myriad.net
Website: www.gcevaluators.com

Global Education Group
407 Lincoln Road, Suite 2H
Miami Beach, FL 33139
Phone: (305) 534-8745
Fax: (305) 534-3487
Email: global@globaledu.com
Website: www.globaledu.com

Globe Language Services
319 Broadway
New York, NY 10007
Phone: (212) 227-1994
Fax: (212) 693-1489

Institute for International Credentials Evaluations*
5150 North Maple Avenue, M/S 56
Joyal Administration, Room 211
California State University, Fresno
Fresno, CA 93740-8026
Phone: (559) 278-7622
Fax: (559) 278-7879
Email: iicecsufresno@cvip.net

International Credentialing Associates, Inc.
7245 Bryan Dairy Road
Largo, FL 33777
Phone: (727) 549-8555
Fax: (727) 549-8554
Email: info@icaworld.com
Website: www.icaworld.com

CANADA

International Credential Evaluation Service
4355 Mathissi Place
Burnaby, BC V5G 4S8, Canada
Phone: (604) 431-3402
Fax: (604) 431-3382
Email: icesinfo@ola.bc.ca
Website: www.ola.bc.ca/ices

International Qualifications Assessment Service
Ministry of Learning
Government of Alberta
Fourth Floor, Sterling Place
9940-106 Street
Edmonton, Alberta T5K 2N2, Canada
Phone: (780) 427-2655
Fax: (780) 422-9734
Email: iqas@aecd.gov.ab.ca
Website: www.aecd.gov.ab.ca/iqas

University of Toronto
Comparative Education Service
214 College Street, Room 202
Toronto, ON M5T 2Z9, Canada
Phone: (416) 978-2185

The Credit Bank Service

A lot of people have very complicated educational histories. They may have taken classes at several different universities and colleges, taken some evening or summer school classes, perhaps taken some company-sponsored seminars or some military training classes, and possibly had a whole raft of other informal learning experiences. They may have credits or degrees from schools that have gone out of business or whose records have been destroyed by war or fire. When it comes time to present a cohesive educational past, they may need to assemble dozens of transcripts, certificates, diplomas, job descriptions, and the like, often into a rather large and unwieldy package.

There is, happily, an ideal solution to this problem: the Excelsior College Credit Bank, operated by the enlightened Excelsior College in New York and available to people anywhere in the world.

Excelsior College Credit Bank
Excelsior College
7 Columbia Circle
Albany, NY 12203
Phone: (518) 464-8500
Email: crbank@excelsior.edu
Website: www.excelsiorcollege.edu

The Credit Bank is an evaluation and transcript service for people who wish to consolidate their academic records, perhaps adding credit for nonacademic career and learning experiences (primarily through equivalency examinations). The Credit Bank issues a single widely accepted transcript on which all credit is listed in a simple, straightforward, comprehensible form.

The Credit Bank works like a money bank, except that you deposit academic credits as they are earned, whether through local courses, correspondence courses, equivalency exams, or other methods. Seven basic categories of learning experience can qualify to be "deposited" in a Credit Bank account, and various elements of these seven can be combined.

The Seven Kinds of Deposits That Can Be Made

1. College courses taken either in residence or by distance learning from regionally accredited schools in the United States, or their equivalent in other countries.

2. Scores earned on a wide range of equivalency tests, both civilian and military.

3. Courses taken at military service schools and military occupational specialties that have been evaluated for credit by the American Council on Education.

4. Workplace-based learning experiences, such as company courses, seminars, or in-house training from many large and smaller corporations, evaluated by the ACE or the New York National Program on Noncollegiate Sponsored Instruction.

5. Pilot training licenses and certificates issued by the Federal Aviation Administration.

6. Approved nursing performance examinations.

7. Special assessments of knowledge gained from experience or independent study.

The first six categories have predetermined amounts of credit. The CLEP basic science exam is always worth six semester units, for example. Fluency in Spanish is always worth twenty-four semester units. Xerox Corporation's course in repairing the 9400 copier is always worth two semester units. The U.S. Army course in becoming a bandleader is always worth twelve semester units. And so it goes, for thousands of already-evaluated nonschool learning experiences.

Although the Credit Bank offers an excellent option for many clients, it may not be as useful in the case of two sorts of learning experiences.

The first case is when a person has extensive learning in a field for which no standard test exists. You may be the world's leading expert in Persian military history, or be fluent in five Asian languages, but because there are no readily available tests of these areas, credit may not be given. The Credit Bank used to offer a special assessment service, in which people with such specialized knowledge could come to New York for an oral examination by two or more experts in the field, at the end of which credit was awarded. This option is not listed in current literature, however.

The other sometimes-problematic situation arises when a person has earned credits and/or degrees at schools accredited by agencies other than the regional agencies—such as the recognized but not regional Distance Education and Training Council. If, for instance, a student earns a bachelor's degree at American Military University or the California College for Health Sciences, that degree is not acceptable to Excelsior. Recent research shows that just over half of all regionally accredited schools similarly do not accept DETC-accredited credits, so this does put Excelsior in the majority, but it's still a factor that prospective clients should be aware of.

One more caution: the Credit Bank literature states that foreign academic credentials must be evaluated by a company called Educational Credential Evaluators (ECE) in Wisconsin, except for Israeli credentials, which are to be evaluated by a company called Josef Silny and Associates. As we suggested in the previous chapter on credential and transcript evaluation services (see "Foreign Academic Experience"), the various agencies that provide this service may differ widely in how they evaluate the same credentials. When we pointed out one of these anomalies to Excelsior, it agreed to accept the evaluation of an agency other than the two it lists; unfortunately, they do not do this anymore.

A $200 fee is required to set up a Credit Bank account. A $25 fee is required each time a new "deposit" is made. (These rates are dramatically lower than those charged a few years ago.)

Work that is deemed not credit worthy, for whatever reason, may still be listed on the transcript as "noncredit work." Further, the Credit Bank will only list those traditional courses from other schools that the depositor wishes included. Thus any previous academic failures, low grades, or other embarrassments may be omitted from the Credit Bank report.

Students who enroll in Excelsior College automatically get Credit Bank service and do not need to enroll separately.

One Hundred Accredited Schools That Offer Degrees Entirely or Almost Entirely by Distance Learning

Information on one hundred (actually one hundred and one!) accredited schools follows. We think it is all self-explanatory.

Information in this book, especially the school listings, changes fast: there are always new names, new area codes, new degree programs, and so on. We do our best to stay on top of things, but remember, our readers play a huge role in this ongoing process. Please, whether it's a defunct email address or a hot new distance-learning program, bring it to our attention at

Bears' Guide to College Degrees by Mail and Internet
Ten Speed Press
Post Office Box 7123
Berkeley, CA 94707
bearsguide@degree.net

If a school is listed but you can't get in touch with it, see appendix B: "For More Information on Schools in This Book."

If a school is not listed and you want to know about it, see appendix C: "For Information on Schools Not in This Book."

American College

Degrees and credentials for insurance professionals, employee-benefit professionals, and financial consultants through distance learning plus two one-week residency sessions in Pennsylvania

270 South Bryn Mawr Avenue
Bryn Mawr, PA 19010

WEBSITE www.amercoll.edu
EMAIL studentservices@amercoll.edu
TELEPHONE (610) 526-1490 • (888) AMERCOLL
FAX (610) 526-1465
YEAR ESTABLISHED 1927
OWNERSHIP STATUS Nonprofit, independent
RESIDENCY Two weeks per year
COST Average
DEGREE LEVEL Master's

FIELDS OF STUDY OR SPECIAL INTEREST Professional, mostly financial planning

OTHER INFORMATION American College offers an external Master of Science in financial services through a combination of distance-learning courses and two one-week intensive residency sessions. It also offers the Certified Financial Planner, Chartered Life Underwriter, Chartered Financial Consultant, Registered Health Underwriter, Registered Employee Benefits Counselor, and Life Underwriter Training Council Fellow designation programs. Courses are developed by resident faculty and taken by students around the world. Students study independently or in classes sponsored by local chapters, as well as by other universities and professional associations. Examinations of the Society of Financial Service Professionals are given online whenever possible.

The college operates an office of student services, with counselors available to give advice by phone or email. The purpose is to eliminate some of the problems that arise in distance education by providing a stronger relationship between the student and the college.

The American College accepts up to nine credits in transfer. Most students are fully employed adults. The average student takes two-and-a-half to three years to complete a program.

Antioch University

Student-designed M.A., M.F.A. in writing, and Ph.D. in leadership and professional studies from one of America's higher-education pioneers

800 Livermore Street
Yellow Springs, OH 45387

WEBSITE www.antioch.edu
EMAIL sas@mcgregor.edu
TELEPHONE (937) 769-1800
FAX (937) 769-1805
YEAR ESTABLISHED 1852
OWNERSHIP STATUS Nonprofit, independent
RESIDENCY Short
COST High average
DEGREE LEVEL Master's, doctorate

FIELDS OF STUDY OR SPECIAL INTEREST Individualized, leadership and professional studies, writing

OTHER INFORMATION The individualized M.A. is based around a student-designed, faculty-approved program of study. All U.S. students are required to come to Antioch's Yellow Springs, Ohio, campus for a five-day orientation seminar during the first quarter they're enrolled and to attend a four-day thesis seminar toward the end of their program. European students need only come to Yellow Springs for the thesis seminar; their orientation seminar is held in Germany.

Each student develops an individualized curriculum under the direction of two degree committee members who are recruited by the student and approved by Antioch University. Students then complete the coursework in their own community. Coursework may include independent study, research, practicums, workshops, conferences, tutorials, and traditional courses at other institutions.

A thesis is required. Popular fields include counseling, applied psychology, creative writing, environmental studies, women's studies, education, peace studies, performing arts, visual arts, and organizational development. A maximum of fifteen quarter credits from prior learning experiences can be applied to this program.

The M.F.A. in writing takes place primarily over the Internet, with five required ten-day intensive workshops in Los Angeles.

Antioch also offers a low-residency (four seminars per year) Ph.D. in leadership and professional studies. Students may fulfill residency requirements at any of Antioch's campuses (Los Angeles or Santa Barbara, California; Keene, New Hampshire; Yellow Springs, Ohio; or Seattle, Washington).

Argosy University

Bachelor's, master's, specialist, and doctorate degrees in a range of fields focusing primarily on business, education, and psychology

5250 Seventeenth Street
Sarasota, FL 34235

WEBSITE www.argosyu.edu
TELEPHONE (941) 379-0404 • (800) 331-5995
FAX (941) 379-9464
YEAR ESTABLISHED 1969
OWNERSHIP STATUS Proprietary
RESIDENCY Eight weeks
COST High average
DEGREE LEVEL Bachelor's, master's, doctorate

FIELDS OF STUDY OR SPECIAL INTEREST *See* Other Information

OTHER INFORMATION Argosy University offers a B.S. in business administration and organizational management; M.A.'s in counseling psychology, education, guidance counseling, and mental health counseling; an M.B.A. specializing in finance, health care administration, human resources, international business, international trade, or marketing; the Educational Specialist credential (Ed.S.) in curriculum and instruction, educational leadership, and school counseling; a D.B.A specializing in accounting, information systems, international business, management, or marketing; and Ed.D.'s in counseling psychology, curriculum and instruction, educational leadership, and pastoral community counseling.

For all of these programs, eight weeks of intensive coursework are required at one of Argosy's three campuses (Sarasota, Florida; Tampa, Florida; or Orange, California); these intensive courses are divided into one-week blocks offered during traditional winter, summer, and spring break periods. The university's programs consist of seminars, supervised individual research, and writing. The average student takes two to four years to earn a degree. Many of the students are teachers, school administrators, professors, university administrators, or professionals in the behavioral sciences.

Master's candidates must write a thesis or complete a directed independent study project; doctoral students must write a dissertation.

International students are welcome; a Test of English As a Foreign Language (TOEFL) score of 550 is required for doctorate and Ed.S. candidates, and a score of 500 is required for master's candidates.

Athabasca University

Recognized degrees being earned by more than twenty-two thousand students worldwide through this Canadian school's many sophisticated home study programs

1 University Drive
Athabasca, AB T9S 3A3
Canada

WEBSITE www.athabascau.ca
EMAIL www.askau.ca
TELEPHONE (780) 675-6100 • (800) 788-9041
FAX (780) 675-6145
YEAR ESTABLISHED 1970
OWNERSHIP STATUS Nonprofit, independent
RESIDENCY None
COST Average
DEGREE LEVEL Bachelor's, master's

FIELDS OF STUDY OR SPECIAL INTEREST Administration, arts and sciences, business administration, commerce, computing and information systems, counseling, distance learning, general studies, health studies, integrated studies, nursing

OTHER INFORMATION Athabasca University offers bachelor's degrees in administration, arts, commerce, general studies, nursing (for registered nurses), professional arts (with emphasis on communications or criminal justice), science, and computing and information systems, as well as certificates in a number of fields, from accounting to labor studies to public administration.

Distance-learning master's degrees include an M.A. in integrated studies, an M.B.A. (requiring three short campus visits), a Master of Counseling, a Master of Distance Education, and a Master of Health Studies. Advanced diplomas are offered in community nursing practice, health studies (with emphasis on advanced nursing practice or leadership), and information technology management.

Distance-education courses are offered through sophisticated home-study packages. Students can register any month throughout the year for undergraduate courses. All students are assigned telephone tutors (with toll-free access for students in North America) with whom they can discuss course content. Some courses are also supplemented by radio, television, audio- and videocassettes, computer components, seminars, laboratories, or teleconference sessions. Many courses are now offered electronically, and all university services can be contacted through email.

Auburn University

Almost entirely nonresident master's degrees in business-related and engineering-related fields

Distance Learning and Outreach Technology
Admin and Development
171 South College Street
O. D. Smith Hall
Auburn University, AL 36849-5611

WEBSITE www.auburn.edu/outreach
EMAIL audl@auburn.edu
TELEPHONE (334) 844-3103 • (888) 844-4700
FAX (334) 844-3118
YEAR ESTABLISHED 1856
OWNERSHIP STATUS Nonprofit, state
RESIDENCY One to three days, depending on the program
COST Average
DEGREE LEVEL Master's

FIELDS OF STUDY OR SPECIAL INTEREST Accounting, business administration, computer science, many engineering-related fields

OTHER INFORMATION Auburn offers an almost totally nonresident Master of Accounting, an M.B.A. (with concentrations in finance, health care administration, human resource management, marketing, operations management, management of information systems, and management of technology), and an M.Eng. (in aerospace engineering, chemical engineering, civil and environmental engineering, computer science, industrial engineering, materials science and engineering, or mechanical engineering). Graduate courses are taped in on-campus classrooms and mailed to distance students, who must keep the same pace as resident students. Class assignments and group work are facilitated by Internet interaction.

Faculty members set aside special telephone "office hours" for external students. They generally answer questions over the phone and then restate those questions and the answers in the next videotaped class for the benefit of all students.

Limited credit is available for prior learning. A student must earn at least thirty-five quarter hours, or half of the total hours required for a master's degree, whichever is greater, at Auburn University. A program that requires only forty-five hours of credit is limited to ten quarter hours of transfer credit. No course for which a grade lower than B was earned may be transferred. The program is limited to U.S. and Canadian residents and overseas U.S. military personnel.

The M.B.A. requires three days on campus for group presentation; engineering degrees require one or two days for exams.

Students generally complete the program in two-and-a-half years, but they have up to five years to earn their degree. Career counseling and job placement assistance are available.

Baker College

Associate's, bachelor's, and master's degrees in business administration entirely through online study

1050 West Bristol Road
Flint, MI 48507-5508

WEBSITE www.baker.edu
EMAIL adm-ol@baker.edu
TELEPHONE (810) 766-4242 • (800) 469-4062
FAX (810) 766-4381
YEAR ESTABLISHED 1888
OWNERSHIP STATUS Nonprofit, independent
RESIDENCY None
COST High average
DEGREE LEVEL Associate's, bachelor's, master's

FIELDS OF STUDY OR SPECIAL INTEREST Business administration

OTHER INFORMATION Part of Michigan's largest private, nonprofit college (with thirteen campuses), Baker College offers an Associate of Business Administration, a B.B.A., and an M.B.A. entirely through online study. M.B.A. specializations include accounting, computer information systems, finance, health care management, human resource management, industrial management, international business, leadership studies, and marketing.

Each class takes place in a "virtual classroom," and every student is provided with twenty-four-hour access to "classes," as well as a private mailbox. Interaction between students and instructors occurs through Web-based bulletin boards. Each course takes six weeks to complete. The master's can be completed in eighteen months.

Bellevue University

Undergraduate and graduate programs in business, computing, and criminal justice through an interactive online site

1000 Galvin Road South
Bellevue, NE 68005

WEBSITE www.bellevue.edu
EMAIL online-u@scholars.bellevue.edu (undergraduates) or online-g@scholars.bellevue.edu (graduates)
TELEPHONE (402) 293-2000 • (800) 756-7920
FAX (402) 293-2020
YEAR ESTABLISHED 1965
OWNERSHIP STATUS Nonprofit, independent
RESIDENCY None
COST Average
DEGREE LEVEL Bachelor's, master's

FIELDS OF STUDY OR SPECIAL INTEREST Business administration, business information systems, criminal justice administration, e-business, leadership, management, management information systems, management of human resources

OTHER INFORMATION Bellevue University Online is the distance-education component of this otherwise traditional university. The university is dedicated to providing an online classroom community and support. Internet students can open the online classroom, interact with professors and other students, use online library services, and receive online advising. For a demonstration of this environment, go to the school's Website.

At the undergraduate level, Bellevue offers the B.S. in business information systems, criminal justice administration, e-business, leadership, management, management information systems, and management of human resources.

At the graduate level, an online M.B.A. and an M.A. in leadership are offered, both requiring thirty-six credit hours and about eighteen months of study.

Credit can also be earned through self-study, life-experience assessment, video courses, and examination.

Brigham Young University

Bachelor of General Studies through independent study

315 Harman Building
Provo, UT 84602-1515

WEBSITE www.ce.byu.edu/bgs
EMAIL bgs@byu.edu
TELEPHONE (801) 378-4351 • (888) 298-3137
FAX (801) 378-2270
YEAR ESTABLISHED 1875
OWNERSHIP STATUS Nonprofit, church
RESIDENCY Thirty credit hours
COST High average
DEGREE LEVEL Bachelor's

FIELDS OF STUDY OR SPECIAL INTEREST Independent studies

OTHER INFORMATION Brigham Young University's (BYU's) Bachelor of General Studies is a flexible, external program that uses the same BYU curriculum offered on campus. Up to 90 of the required 120 credits can be earned through independent study. At least 30 hours must be completed on campus at BYU. Although the major is in general studies, the student must have an emphasis on one of eight study areas: American studies, English and American literature, family history, family life, history, management, psychology, or writing.

The 120 semester hours required for graduation are roughly broken down as follows: general education requirements (30–60 hours), general electives (10–40 hours), religious education (14 hours), and emphasis (30 hours). Transfer credits from other accredited colleges and universities are accepted and evaluated upon application.

Although intended primarily for former BYU students who have been away from the university for some time and are not able to return, the program is also available to other qualified students who can meet the thirty-credit BYU campus residency requirement.

The Church of Jesus Christ of Latter-Day Saints owns and operates BYU, but admission is open to all who will abide by BYU's nonsectarian code of honor and receive an annual ecclesiastical endorsement.

Burlington College

Bachelor's degrees in the liberal arts, almost entirely by independent study; formerly Vermont Institute of Community Involvement

95 North Avenue
Burlington, VT 05401

WEBSITE www.burlingtoncollege.edu
EMAIL admissions@burlcol.edu
TELEPHONE (802) 862-9616 • (800) 862-9616
FAX (802) 660-4331
YEAR ESTABLISHED 1972
OWNERSHIP STATUS Nonprofit, independent
RESIDENCY Four days per semester
COST High average
DEGREE LEVEL Bachelor's

FIELDS OF STUDY OR SPECIAL INTEREST Cinema studies, fine arts, individualized major, literature, psychology, social ecology, transpersonal psychology, writing

OTHER INFORMATION Burlington offers a liberal arts–centered B.A. through the school's primarily nonresident Independent Degree Program (IDP). Applicants to the IDP must have already completed forty-five college credits, have "strong writing skills," and be able to spend four days on the Vermont campus at the beginning of each semester.

Those forty-five credits can come from prior traditional college learning, proficiency exams, or experiential learning. In addition to the required units, students can transfer in a maximum of ninety credits. All students must complete a minimum of thirty credits through the program, regardless of prior experience.

Although Burlington's programs are highly individualized, the school specifically encourages applicants whose interests fall in the fields of fine arts, humanities, psychology, transpersonal psychology, or "almost any liberal area(s) of study."

During the four-day residency, the student works with faculty to plan out the semester of independent study, then returns home to carry out the plan, communicating with faculty by telephone, mail, fax, or modem.

The social ecology degree is offered in partnership with the Institute for Social Ecology in Plainfield, Vermont.

Caldwell College

Bachelor's degrees in a wide range of fields, with only one day per semester on campus

9 Ryerson Avenue
Caldwell, NJ 07006-6195

WEBSITE www.caldwell.edu/adult-ed
EMAIL agleason@caldwell.edu
TELEPHONE (973) 618-3385 • (888) 864-9518
FAX (973) 618-3660
YEAR ESTABLISHED 1939
OWNERSHIP STATUS Nonprofit, church
RESIDENCY First Saturday of each semester
COST High average
DEGREE LEVEL Bachelor's

FIELDS OF STUDY OR SPECIAL INTEREST Accounting, art, business administration, communication arts, computer information systems, criminal justice, English, French, history, international business, management, marketing, political science, psychology, religious studies, social studies, sociology, Spanish

OTHER INFORMATION Caldwell's mission statement speaks of "a commitment to assist adult learners in their pursuit of lifelong learning," and the school prides itself on its flexibility in meeting the needs of fully employed students. Bachelor's degrees are offered.

This is primarily an off-campus, independent study program that utilizes tutorial relationships with professors. Students spend one day per semester on campus. (The computer information systems major may also require a few on-campus workshops.) The school estimates that part-time students will take five to seven years to complete the bachelor's degree. Applicants must be twenty-three years of age or older.

Up to seventy-five credits of prior learning can be applied toward the degree; these credits can come from prior schooling, exams (CLEP, DANTES, and other standardized subject examinations), and life experience. Credit is granted for military and nonacademic training through portfolio assessment.

A wide range of student support services is offered, including assistance with financial aid, academic and career counseling, and tutoring in a range of subjects.

California College for Health Sciences

Associate's, bachelor's, and master's degrees in a variety of health and human service disciplines, entirely through distance learning

2423 Hoover Avenue
National City, CA 91950

WEBSITE www.cchs.edu
EMAIL cchsinfo@cchs.edu
TELEPHONE (619) 477-4800 • (800) 221-7374
FAX (619) 477-4360
YEAR ESTABLISHED 1979
OWNERSHIP STATUS Proprietary
RESIDENCY None
COST Average
DEGREE LEVEL Associate's, bachelor's, master's

FIELDS OF STUDY OR SPECIAL INTEREST Health and human services

OTHER INFORMATION With no residency requirements, California College's degree programs in the health and human service disciplines are geared toward adults juggling work, family, and community commitments.

Associate's degrees are available in business, early childhood education, electroencephalographic technology, medical transcription, and respiratory therapy. Bachelor's degrees are available in business, health services management, and respiratory care.

Master's programs in health care administration, health services, and public health, as well as an M.B.A. specializing in health care, are designed particularly for those already employed in a health care setting. The core of each program is a series of correspondence courses. Texts and syllabi are mailed to students, who complete assignments and mail them back. Students are expected to complete one credit per month; thus, a three-credit course is expected to take three months and must normally be completed within six months. Exams can be taken anywhere but must be supervised by an approved proctor.

In addition to the college's many student services, students have instant access to the college's Website twenty-four hours a day and can visit the student services tutorial help center, quickly get feedback from faculty online, and review course catalogs at any time.

California College for Health Sciences is a division of Harcourt Higher Learning; the school's accreditation comes from the DETC.

California State University—Dominguez Hills

A variety of nonresident degrees (including an M.A. in humanities) offered through a state university

Division of Extended Education
1000 East Victoria Street
Carson, CA 90747

WEBSITE www.csudh.edu
EMAIL eereg@csudh.edu
TELEPHONE (310) 243-3741
FAX (310) 516-3971
YEAR ESTABLISHED 1960
OWNERSHIP STATUS Nonprofit, state
RESIDENCY None
COST Low to average
DEGREE LEVEL Bachelor's, master's

FIELDS OF STUDY OR SPECIAL INTEREST Business administration, humanities, negotiation and conflict management, nursing, quality assurance

OTHER INFORMATION Dominguez Hills's Division of Extended Education offers eight nonresident degree programs through online study, correspondence, or a combination of the two.

Both B.S. and M.S. degrees are offered in nursing and quality assurance. These programs can be completed through a mix of online coursework and prior study.

The school also offers an M.A. in the humanities via correspondence, a rare opportunity to earn an accredited, nonresident master's degree in art, history, literature, music, or philosophy. (We are biased. The authors' wife and mother, respectively, Marina Bear, completed her M.A. here in 1985 while living in a remote location and taking care of three young children.) This M.A. requires thirty semester hours of credit.

Other master's degrees offered nonresidentially include an M.B.A., a Master of Public Administration, and an M.A. in behavioral science (focusing on negotiation and conflict management).

Capella University

Online degrees, including doctorates, in business, education, human services, information technology, and psychology—from a school dedicated entirely to adult learners

222 South Ninth Street, Twentieth Floor
Minneapolis, MN 55402-3389

WEBSITE www.capellauniversity.edu
EMAIL info@capella.edu
TELEPHONE (612) 339-8650 • (888) 227-3552
FAX (612) 339-8022
YEAR ESTABLISHED 1993
OWNERSHIP STATUS Proprietary
RESIDENCY None for bachelor's and most master's; short sessions for doctorates
COST High average
DEGREE LEVEL Bachelor's, master's, doctorate

FIELDS OF STUDY OR SPECIAL INTEREST Business, education, human services, information technology, psychology

OTHER INFORMATION Capella University began as the Graduate School of America, a major, well-funded, ambitious effort to create an important nontraditional institution that meets the needs of busy professionals seeking a master's or doctorate degree. It now offers degree programs at all levels, as well as a number of certificates.

Capella University's student body currently comprises more than five thousand learners from all fifty states and more than forty countries. The majority of Capella's learners are working adults who often are balancing family, work, and educational achievement.

Online master's and doctorate programs are offered by the schools of business, education, human services, psychology, and technology. A wide range of specializations is available in each of these fields. All of the doctorate programs require some residency; none of the master's degrees do, except for the more clinically oriented specializations within the M.S. programs in psychology and human services.

The B.S. completion program in information technology is designed for students who have already earned sixty semester hours through another regionally accredited institution; the remaining coursework (including the information technology major) is completed online through Capella. Students may specialize in e-business, project management, or Web application development.

Graduate certificate programs are available in most of the degree specialization areas; an undergraduate certificate in information technology is also available.

Capital University

Bachelor's degrees in an array of fields through a venerable private university

Columbus Center
2199 East Main Street
Columbus, OH 43209-2394

WEBSITE www.capital.edu
EMAIL nneidhar@capital.edu
TELEPHONE (614) 236-6996
FAX (614) 236-6171
YEAR ESTABLISHED 1850
OWNERSHIP STATUS Nonprofit, independent
RESIDENCY None
COST High average
DEGREE LEVEL Bachelor's

FIELDS OF STUDY OR SPECIAL INTEREST Accounting, computer science, criminology, economics, English, general studies, international studies, management, nursing, organizational communications, philosophy, political science, psychology, public relations, religion, social work, sociology

OTHER INFORMATION This program, begun in 1976 under the auspices of the Union for Experimenting Colleges and Universities (now the Union Institute and University), was taken over in 1979 by the venerable Capital University. Bachelor's degrees are available in the previously mentioned fields or, with faculty approval, in an individualized field of the student's choice.

Students must complete 124 semester hours' worth of course requirements, largely through guided independent study and online coursework. Each student must complete a senior project in his or her field showing bachelor's-level abilities and serving as a capstone learning experience. Some transfer credit is accepted, and credit for experiential learning is available through portfolio assessment.

Central Michigan University (CMU)

Off-campus bachelor's, master's, and doctorate degrees in various fields

CMU-DDL
CEL-North
Mount Pleasant, MI 48859

WEBSITE www.ddl.cmich.edu
EMAIL help-ddl@cel.cmich.edu
TELEPHONE (517) 774-3505 • (800) 688-4268
FAX (517) 774-3491
YEAR ESTABLISHED 1892
OWNERSHIP STATUS Nonprofit, state
RESIDENCY Short or none
COST Low average to average, depending on the program
DEGREE LEVEL Bachelor's, master's, doctorate

FIELDS OF STUDY OR SPECIAL INTEREST Administration, audiology, community development, health sciences, industrial administration, nutrition and dietetics

OTHER INFORMATION Central Michigan University offers degrees at all levels through online study and other non-traditional methods.

The B.S. is available in administration, community development, health sciences, or industrial administration. The program requires 124 semester hours of credit; up to 94 hours may consist of prior learning (transfer credit and/or portfolio evaluation). Students may fulfill remaining requirements through residential coursework, courses taken at off-campus sites (CMU will consider setting up a corporate extension site whenever the demand justifies it), online classes, telecourses, or correspondence.

The M.S. programs in administration and in nutrition and dietetics each involve thirty-six semester hours of credit; twenty-one hours must be taken through CMU, but the remaining fifteen can consist of transfer credit and evaluation of prior work. A full-time student can finish the program in about two years.

The online Doctor of Audiology, designed in consultation with Vanderbilt University, is a course-based program designed for professional audiologists. No dissertation is required, and the program can usually be completed in about three years.

Charles Sturt University

Hundreds of rigorous, inexpensive programs offered to students worldwide by Australia's largest distance-learning provider

International Division
Locked Bag 676
Wagga Wagga, NSW 2678
Australia

WEBSITE www.csu.edu.au
EMAIL inquiry@csu.edu.au
TELEPHONE 61 (2) 6933-4334
FAX 61 (2) 6933-2063
YEAR ESTABLISHED 1989
OWNERSHIP STATUS Nonprofit
RESIDENCY None for most programs
COST Low
DEGREE LEVEL Bachelor's, master's, doctorate, law

FIELDS OF STUDY OR SPECIAL INTEREST *See* Other Information

OTHER INFORMATION Charles Sturt is a multicampus university serving the regions of western and southwestern New South Wales and northern Victoria. The major campuses are located in the cities of Albury-Wodonga, Bathurst, Dubbo, and Wagga Wagga.

Bachelor's degree programs are completed through a mix of online and correspondence courses and take an average of six years for a part-time student to complete or three to four years for a full-time student. Offerings include psychology, a variety of agriculture and food-related fields (such as agriculture, ecotourism, environmental agriculture, equine studies, food science, parks and heritage, and viticulture), business (with several specializations, including accounting), education (early childhood, primary, and vocational), health and medicine (complementary medicine, gerontology and aged care, mental health, nursing, prehospital care, and other fields), infor-

mation technology (or spatial information systems), natural science fields (such as analytical chemistry, biotechnology, mathematics, and many others), social sciences (such as emergency management, justice studies, leisure, policing, social work, and other fields), and theology.

Master's degrees tend to involve a series of six to ten modules focusing on a specific area of study within the major; some culminate in a thesis or project, but others do not. The master's is available in a variety of fields related to business (including accounting, applied finance, human resources, and marketing; an M.B.A. is also available with three specializations, including one in global business), education (with numerous specializations), health (including aged services management, asthma education, genetic counseling, medical imaging, medical laboratory science, medical ultrasound, and nursing; a Master of Psychology is also available), religion (both the M.Min. and Th.M.), and social sciences (such as cultural heritage studies, journalism, and organizational communication). Perhaps the widest range of offerings is in the general area of law enforcement, where students may choose from programs in child protection investigations, criminal intelligence, ethics and legal studies, fraud investigations, police negotiation, or other related fields.

CSU also offers the following professional doctorates: the D.B.A (which can be done by coursework alone), the Doctor of Psychology, and the Doctor of Public Policy. In addition, CSU offers research doctorates in the following fields: agricultural economics, agriculture, Australian history, business management, communication and culture, drama, education, environmental and information science, environmental studies, financial and managerial accounting, fine arts, health studies, industry and resource economics, information studies, information technology, justice studies and police studies, professional and applied ethics, psychology, rural social studies, science and technology, social welfare and social policy, social work, and wine and food sciences.

Charter Oak State College

Associate's and bachelor's degrees through any combination of nontraditional credit-earning opportunities; originally known as the Connecticut Board for State Academic Awards and later as Charter Oak College

55 Paul J. Manafort Drive
New Britain, CT 06053-2142

WEBSITE www.charteroak.edu
EMAIL info@charteroak.edu
TELEPHONE (860) 832-3800
FAX (860) 832-3999
YEAR ESTABLISHED 1973
OWNERSHIP STATUS Nonprofit, state
RESIDENCY None
COST Low
DEGREE LEVEL Associate's, bachelor's

FIELDS OF STUDY OR SPECIAL INTEREST Anthropology, applied arts, art history, biology, business, chemistry, child study, communication, computer science studies, criminal justice, economics, engineering studies, fire science technology, French, geography, geology, German, history, human services (specializing in administration, applied behavioral science, or health studies), individualized studies, information systems, information technology, liberal studies, literature, mathematics, music history, music theory, optical business management, organizational management, philosophy, physics, political science, psychology, religious studies, sociology, Spanish, technology studies

OTHER INFORMATION Operated by the Connecticut Board for State Academic Awards, Charter Oak offers associate's and bachelor's degrees in general studies with concentrations in the fields previously mentioned. Charter Oak accepts an unlimited number of transfer credits from other regionally accredited schools, regardless of when they were earned. Students can earn remaining credits to fulfill degree requirements through a variety of means: classroom-based or distance-learning courses taken at any regionally accredited school, military training, standardized college-level examinations such as CLEP or DANTES, portfolio assessment of life experience, and contract learning. With this array of options, including some distance-learning courses and independent study offered through Charter Oak itself, students can complete their degree in a manner that suits their lifestyle.

Enrollment is open to anyone over the age of sixteen who has completed nine college-level credits. Foreign students must show evidence of fluency in English, contract to have foreign credits evaluated by a service chosen by Charter Oak, and earn at least thirty U.S. credits while enrolled.

City University

Nonresident bachelor's and master's degrees through online study or traditional correspondence

335 116th Avenue SE
Bellevue, WA 98004

WEBSITE www.cityu.edu
EMAIL info@cityu.edu
TELEPHONE (425) 637-1010 • (800) 426-5596
FAX (425) 709-5361
YEAR ESTABLISHED 1973
OWNERSHIP STATUS Nonprofit, independent
RESIDENCY None
COST High average
DEGREE LEVEL Bachelor's, master's

FIELDS OF STUDY OR SPECIAL INTEREST *See* Other Information

OTHER INFORMATION Nonresident bachelor's degrees in accounting, business administration, commerce, computer systems (with emphasis on computer programming, Internet working, networking and telecommunications, networking technologies, or student-defined selected studies), e-commerce, general studies, humanities, management, marketing, quantitative studies, and social sciences. Up to 135 of the 180 quarter hours for the bachelor's degree may be transferred in. These credits may come from prior schooling, standardized college-level exams, departmental exams, and military and/or other life-experience learning. Some corporate training may be considered for credit on a case-by-case basis.

City University also offers an M.B.A. (with an emphasis on financial management, information systems, managerial leadership, marketing, or personal financial planning); a Master of Public Administration; M.A.'s in counseling psychology, executive leadership, and management; M.S.'s in computer systems and project management; and M.Ed.'s in curriculum and instruction, educational leadership and principal certification, educational technology, guidance and counseling, and reading and literacy. A Master of Teaching completion program is also available to residents of Washington and California. Up to twelve quarter hours may be transferred into a City University master's program, with faculty approval.

City University also offers a variety of extension programs in ten Washington cities, as well as San Jose, California; Vancouver, British Columbia, Canada; Zurich, Switzerland; Frankfurt, Germany; and two locations in Slovakia.

Some university-sponsored scholarships are available.

Clarkson College

Nonresident bachelor's degrees in health care fields, as well as a low-residency master's degree in nursing

101 South Forty-Second Street
Omaha, NE 68131

WEBSITE www.clarksoncollege.edu
EMAIL admiss@clrkcol.crhsnet.edu
TELEPHONE (402) 552-3041 • (800) 647-5500
FAX (402) 552-6057
YEAR ESTABLISHED 1888
OWNERSHIP STATUS Nonprofit, independent
RESIDENCY None for bachelor's, some for master's
COST High average
DEGREE LEVEL Bachelor's, master's

FIELDS OF STUDY OR SPECIAL INTEREST Business administration (health care related), medical imaging, nursing

OTHER INFORMATION Clarkson offers a B.S. in business administration with a concentration in health service management, entirely through distance-learning methods. The bachelor's degree may be completed entirely through Clarkson or by building on an associate's degree in science or on courses taken for another bachelor's degree.

Bachelor's degree–completion programs are available in medical imaging (for registered technicians) and nursing (for registered nurses). Credit is available for a range of life-experience learning through portfolio evaluation, assessment of military training, and standardized college-level tests. Clarkson's own courses are delivered through a range of media, including the Internet, fax, video- and audiocassettes, and teleconferencing.

In addition, Clarkson offers a distance-learning M.S. in nursing (M.S.N) with a concentration in administration, education, or family nurse practice. A post-master's family nurse practitioner certificate is also available for students who have already earned an M.S.N. Students must come to campus for three weekends total for clinical evaluation and to defend a thesis or complete comprehensive exams (depending on the track chosen).

Students must live at least seventy-five miles from Omaha to qualify for Clarkson's distance-learning programs.

Colorado State University

Graduate programs in scientific, business, education, engineering, and computer fields through Internet study or videocassette-based classes

Division of Educational Outreach
Spruce Hall
Fort Collins, CO 80523-1040

WEBSITE www.learn.colostate.edu
EMAIL questions@learn.colostate.edu
TELEPHONE (970) 491-5288 • (877) 491-4336
FAX (970) 491-7885
YEAR ESTABLISHED 1870
OWNERSHIP STATUS Nonprofit, state
RESIDENCY None for undergraduate and master's programs; varies for doctorates
COST High average
DEGREE LEVEL Undergraduate degree completion, master's and doctorate degrees

FIELDS OF STUDY OR SPECIAL INTEREST Agriculture, business-related fields, computer science, engineering and industrial fields, statistics

OTHER INFORMATION Established in 1967, the Distance Degree Program (formerly called SURGE) was the first video-based graduate education program of its kind in America. Today, courses are delivered through videotape, the Internet, or a combination of the two.

An average of eighty courses are taught at a distance each semester, representing the College of Agricultural Sciences, Applied Human Sciences, Business, Engineering, Natural Sciences, and Veterinary Medicine and Biomedical Sciences. Live Colorado State courses are recorded and sent with available materials to a participating site or directly to a student on videocassette or through Internet streaming video. The student must find a proctor for exams and is not required to return tapes.

Undergraduate programs are oriented to degree completion and build upon an existing associate's or bachelor's degree and professional experience. Bachelor's degrees are available in fire service management and training and social sciences with an emphasis on communication and public affairs. Master's degrees are available in agriculture, business administration, computer science, engineering (agricultural, civil, electrical, environmental, industrial, or mechanical), human resources, industrial hygiene, management, and statistics. Doctorate degrees (which require a variable amount of campus residency) are available in electrical engineering, industrial engineering, mechanical engineering, and systems engineering.

Colorado State's Distance Degree Program is available to residents of the United States and Canada, as well as to overseas U.S. military personnel.

Columbia Union College

Bachelor's degrees in many fields, entirely through correspondence courses

7600 Flower Avenue
Wilkinson Hall, Room 336A
Takoma Park, MD 20912-7796

WEBSITE www.cuc.edu
EMAIL hsi@cuc.edu
TELEPHONE (301) 891-4124 • (800) 835-4212
YEAR ESTABLISHED 1904
OWNERSHIP STATUS Nonprofit, church
RESIDENCY None (except for the respiratory therapy program)
COST High average
DEGREE LEVEL Bachelor's

FIELDS OF STUDY OR SPECIAL INTEREST Business administration, general studies, information systems, psychology, religion, respiratory care, theology

OTHER INFORMATION A maximum of 90 credits (out of 120 required) can be transferred into the program based on prior study. These credits can come from courses taken at or through other schools, standardized examinations, and life-experience evaluation (portfolio credit).

Remaining credits are earned through Columbia Union's correspondence courses. For each course, the student is sent a syllabus, textbook, and assignments. All courses require proctored examinations, which can be taken anywhere. Contact is maintained between students and instructors by mail, phone, and email and through ongoing progress evaluations.

The Seventh-Day Adventist Church owns and operates the school, but nonmembers are welcome. Students may live anywhere in the world, but all work must be done in English.

Columbia University

Nonresidential master's degrees, professional degrees, and certificate programs in many engineering and technology fields from one of the most prestigious schools in the United States

Columbia Video Network
540 Mudd, Mail Code 4719
500 West 120th Street
New York, NY 10027

WEBSITE www.cvn.columbia.edu
EMAIL cvn@cvn.columbia.edu
TELEPHONE (212) 854-6447
FAX (212) 854-2325
YEAR ESTABLISHED 1754
OWNERSHIP STATUS Nonprofit, independent
RESIDENCY None
COST High average to high
DEGREE LEVEL Master's, professional

FIELDS OF STUDY OR SPECIAL INTEREST A good variety of engineering and technology-related fields

OTHER INFORMATION Columbia University offers a solid assortment of degree and certificate programs through the Columbia Video Network (CVN); students watch taped lectures via streaming media through Windows Media Player or on VHS tapes.

Class notes, homework assignments, and syllabi are accessed through the Web. Programs tend to be highly flexible and can generally be tailored to the student's professional and research interests.

M.S. programs are available in computer science, electrical engineering, engineering and management systems, materials science, and mechanical engineering. A thesis for the M.S. program is optional. The M.S. program must be completed within a five-year time frame, with the majority of students completing their degrees within three years.

The Professional Degree (P.D.) is a postgraduate degree designed for students who already hold an appropriate master's degree. Students must complete thirty semester hours of approved coursework beyond the master's to earn this degree. A capstone thesis or project is required only for the P.D. in computer science. Students may major in computer science, electrical engineering, industrial engineering, or mechanical engineering. The P.D. can be expected to involve two to three years of part-time study beyond the master's degree.

The Certificate of Professional Achievement involves twelve semester hours of graduate-level coursework and is available in the following fields: business and technology, civil engineering, computer science, electrical engineering, financial engineering, genomic engineering, industrial engineering and operations research, materials science, and mechanical engineering. Students must complete the program within two years.

De Montfort University

Degrees at all levels from a British university, with minimal time required on campus in England; formerly Leicester Polytechnic

Centre for Independent Study
The Gateway
Leicester LE1 9BH
United Kingdom

WEBSITE www.dmu.ac.uk
EMAIL enquiry@dmu.ac.uk
TELEPHONE 44 (116) 255-1551
FAX 44 (116) 257-7533
YEAR ESTABLISHED 1897
OWNERSHIP STATUS Nonprofit, state
RESIDENCY Short or none
COST Average
DEGREE LEVEL Bachelor's, master's, doctorate, law

FIELDS OF STUDY OR SPECIAL INTEREST *See* Other Information

OTHER INFORMATION De Montfort University offers a variety of programs through independent study, with minimal residence required on the campus in England. Most programs are based on a learning contract, an agreement negotiated between the student and the university. After being accepted into the program, a student is assigned a mentor or supervisor (usually a member of the university staff), who guides the student through the program and assists in the formulation of a research or study proposal. Normally the mentor meets with the student once during each term; the school generally requires foreign (non-U.K.) students to have a local mentor as well as the university mentor.

At the undergraduate level, De Montfort offers B.A. and Honours B.A. programs in business, as well as B.S. and Honours B.S. programs in chemistry, waste and environmental management, and water and environmental management. Undergraduate diplomas are also available in environmental protection and legal practice.

Master's degrees can be earned in clinical pharmacy, conservation science, environmental quality management, health and community development, industrial data modeling, lubricant and hydraulic technology, polymer technology, and law (advanced legal practice, business law, countryside and agriculture law, environmental law, or food law). In lieu of formal examinations, the university conducts continuous assessment through a variety of coursework assignments plus a major project or thesis, which accounts for at least 40 percent of the total.

An oral examination is held in the United Kingdom at the end of each program.

De Montfort may also negotiate a research Ph.D. in fine arts practice on a nonresidential or low-residency basis. Contact the school for details.

Deakin University

Nonresidential and low-residency degrees at all levels from one of Australia's top universities

Deakin International
336 Glenferrie Road
Malvern, Victoria 3144
Australia

WEBSITE www.deakin.edu.au
EMAIL dconnect@deakin.edu.au
TELEPHONE 61 (3) 9244-6100
FAX 61 (3) 9244-5478
YEAR ESTABLISHED 1974
OWNERSHIP STATUS Nonprofit
RESIDENCY Short or none
COST Low average
DEGREE LEVEL Bachelor's, master's, doctorate, law

FIELDS OF STUDY OR SPECIAL INTEREST *See* Other Information

OTHER INFORMATION Deakin University offers programs to students worldwide through Deakin International, its overseas student office. Most instruction takes place online or via correspondence, although the majority of courses also require proctored final examinations (which may be taken anywhere).

Bachelor's degrees are available in international development studies, international relations, journalism, law, and public relations.

Master's degrees are available in aquaculture, commerce (specializing in accounting, economics, law, management information systems, or marketing), computing studies, distance education, education (focusing on curriculum and administration studies or TESOL), environmental engineering, health science (emphasizing human nutrition or nursing), international and community development, international relations, international trade and investment law, law, professional education and training, science and technology studies, and TESOL.

A research-based Doctor of Health Science is available almost completely nonresidentially, and it may be possible to fulfill the residency requirements through one of Deakin's many partner universities located worldwide. Contact the school for details.

Eastern Illinois University

Bachelor of Arts that can be earned completely through distance-learning methods

School of Adult and Continuing Education
600 Lincoln Avenue
Charleston, IL 61920

WEBSITE www.eiu.edu/~adulted
EMAIL cspah@eiu.edu
TELEPHONE (217) 581-2223 • (800) 446-8918
FAX (217) 581-6697
YEAR ESTABLISHED 1895
OWNERSHIP STATUS Nonprofit, state
RESIDENCY None
COST Low average
DEGREE LEVEL Bachelor's

FIELDS OF STUDY OR SPECIAL INTEREST Individualized program of study

OTHER INFORMATION This nontraditional program is designed to allow working adults with family and other responsibilities the chance to complete their degree requirements off campus. No major for the Bachelor of Arts need be declared.

A maximum of 100 of the 120 required credits can be transferred into the program. Those credits can come from prior schooling; correspondence courses; many sorts of life-experience learning, including but not limited to military and job-related training; and ACT, CLEP, DANTES, and departmental exams. The university stresses that skills and knowledge acquired by nonacademic means can be evaluated for academic credit. Applicants without a high school degree or a general equivalency diploma (GED) are considered on a case-by-case basis.

A minimum of twenty credits must be completed through coursework at Eastern Illinois University. These hours may be completed through Internet courses taken from Eastern Illinois University. Students are not required to come to campus to complete degree requirements. All students are required to take EDF 2985, Adults in Transition, within two semesters of being admitted to the program. This course is available via the Internet.

Vocationally oriented coursework completed through a regionally accredited institution may, upon review, be accepted toward meeting degree requirements.

Eastern Oregon University

A number of wholly nonresident undergraduate degrees for students anywhere in the United States or Canada, as well as one low-residency master's program for Oregon residents

Division of Distance Education
One University Boulevard
La Grande, OR 97850-2889

WEBSITE www2.eou.edu/dde
EMAIL dde@eou.edu
TELEPHONE (541) 962-3378 • (800) 544-2195
FAX (541) 962-3627
YEAR ESTABLISHED 1929
OWNERSHIP STATUS Nonprofit, state
RESIDENCY None for associate's or bachelor's, short for master's
COST Low average
DEGREE LEVEL Associate's, bachelor's, master's

FIELDS OF STUDY OR SPECIAL INTEREST Business administration, business economics, fire services administration, liberal studies, philosophy, physical education, politics, teacher education

OTHER INFORMATION Eastern Oregon offers wholly nonresident B.A.'s and B.S.'s in business administration and business economics, fire services administration, liberal studies (with a concentration in virtually anything), philosophy/politics/economics (combined program), and physical education and health. An A.S. in office administration is also available. Credit is given for independent study, cooperative work experience, assessment of prior learning, weekend college, and examination. Coursework is accomplished via correspondence courses (with video- and audiotapes), computer conferencing courses, Web-based courses, and weekend classes.

A Master of Teacher Education degree is available by distance learning to Oregon residents.

The school currently limits itself to working with English-speaking students in the United States and Canada because of the logistics involved in negotiating postage costs, delays, and test proctoring for students in other countries.

Eastern does not charge additional tuition to out-of-state students but does require that these students have full Internet communication capabilities (email and Web access).

Edith Cowan University

Many nonresident degrees from a major university named after the first woman to serve in Australia's parliament; formerly Western Australian College of Advanced Education

International Students Office
Goldsworthy Road
Claremont, WA 6010
Australia

WEBSITE www.cowan.edu.au
EMAIL iso@ecu.edu.au
TELEPHONE 61 (8) 9442-1333
FAX 61 (8) 9383-1786
YEAR ESTABLISHED 1990
OWNERSHIP STATUS Nonprofit, state
RESIDENCY Short or none
COST Low average
DEGREE LEVEL Bachelor's, master's, doctorate

FIELDS OF STUDY OR SPECIAL INTEREST *See* Other Information

OTHER INFORMATION Edith Cowan University offers programs through a variety of distance-learning methods, including guided independent research, correspondence, audiovisual materials, online study, and other appropriate instructional media.

Bachelor's degrees are offered in aboriginal studies, accounting, addiction studies, advertising, applied anthropology and sociology, applied women's studies, children and family studies, disability studies, education (with optional specialization in special education), gerontology, health promotion, human services, indigenous studies, information systems, justice studies, leisure studies, management, marketing, nursing (for registered/licensed nurses), police studies, psychology, and youth work.

Master's degrees are offered in accounting, applied linguistics, business administration with an optional specialization (in health services management, justice administration, or sports management), education with an optional specialization (in any of the fields listed for the Ed.D; see next paragraph), health science (with an optional emphasis on health promotion or occupational safety and health), information science, medicine for practicing physicians (in family medicine, palliative care, or sports medicine), nursing, public health, social science (with an optional emphasis on development studies or leisure studies), and sports management.

Research Ph.D.'s are available in development studies, education, interdisciplinary studies, nursing, and occupational health and safety. An Ed.D. is also available with specialization in one of the following fields: career education, children with special needs, early-childhood studies, educational computing, educational policy and adminis-

trative studies, interactive multimedia, language and literacy, mathematics education, music education, religious education, science education, society and environmental education, teaching and learning, or technology and enterprise education.

Empire State College

Associate's, bachelor's, and master's degrees from a longtime leader in individualized academic programs

Center for Distance Learning
3 Union Avenue
Saratoga Springs, NY 12866-4391

WEBSITE www.esc.edu
EMAIL cdl@esc.edu
TELEPHONE (518) 587-2100 • (800) 847-3000
FAX (518) 587-2660
YEAR ESTABLISHED 1971
OWNERSHIP STATUS Nonprofit, state
RESIDENCY None for associate's or bachelor's, some for master's
COST Low
DEGREE LEVEL Associate's, bachelor's, master's

FIELDS OF STUDY OR SPECIAL INTEREST Accounting, business, criminal justice, emergency management, fire service, health services, human services, interdisciplinary studies, labor studies, management, public affairs

OTHER INFORMATION Part of the State University of New York (SUNY), Empire State College offers totally nonresident associate's and bachelor's degrees and several low-residency master's programs.

Through SUNY's Center for Distance Learning, students can develop an individualized associate's or bachelor's degree program that builds upon their interests, life experiences, needs, and goals in one of the general areas listed here. The primary mode of study is independent study guided by faculty mentors. Credit is given for CLEP, DANTES, and other exams, as well as for college-level learning gained from work and other life experience. (The school provides help in creating a life-experience portfolio for evaluation.) In addition, Empire State offers structured online and correspondence courses.

At the graduate level, Empire State offers an M.B.A. that allows distance learners to test out of almost half of the required credits through assessment of prior knowledge, workplace training, and managerial experience. Remaining credits are earned through Internet courses, independent studies, and two weekend residencies in New York.

Empire State also offers M.A. programs in business and policy studies, labor and policy studies, liberal studies, and social policy. These degrees are earned primarily through independent study, with three weekend residencies per year at one of forty-five locations across New York state.

Excelsior College

Undergraduate and graduate degrees from a pioneer in nontraditional education; formerly Regents College

7 Columbia Circle
Albany, NY 12203-5159

WEBSITE www.excelsiorcollege.edu
EMAIL info@excelsiorcollege.edu
TELEPHONE (518) 464-8500 • (888) 647-2388
FAX (518) 464-8777
YEAR ESTABLISHED 1971
OWNERSHIP STATUS Nonprofit, independent
RESIDENCY None
COST Low to low average
DEGREE LEVEL Associate's, bachelor's, master's

FIELDS OF STUDY OR SPECIAL INTEREST Business, liberal arts, liberal studies, nursing, science, technology

OTHER INFORMATION Among the largest and most popular nonresident degree programs in the United States, Excelsior College has no campus and offers no undergraduate courses of its own; rather, it evaluates work done elsewhere and awards its own degrees to students who have accumulated sufficient credits by a broad variety of means.

Those means include course credit from any regionally accredited college (either correspondence or classroom based); many equivalency exams (CLEP, DANTES, GRE, etc.), including, of course, Excelsior's own nationally recognized exam program (see Equivalency Examinations in the "Ways to Earn Credit" section); and life-experience portfolios as evaluated through partnerships with Ohio University, Charter Oak State College, and Empire State College. Excelsior offers credit for many noncollege learning experiences, including corporate training programs, military training, and professional licenses. (The technology degree program offers credit for Microsoft certifications, for example.) If nonschool learning experiences cannot be assessed easily at a distance or by exam, the student may go to Albany, New York, for an oral examination.

Excelsior offers associate's and bachelor's degrees in the arts, business (including accounting, finance, management, and marketing), nursing, science, and technology (including computer information systems, nuclear engineering, and electronics engineering).

At the graduate level, Excelsior does offer some of its own courses for an M.A. in liberal studies and an M.S. in nursing.

Excelsior was formerly known as Regents College. It began as an integral part of the University of the State of New York, with the university awarding the degrees. In a controversial move in 1998, Regents College purchased its independence and became a private institution. As part of the separation, it was required to change its name—thus the switch from Regents to Excelsior.

Fielding Graduate Institute

A variety of social science–oriented master's and doctorate programs, including the only APA-approved distance-learning Ph.D. in clinical psychology

2112 Santa Barbara Street
Santa Barbara, CA 93105

WEBSITE www.fielding.edu
EMAIL admissions@fielding.edu
TELEPHONE (805) 687-1099 • (800) 340-1099
YEAR ESTABLISHED 1974
OWNERSHIP STATUS Nonprofit, independent
RESIDENCY Short
COST High average
DEGREE LEVEL Master's, doctorate

FIELDS OF STUDY OR SPECIAL INTEREST Clinical psychology, education, human and organizational development, leadership and change, neuropsychology, organizational development, organizational management

OTHER INFORMATION Fielding's flexible, student-centered distributed-learning format is founded on the principles of adult learning. Its competency-based scholar-practitioner model is designed to serve midcareer professionals who must maintain multiple commitments to family, work, and community while earning an advanced degree. An electronic virtual learning community known as the Fielding Electronic Information Exchange (FELIX) is combined with periodic face-to-face events at various locations throughout the United States.

The Ph.D. in clinical psychology is the only distributed-learning Ph.D. program in its field to be approved by the APA. Other programs offered include Ph.D.'s in human and organizational systems and human development, the Ed.D. in educational leadership and change, and the M.A. in organizational management and organizational development. A graduate-level certificate program is also available in neuropsychology. Fielding also offers a special clinical psychology "retooling" program for students who hold a non-APA-approved Ph.D. and would like to fulfill remaining curricular requirements. Fielding's Ph.D. program in media studies is a nonclinical degree designed for individuals in the entertainment, education, health care, government, and corporate areas.

For the psychology and organizational development programs, students must attend a five-day orientation workshop (held each March and September) before enrolling. Students must also attend regional research sessions and academic seminars held throughout the year in various parts of the country.

Coursework is competency based, individualized, and accomplished through academic study, research, and practical field experience and training, according to an approved learning contract.

George Washington University

Nonresidential and low-residency programs in educational technology, health sciences, and project management

GWTV—Distance Learning
801 Twenty-Second Street NW, Suite 350
Washington, DC 20052

WEBSITE www.gwu.edu/~distance
EMAIL webmaster@gwtv.gwu.edu
TELEPHONE (202) 994-8233
FAX (202) 994-5048
YEAR ESTABLISHED 1821
OWNERSHIP STATUS Nonprofit, independent
RESIDENCY Short or none
COST High average
DEGREE LEVEL Bachelor's, master's

FIELDS OF STUDY OR SPECIAL INTEREST Educational technology, health sciences (with four specializations), project management

OTHER INFORMATION George Washington University offers a totally nonresident degree through its Graduate School of Education and Human Development: the M.A. in educational technology. Instruction takes place through a range of nontraditional learning methods, including cable television, the Internet, and videocassettes.

For working professionals in health-related fields, a bachelor's program in health sciences is available with the following specializations: clinical health sciences, clinical management and leadership, clinical research administration, and EMS management. An M.S. in health sciences (specializing in clinical leadership) is also offered for certified physician assistants.

A low-residency M.S. in project management is also available. Students attend a one-week residency in Washington, DC, at the beginning of the program and complete all remaining work via distance learning.

Georgia Institute of Technology

Technology-oriented degrees from a highly respected institution

Center for Distance Learning
Atlanta, GA 30332

WEBSITE www.conted.gatech.edu/distance
EMAIL cdl@conted.gatech.edu
TELEPHONE (404) 894-8572 • (800) 225-4656
FAX (404) 894-8924
YEAR ESTABLISHED 1885
OWNERSHIP STATUS Nonprofit, state
RESIDENCY None
COST High; $594 per credit hour
DEGREE LEVEL Master's

FIELDS OF STUDY OR SPECIAL INTEREST Engineering, health physics

OTHER INFORMATION Georgia Tech is one of the more highly respected schools of its kind in the United States and is consistently ranked as one of the top five engineering schools in the country by *U.S. News & World Report*. The Georgia Tech distance-learning program, started in 1977, is as rigorous as its on-campus counterpart, but the effort has been worth it for the many working professionals who have completed it. Those interested should look into whether their company is one of the many that reimburse tuition for employees.

The school's Internet-based instruction system allows people who are working in technological fields to earn an M.S. in electrical and computer engineering, environmental engineering, health physics, industrial engineering, or mechanical engineering entirely through online courses (or videotaped classes that can be sent anywhere in the United States and, in some cases, to other countries).

Proctored examinations are required and may be taken in a student's local area with a school-approved proctor supervising.

Goddard College

Student-designed bachelor's and master's degrees in a range of innovative fields

123 Pitkin Road
Plainfield, VT 05667 .

WEBSITE www.goddard.edu
EMAIL admissions@goddard.edu
TELEPHONE (802) 454-8311 • (800) 468-4888
FAX (802) 454-8017
YEAR ESTABLISHED 1938
OWNERSHIP STATUS Nonprofit, independent
RESIDENCY Short (twice per year)
COST Average to moderately high, depending on program
DEGREE LEVEL Bachelor's, master's

FIELDS OF STUDY OR SPECIAL INTEREST Individualized, writing

OTHER INFORMATION Goddard has been a pioneer in non-traditional progressive education for more than sixty years. Students design an individualized B.A. or M.A. program in virtually any field based on a faculty-approved learning contract. Or they can follow a predesigned track in business and organizational leadership, education, feminist studies, literature and writing, natural and physical sciences, psychology and counseling, social and cultural studies, or visual and performing arts. An M.F.A. in writing is also available.

The first seven days of each semester are spent in residency, where the work of the coming semester is planned. Students may choose to do the majority of their coursework off campus if they maintain contact by mail every three weeks. Both bachelor's and master's programs require a minimum enrollment: two semesters for the bachelor's, three for the master's.

Students design their own course of study, which may involve research projects, reading assignments, various types of creative projects, a practicum and/or internship, and, in the master's programs, a thesis or other major final project. The exact format is tailored to each student's individual needs. At the end of a planned course of study, the student and mentor meet to translate the student's accomplishments into course equivalents and to assign credits.

Credit is available for examinations and prior learning, although life-experience credit is only awarded at the undergraduate level. Students are expected to devote a minimum of twenty-six hours per week to their studies.

Non-U.S. students are welcome.

Golden Gate University

Many online master's programs and a bachelor's in public administration, delivered entirely over the Internet

536 Mission Street
San Francisco, CA 94105-2968

WEBSITE cybercampus.ggu.edu
EMAIL cybercampus@ggu.edu
TELEPHONE (415) 369-5250 • (888) 874-2923
FAX (415) 227-4502
YEAR ESTABLISHED 1901
RESIDENCY None
COST High average
DEGREE LEVEL Bachelor's, master's

FIELDS OF STUDY OR SPECIAL INTEREST Accounting, business administration, health care administration, finance, financial planning, marketing, public administration, taxation, telecommunications management

OTHER INFORMATION Golden Gate University's CyberCampus delivers degree programs entirely over the Internet. Courses are taught on a more-or-less open-ended (asynchronous) basis through study modules and interactive conferences.

Online master's degree programs are available in the fields listed previously. Each program generally involves two to four years of part-time study.

The Bachelor of Public Administration completion program is designed for students who have already completed two years (fifty-six semester hours) of undergraduate coursework through another institution (traditionally or otherwise); the remaining two years are completed through Golden Gate University.

Undergraduate certificates are available in finance, financial planning, and technology management. Graduate certificates are available in accounting, arts administration, finance, financial planning, health care administration, information systems, marketing, and taxation. Each certificate involves four to six courses (twelve to eighteen semester hours) and takes an average of eighteen months to complete.

Governors State University

Bachelor of Arts tailored to the individual interests of students, earned entirely through distance learning

Board of Governors Program
University Park, IL 60466

WEBSITE www.govst.edu/bog
EMAIL bog@govst.edu
TELEPHONE (708) 534-4092 • (800) 478-8478, ext. 4092
FAX (708) 534-1645
YEAR ESTABLISHED 1969
OWNERSHIP STATUS Nonprofit, state
RESIDENCY None
COST Low average
DEGREE LEVEL Bachelor's

FIELDS OF STUDY OR SPECIAL INTEREST Individualized studies; no major required

OTHER INFORMATION Governors State University (GSU) offers a B.A. in individualized studies through a nontraditional program designed to allow working adults with family and/or career responsibilities the chance to complete their degree requirements off campus. The program offers no majors.

A maximum of 96 of the required 120 credits can be transferred into the program from regionally accredited institutions; up to 80 of these may be lower-level credits. These credits may come from prior schooling, correspondence courses, life-experience learning (including but not limited to military and job-related training), and ACT, CLEP, and DANTES exams. The university stresses that skills and knowledge acquired by nonacademic means can be evaluated for academic credit.

The time to complete this degree depends on the amount of prior credit.

The credits earned at GSU must be completed with a final grade of C or higher. Governors State University offers more than fifty media-based courses in a broad range of fields.

"Guerrilla Marketing" M.B.A.

Jay Conrad Levinson, author of the best-selling marketing series in history, *Guerrilla Marketing,* plus twenty-eight other business books, is developing a distance-learning M.B.A. based on his approach and principles. It will be offered in association with a major regionally accredited university, which will award the degree. At press time, talks were in progress with several schools. If all goes well, the program should launch later in 2003. Since John Bear, best-selling author of this and many other books and long-time friend of Jay Levinson, is involved in the process, we decided to do a little guerrilla marketing of our own and put this "early warning" notice into this book.

WEBSITE www.jayconradlevinson.com
EMAIL guerrillamarketingmba@ursa.net
TELEPHONE (800) 748-6444
FAX (415) 456-2701
YEAR ESTABLISHED 2003
OWNERSHIP STATUS Undecided at press time
RESIDENCY Probably one annual conference with Jay Levinson
COST Undecided at press time
DEGREE LEVEL M.B.A.

FIELDS OF STUDY OR SPECIAL INTEREST The Guerrilla Marketing approach to a marketing-oriented M.B.A.

OTHER INFORMATION These words were written by John Bear in December 2002, just before this book went to press. Things will inevitably be different by the time you are reading them. To find out more, either go to the Website or call, write, fax, or email—with no cost and no obligation, of course.

There are more than twelve hundred M.B.A.'s in the world. In some ways, they are all the same: they cover the basics of a graduate education in business, including marketing, economics, organizational behavior, and so on.

Some M.B.A.'s have a content specialization (e.g., for health care professionals or for engineers). Some have a philosophical approach throughout (e.g., for global businesspeople or for Christians). The Guerrilla Marketing M.B.A. will be the first based on a long-established series of best-selling books with a proven approach to success in the field. It will probably involve one annual conference, with the rest of the study done online or through other distance-learning methods.

Forty-seven fine schools in this book offer degrees in business. Check them out and compare them with this one to make the choice that is best for you. (Note: Whereas Mariah and I have no connection with any other school in this book, I may well have an involvement with this program. I've read *Guerrilla Marketing,* after all.)

Henley Management College

Largely nonresident graduate degrees in business administration and project management, geared to experienced managers, from a respected British school

Greenlands
Henley-on-Thames
Oxfordshire RG9 3AU
United Kingdom

WEBSITE www.henleymc.ac.uk
EMAIL enquiries@henleymc.ac.uk
TELEPHONE 44 (1491) 571-454
FAX 44 (1491) 571-635
YEAR ESTABLISHED 1945
OWNERSHIP STATUS Nonprofit, independent
RESIDENCY Periodic weekends
COST Variable
DEGREE LEVEL Master's, doctorate

FIELDS OF STUDY OR SPECIAL INTEREST Business administration, project management

OTHER INFORMATION Henley bills itself as the oldest independent management college in Europe. It has about seven thousand distance-learning M.B.A. students in some eighty countries.

The M.B.A. program is delivered through a range of methods, including printed correspondence texts and courses prepared by and for the institution, interactive online workshops (using Lotus Notes), and local tutorial support (offered at many locations in the United Kingdom and abroad). The program's stated objective is "to help students to develop their management skills and self-awareness to enable them to gain an in-depth knowledge of how organizations operate and how they can function most effectively to achieve their goals." Three years of relevant managerial experience are required for admission to the course of study. Generally, a residential weekend is required every six months; international students may group their residencies into weeklong blocks. The program takes three years to complete and requires a substantial master's dissertation (thesis of about fifteen thousand words). Specializations in project management and telecommunications are available.

In recent years, Henley has also added a D.B.A. that can be completed in a low-residency mode. Students must attend an annual residential study week at one of the school's centers in the United Kingdom, France, or Singapore.

Heriot-Watt University

International M.B.A. from a respected British university entirely through home study and proctored examinations; no entrance exams or bachelor's degree required for admission; also offers a bachelor's degree in management and a diploma in malting and brewing

M.B.A. Student Services
Pearson Plc
1330 Avenue of the Americas
New York, NY 10019

WEBSITE www.ebsmba.com
EMAIL mbainquiries@nyif.com
TELEPHONE (212) 641-6616 • (800) 622-9661
FAX (800) 843-9288
YEAR ESTABLISHED 1821
OWNERSHIP STATUS Nonprofit, state
RESIDENCY None
COST Average to high average
DEGREE LEVEL Bachelor's, master's

FIELDS OF STUDY OR SPECIAL INTEREST Business administration, malting and brewing, management

OTHER INFORMATION Heriot-Watt offers the only internationally recognized M.B.A. program that explicitly does not require a bachelor's degree and can be done entirely by home study and proctored examinations. With more than eight thousand students in more than 120 countries (including more than four thousand students in the United States and Canada), it is by far the largest M.B.A. program in the world. The only requirement for earning the degree is passing nine rigorous three-hour examinations, one for each of the required nine courses (marketing, economics, accounting, finance, strategic planning, etc.). The exams are given four times per year on hundreds of college campuses worldwide (some one hundred in the United States and Canada).

Students buy the courses one or more at a time, as they are ready for them. The courses consist of looseleaf textbooks (averaging five hundred pages) written by prominent professors specifically for this program. Courses are not interactive, and there are no papers to write, quizzes, other assignments, or theses or capstone projects. Each course averages about 160 hours of study time. The entire M.B.A. can technically be completed in a year, although eighteen to thirty-six months is more common.

A bachelor's degree in management, available through a similar examination-based model, is also available, as is a postgraduate diploma in malting and brewery.

For more information on the malting and brewery program, contact Heriot-Watt directly at Heriot-Watt University, Edinburgh EH14 4AS, Scotland (www.hw.ac.uk).

Heriot-Watt University has a 350-acre campus in Edinburgh, Scotland, with more than ten thousand on-campus students pursuing bachelor's, master's, and doctorate degrees in many scientific, technical, and business fields.

Indiana University

Independent study program, three flexible associate's degree programs, two bachelor's degree programs, seven master's programs, one certificate program, and a high school diploma—all entirely by distance learning

Office of Distributed Education
Indiana University
Bloomington, IN 47405-7101

WEBSITE www.scs.indiana.edu
EMAIL scs@indiana.edu
TELEPHONE (812) 855-2292 • (800) 334-1011
FAX (812) 855-8680
YEAR ESTABLISHED 1912
OWNERSHIP STATUS Nonprofit, state
RESIDENCY None
COST Average
DEGREE LEVEL Associate's, bachelor's, master's, certificate, high school diploma

FIELDS OF STUDY OR SPECIAL INTEREST Adult education, business administration, distance education, general studies, industrial systems technology, labor studies, language education, nursing, therapeutic recreation

OTHER INFORMATION Indiana University (IU) offers the Bachelor of General Studies entirely through nonresidential study and now entirely online. Students in this interdisciplinary program study several fields of knowledge, including the humanities, social studies, natural sciences, and behavioral sciences. It is possible to specialize in one field as a concentration within the general studies major. The average student takes four to six years to complete this degree, but the program can be completed more quickly if the student has substantial prior credit. Of the 120 semester units required for the degree, 90 can be transfer units. The remaining 30 must be earned through Indiana University, usually online or by correspondence. One-quarter of the units earned must be upper division (junior or senior level). Transfer credit is awarded for prior schooling, including correspondence courses, military and other noncollegiate training, a range of proficiency exams, and life-experience learning. Indiana offers a course that assists students in developing a life-experience portfolio. Persons over twenty-one years of age without a high school diploma (or equivalent) may be admitted provided that they can show a fair prospect of success.

A B.S. in labor studies is also available.

An Associate of General Studies is also available entirely through nonresidential study and now entirely online.

An A.S. is also available in histotechnology and in labor studies.

Master's programs are available in adult education, business administration, industrial systems technology, language education, music technology, nursing (B.S. in nursing required), and therapeutic recreation.

An undergraduate certificate in distance education is available.

The IU School of Continuing Studies also offers at a distance a fully accredited diploma through Indiana University High School.

ISIM University

Master's degrees in business administration, information management, and information technology earned entirely over the Internet; formerly the International School of Information Management

Admissions Office
501 South Cherry Street, Suite 350
Denver, CO 80246

WEBSITE www.isim.edu
EMAIL admissions@isim.edu
TELEPHONE (303) 333-4224 • (800) 441-4746
FAX (303) 336-1144
YEAR ESTABLISHED 1987
OWNERSHIP STATUS Proprietary
RESIDENCY None
COST Average
DEGREE LEVEL Master's

FIELDS OF STUDY OR SPECIAL INTEREST Business administration, information management, information technology, project management

OTHER INFORMATION This school offers an M.B.A. and an M.S. in information management and information technology. Education takes place via ISIM's "electronic campus"—instructor-guided learning that uses the school's interactive virtual classroom, accessible through the Internet.

ISIM has won numerous awards from the United States Distance Learning Association (USDLA) for its graduate degree courses.

ISIM requires the following for admission into its programs: a bachelor's degree from an accredited or good state-approved institution, a resumé demonstrating professional accomplishments, a goals statement, transcripts indicating undergraduate and/or postgraduate work, three letters of recommendation, and a $75 application fee.

A maximum of fifteen credits out of a total of thirty-six can be earned through a combination of transfer credits, credit by examination, or prior experience. A capstone project is required of every student. The average student takes two years to complete an ISIM master's program. No financial aid is available. Foreign students are welcome.

ISIM University's accreditation comes from the DETC. ISIM is a division of Cardean University, a subsidiary of UNext.com (a large education corporation).

Jones International University

Distance-learning master's and bachelor's degrees and certificate programs from the first fully online, accredited university

9697 East Mineral Avenue
Englewood, CO 80112

WEBSITE www.jonesinternational.edu
EMAIL info@international.edu
TELEPHONE (303) 784-8045 • (800) 811-5663
FAX (303) 784-8547
YEAR ESTABLISHED 1995
OWNERSHIP STATUS Proprietary
RESIDENCY None
COST Average; $308/graduate credit hour; $250/undergraduate credit hour
DEGREE LEVEL Bachelor's, master's

FIELDS OF STUDY OR SPECIAL INTEREST Administration, business communications, corporate finance, corporate training and knowledge management, designing enterprise databases, e-commerce, enterprise systems, entrepreneurship, global business management, global enterprise management, global leadership and administration, health care management, human resources administration, information technology management, Internet work design and administration, library and resource management, marketing, negotiation and conflict management, Platform Independent Enterprise Programming, project management, research and assessment, technology and design

OTHER INFORMATION Jones International University (JIU) offers all degree programs, certificate programs, and individual courses entirely online. As such, JIU is "The World's University," an international institution that brings together a diverse and rich faculty and student population from more than a hundred countries around the globe, creating a community of highly motivated students, business executives, and instructors. This collection of perspectives, cultures, and experiences offers an unprecedented education and global perspective like no other university, from the convenience and comfort of your own home.

JIU offers fourteen graduate degrees, including M.B.A. (with seven degree specializations), M.Ed. in e-learning (with six degree specializations), and M.A. in business communication. Thirteen bachelor's degrees are also available, including business administration (with seven degree specializations), information technology (with five degree specializations), and business communication. World-class faculty from institutions such as Carnegie Mellon, Tulane, and Oxford Universities design all JIU courses specifically for the Internet.

More than fifty certificate programs in high-demand areas—such as project management, advanced public relations, e-commerce, team strategy, health care administration, quality software management, and e-learning—are also available.

Judson College

Nonresidential bachelor's degrees in a dozen different fields from a venerable southern women's college

Distance Learning Program
Post Office Box 120
302 Bibb Street
Marion, AL 36756

WEBSITE www.judson.edu
EMAIL ateague@future.judson.edu
TELEPHONE (334) 683-5169 • (800) 447-9472
FAX (334) 683-5158
YEAR ESTABLISHED 1838
OWNERSHIP STATUS Nonprofit, church
RESIDENCY None
COST Average
DEGREE LEVEL Bachelor's

FIELDS OF STUDY OR SPECIAL INTEREST Business, criminal justice, education, English, history, music, psychology, religious studies

OTHER INFORMATION This Baptist women's college offers entirely nonresident bachelor's degrees to women and men. Individualized study programs are based on learning contracts between the student and the school. The learning contract details the learning to be accomplished and the means of learning.

Of the 128 hours required for the bachelor's degree, 32 hours must be completed through Judson. Up to 96 hours of credit may be awarded for work done at other regionally accredited schools and for ACE courses. Up to 30 hours of credit may be awarded based on portfolio, challenge exams, and standardized equivalency exams.

Student services include academic advising and assistance with state and federal financial aid procedures.

Foreign students are not eligible for this program.

Kansas State University

Totally nonresident bachelor's and master's programs from a large state university

13 College Court Building
Manhattan, KS 66506-6001

WEBSITE www.dce.ksu.edu
EMAIL info@dce.ksu.edu
TELEPHONE (785) 532-5575 • (800) 622-2578
FAX (785) 532-5637
YEAR ESTABLISHED 1863
OWNERSHIP STATUS Nonprofit, state
RESIDENCY None for most programs; short for some master's programs (*see* Other Information)
COST Average
DEGREE LEVEL Bachelor's, master's

FIELDS OF STUDY OR SPECIAL INTEREST Agribusiness, animal sciences and industry, business, chemical engineering, civil engineering, electrical engineering, engineering management, family financial planning, food science and industry, industrial/organizational psychology, interdisciplinary social science, software engineering

OTHER INFORMATION Kansas State University (KSU) offers four bachelor's degree-completion programs: the B.S. in interdisciplinary social science, the B.S. in animal sciences and industry, the B.S. in food science and industry, and the B.S. in business. Applicants to the social science, food science, or animal science programs must already have earned at least sixty semester hours from an accredited institution that can be applied toward the degree. Applicants to the business degree program must have earned at least forty-five hours of general credit courses and must have a 2.5 grade-point average. Assessment of prior learning is available after acceptance into the program. Credit is awarded for military experience and for a wide range of equivalency examinations. Students must earn at least thirty KSU credits after acceptance into the program. Courses are delivered by videotape, audiocassette, print, CD-ROM, and the Internet. Foreign students are admitted if they live in the United States and provide evidence of English fluency.

The Master in Agribusiness (M.A.B.) takes place largely over the Internet, with two one-week residential sessions required each year. The M.S. in industrial and organizational psychology involves Internet coursework, two two-week summer residencies, and a guided capstone practicum. The M.S. in family financial planning, approved by the Certified Financial Planner Board of Standards, can be completed entirely online; the program generally takes about three years of part-time study. The master's programs in engineering-related fields—engineering management, software engineering, chemical engineering, and civil engineering—can be completed entirely nonresidentially through a mix of online classes and video courses.

For Kansas residents only, an online bachelor's completion program in early-childhood education is also available.

Laurentian University

Nonresident bachelor's degrees and certificate programs in a variety of fields from one of Canada's largest bilingual distance-education providers

Centre for Continuing Education
935 Ramsey Lake Road
Sudbury, Ontario P3E 2C6
Canada

WEBSITE cce.laurentian.ca
EMAIL cce_l@laurentian.ca
TELEPHONE (705) 673-6569
FAX (705) 675-4897
YEAR ESTABLISHED 1913
OWNERSHIP STATUS Nonprofit
RESIDENCY None
COST Average
DEGREE LEVEL Bachelor's

FIELDS OF STUDY OR SPECIAL INTEREST Family life studies and human sexuality, folklore et ethnologie de l'amérique française, français—langue et linguistique, gerontology, history (in development), law and justice (in development), liberal science, Native studies, nursing, psychology, religious studies, social work (Native human services/service social), sociology, women's studies

OTHER INFORMATION Established in 1913 as a Jesuit institution (later adopted by an interdenominational coalition), this bilingual English-French university offers entire bachelor's degree programs, bachelor's completion programs, and certificates through correspondence. In addition to its English-French support, Laurentian maintains a commitment to become a "trilingual" institution through special courses designed for speakers of First Nation languages.

Bachelor's completion programs are available in nursing (for registered nurses).

An Honours Bachelor of Social Work in French and an Honours Bachelor of Social Work with a focus on Native human services is also available via distance education.

Certificate programs are available in family life studies and human sexuality, gerontology, and law and justice.

U.S. and Canadian residents are eligible for Laurentian's distance-learning programs. Residents of other countries may be accepted on a case-by-case basis.

Murdoch University

Nonresidential bachelor's and master's programs offered to students worldwide by a large Australian university

External Studies Unit
90 South Street
Murdoch, WA 6150
Australia

WEBSITE www.murdoch.edu.au
EMAIL p.martin@murdoch.edu.au
TELEPHONE 61 (8) 9360-2498
FAX 61 (8) 9360-6491
YEAR ESTABLISHED 1973
OWNERSHIP STATUS Nonprofit, state
RESIDENCY Short or none
COST Low average
DEGREE LEVEL Bachelor's, master's

FIELDS OF STUDY OR SPECIAL INTEREST *See* Other Information

OTHER INFORMATION Murdoch University offers many bachelor's and master's programs through a mix of correspondence and online classes. Some (most notably engineering and health programs) generally require short on-campus workshop sessions, but these may sometimes be negotiated.

B.A. programs are available in aboriginal and islander studies, Asian studies, communication studies, education, English and comparative literature, general studies, history, philosophy, politics and international relations, theology, and women's studies. B.S. programs are available in applied computational physics, chemistry, computer science, education, environmental science, general studies, mathematics and statistics, mineral science (with emphasis on extractive metallurgy), and sustainable development. A B.Ed. is available with emphasis on primary or secondary education. Bachelor's programs of various other denominations are available in applied science, computer studies, development studies, ecological public health, ecologically sustainable development, economics, education studies (with optional emphasis on teaching languages other than English), engineering, environmental impact assessment, environmental science, policy studies (specializing in city, public, or science and technology policy), professional studies, renewable energy technology, social research and evaluation, sociology, software engineering, telecommunications management, and theology.

Master's programs are available in Asian studies, city policy, development studies, ecological public health, ecologically sustainable development, education with an emphasis on primary or secondary education, environmental science, renewable energy technology, science and technology policy, software engineering, telecommunications management, and veterinary studies (with emphasis on small-animal medicine).

Certificate and diploma programs are also available in some of the fields listed here.

Murray State University

Bachelor of Independent Studies with one day of residency and a master's for registered nurses through satellite programs

Post Office Box 9
Murray, KY 42071

WEBSITE www.mursuky.edu
EMAIL marla.poyner@murraystate.edu
TELEPHONE (270) 762-5322 • (800) 669-7654
FAX (270) 762-3780
YEAR ESTABLISHED 1922
OWNERSHIP STATUS Nonprofit, state
RESIDENCY Minimum of one day for bachelor's program
COST Low average
DEGREE LEVEL Bachelor's, master's

FIELDS OF STUDY OR SPECIAL INTEREST Independent studies, nursing

OTHER INFORMATION Murray State offers a Bachelor of Independent Studies through a range of methods including online study, correspondence, television, contract learning courses, and traditional classes. Some evening and weekend classes are also available. All distance-learning students must attend a daylong seminar, held on Saturdays in April, August, and December. Admission to the program is based on satisfactory completion of the seminar. All students must earn credit in basic skills, humanities, science, social sciences, and electives and complete a senior thesis. The school feels that it is best suited to adults who are already established in their field.

Students must take 32 of the 128 required semester hours through Murray State. Credit is awarded for military and other prior learning (Murray State charges a relatively low fee for portfolio assessment), as well as CLEP, College Board, and DANTES exams. In addition, departmental challenge exams are available in some fields; credit is awarded for the exam, if passed.

Murray State also offers a Master of Science of Nursing for registered nurses who already have a B.S. in nursing. Courses are delivered by remote television to three sites within a hundred-mile radius of the campus.

Financial aid, academic advising, and job placement assistance are offered. Students living outside of the United States are not admitted.

Naropa University

Low-residency master's programs in contemplative education and transpersonal studies, a certificate in ecopsychology, and a variety of online graduate-level courses in creative writing from an established university with a strong progressive history

909 Fourteenth Street
Boulder, CO 80302

WEBSITE www.naropa.edu/distance
EMAIL registrar@ecampus.naropa.edu
TELEPHONE (303) 245-4800 • (800) 603-3117
FAX (303) 245-4819
OWNERSHIP STATUS Nonprofit, independent
RESIDENCY Ten- to fourteen-day annual summer residency
COST Average
DEGREE LEVEL Master's

FIELDS OF STUDY OR SPECIAL INTEREST Buddhist studies, contemplative education, creative writing, ecopsychology, poetry, transpersonal studies

OTHER INFORMATION Naropa University offers an M.A. in contemplative education and an M.A. in transpersonal studies through a low-residency format. Students complete coursework through online study and attend a yearly two-week summer residency in Boulder. Each program can be completed in about three years of serious part-time study.

A certificate in ecopsychology is also available through online study.

At present, students are required to complete a few intensive classes on campus, but all required courses for this program are expected to eventually be available online. A vast number of graduate-level courses are available, and Naropa is developing more degree and certificate programs to become available over the next few semesters. Naropa's Jack Kerouac School of Disembodied Poetics may eventually adapt its M.F.A. program to a low-residency format, and judging by the number of courses in this field now available online, a substantial portion of the program can already be completed off campus. Contact the school for details.

National Technological University

Nonresidential master's programs in many technology-related and management-related fields, earned entirely through online study or televised courses

700 Centre Avenue
Fort Collins, CO 80526

WEBSITE www.ntu.edu
EMAIL admissions@ntu.edu
TELEPHONE (970) 495-6400 • (800) 582-9976
FAX (970) 484-0668
YEAR ESTABLISHED 1984
OWNERSHIP STATUS Nonprofit, independent
RESIDENCY None
COST High average
DEGREE LEVEL Master's

FIELDS OF STUDY OR SPECIAL INTEREST Business administration, chemical engineering, computer engineering, computer science, electrical engineering, engineering management, environmental systems management, individualized major, information systems, international business, management of technology, manufacturing systems engineering, materials science and engineering, mechanical engineering, optical science, project management, software engineering, systems engineering

OTHER INFORMATION National Technological University (NTU) offers a wide range of graduate courses and non-credit courses in technological subjects, transmitted by satellite digital compressed video from forty-six university campuses (in locations from Alaska to Florida) to corporate, government, community, and university work sites. Working professionals and technical managers may take the classes, often in "real time" (as they are being taught on the campuses), with telephone, fax, and email links to the classrooms. NTU offers master's programs using this approach in all of the fields previously listed.

It is now also possible to complete an M.S. in computer engineering, computer science, software engineering, or systems engineering entirely through online study without relying on the telecourse network.

No credit is awarded for any prior learning, traditional or nontraditional.

Geared toward working professionals and managers, all studies are conducted on a part-time basis. The degree is awarded after completion of thirty to forty-five credit hours, depending on the program of study; this generally takes about three years.

Foreign students are admitted.

The New Jersey Institute of Technology

Bachelor's and master's programs entirely through the Internet

Office of eLearning
University Heights, NJ 07102

WEBSITE www.cpe.njit.edu/
EMAIL dl@njit.edu
TELEPHONE (973) 596-3061 • (800) 624-9850
FAX (973) 596-3203
YEAR ESTABLISHED 1881
OWNERSHIP STATUS Nonprofit, state
RESIDENCY None
COST *See* www.cpe.njit.edu/ for details
DEGREE LEVEL Bachelor's, master's

FIELDS OF STUDY OR SPECIAL INTEREST Computer science, engineering management, human-computer interaction, information systems, information technology, professional and technical communication, and more

OTHER INFORMATION The New Jersey Institute of Technology offers bachelor's programs in computer science, human-computer interaction, and information systems.

The New Jersey Institute of Technology offers master's programs in engineering management, information systems, and practice of technical communication. Study takes place through a variety of media, including online conferencing (WEBCT), CD ROM, videocassettes, telephone, fax, and email.

Students must have Internet access. Online students study on the same schedule as on-campus students. Examinations can be administered in remote locations through an approved proctor.

The New Jersey Institute of Technology also offers graduate certificate programs that can be applied directly to the appropriate master's degree upon completion. Most of these programs (including computer networking, enterprise modelling and design, information systems design, information systems implementation, Internet application development, Internet systems engineering, management of technology [partially via eLearning], practice of technical communications, project management, and telecommunications networking) can be completed via eLearning.

A noncredit Webmaster certification program is also available and can be completed entirely through online study. See this link for more information: http://cpe.njit.edu/webmaster/.

Northwood University

Bachelor's in management with several concentrations, with only two three-day seminars required on campus

University College
4000 Whiting Drive
Midland, MI 48640

WEBSITE www.northwood.edu
EMAIL uc@northwood.edu
TELEPHONE (517) 837-4411 • (800) 445-5873
FAX (517) 837-4600
YEAR ESTABLISHED 1959
OWNERSHIP STATUS Nonprofit, independent
RESIDENCY Six days total
COST Average
DEGREE LEVEL Bachelor's

FIELDS OF STUDY OR SPECIAL INTEREST Management (automotive management, computer science, marketing)

OTHER INFORMATION Northwood University is a private, nonprofit, professional school of management. Through its University College, it offers a B.S. in management that can be completed entirely by distance learning. Targeted to students twenty-five years of age and older, the college tailors the program to suit individual student needs. Preapproved specializations are available in automotive management, computer science, and marketing.

The school has campuses and outreach centers in Midland, Michigan; Cedar Hills (Dallas), Texas; and West Palm Beach, Florida. Additional outreach centers are located in Carlsbad, New Mexico; Indianapolis, Indiana; Chicago, Illinois; Lansing, Michigan; Fort Worth, Texas; Louisville, Kentucky; Detroit, Michigan; New Orleans, Louisiana; Flint, Michigan; Selfridge ANG Base, Michigan; and Tampa, Florida.

Students who cannot attend class at any of the outreach centers may complete coursework through correspondence or online study. Two three-day seminars on campus are required, and students must complete an oral/written comprehensive examination.

Nova Southeastern University

Nontraditional bachelor's, master's, and doctorate degrees in a wide range of fields, designed for working adults; formerly Nova University, before merging with Southeastern Medical School (hence the name change)

3301 College Avenue
Fort Lauderdale, FL 33314

WEBSITE www.nova.edu
EMAIL bowersb@nova.edu
TELEPHONE (954) 262-8061 • (800) 338-4723
YEAR ESTABLISHED 1964
OWNERSHIP STATUS Nonprofit, independent
RESIDENCY Varies by program
COST High average
DEGREE LEVEL Bachelor's, master's, doctorate

FIELDS OF STUDY OR SPECIAL INTEREST *See* Other Information

OTHER INFORMATION Class schedules, research requirements, and residency requirements vary by program; in general, required research activities emphasize direct application to the workplace. Nova Southeastern University full-time faculty and part-time faculty from institutions around the country teach the classes.

At the bachelor's level, B.S. completion programs, consisting of online study supplemented with intensive seminars, are available in professional studies and education (with emphasis on early-childhood education, elementary education, exceptional education, middle school science, or secondary education).

At the master's level, most programs require some residency in the form of cluster groups; others (most notably those offered through the School of Computer and Information Sciences) can be completed entirely through online study. Programs are as follows: Master of Accounting, M.B.A. (with an emphasis on finance, management information systems, or marketing), Master of Medical Science, and M.S. degrees in child and youth studies, computer information systems, computer science, computing technology in education, curriculum instruction and technology, dispute resolution, educational media, education with emphasis on teaching in learning, instructional technology and distance education, management and administration of educational programs, management information systems, and social studies education.

Nova Southeastern University also offers some of the more nontraditional doctorate programs ever to achieve regional accreditation. The typical student attends one group meeting each month (generally two or three days in duration), two one-week residential sessions, and three to six practicums, which emphasize direct application of research to the workplace. Total time is generally about three and a half years. A major part of instruction programs is through teleconferencing and Web study. Residential work is available in twenty-three states. Nova will consider offering the program anywhere in the continental United States where a cluster of twenty to twenty-five students can be formed. Ed.D. programs are available in computing technology in education and educational leadership. Ph.D. programs are available in child and youth studies, computer information systems, computer sciences, computing technology in education, dispute resolution, information science, information systems, instructional technology and distance education, occupational therapy, and physical therapy. The degrees of Doctor of Occupational Therapy and Doctor of Physical Therapy are also available.

Ohio University

A quite inexpensive Bachelor of Specialized Studies entirely through home study

External Student Program
Haning Hall 018
Athens, OH 45701

WEBSITE www.cats.ohiou.edu
EMAIL external.student@ohiou.edu
TELEPHONE (740) 593-2150 • (800) 444-2420
FAX (740) 593-0452
YEAR ESTABLISHED 1804
OWNERSHIP STATUS Nonprofit, state
RESIDENCY None
COST Low average
DEGREE LEVEL Bachelor's, master's

FIELDS OF STUDY OR SPECIAL INTEREST Specialized studies, business administration

OTHER INFORMATION This extremely flexible self-paced program leads to a Bachelor of Specialized Studies that can easily be earned entirely through nonresidential study. Students define their own subject areas and design their own interdisciplinary degrees.

Credit toward the degree can come from portfolio assessment of military and other noncollegiate learning experiences, correspondence courses, independent study projects, and CLEP exams. For many correspondence courses, only an examination is required; a grade is given for the course if the examination is passed. These exams can be administered anywhere in the world but must be supervised by an Ohio University–approved proctor. A maximum of 144 quarter hours can be transferred into the program from prior schooling or from the previously mentioned sources; 48 credits must be completed after enrolling at Ohio.

The External Student Program provides an advising service, including some career counseling, and also acts as a liaison in dealing with other university offices.

The university also offers a college program for the incarcerated at unusually low cost.

Foreign students are admitted but must be fluent in English to successfully complete coursework.

An M.B.A. is also available through a mix of extension coursework and weeklong intensive sessions on campus.

Open University

Nonresident degrees at all levels, from one of the largest nontraditional programs in the world

Walton Hall
Milton Keynes MK7 6AA
United Kingdom

WEBSITE www.open.ac.uk
EMAIL general-enquiries@open.ac.uk
TELEPHONE 44 (1908) 274-066
FAX 44 (1908) 653-744
YEAR ESTABLISHED 1969
OWNERSHIP STATUS Nonprofit, state
RESIDENCY None
COST Low average
DEGREE LEVEL Bachelor's, master's, doctorate, law

FIELDS OF STUDY OR SPECIAL INTEREST Arts, business, computing, education, health and social welfare, languages, law, mathematics, social science, technology

OTHER INFORMATION Established in 1969, Open University is now one of the largest distance-education institutions in the world. There are currently 200,000 undergraduate students registered, as well as some 9,000 higher-degree students. Similar ventures around the globe now model themselves on this highly successful educational experiment.

As at other British universities, the earning of credit is based entirely on a combination of achieving a specified level of continuous assessment and passing the course examination. Open University students study in their own homes and on their own schedules, using correspondence texts, audio- and videocassettes, and sometimes online supplementary material. Study can lead to a degree, certificate, or diploma.

Some courses have weeklong summer schools or weekend residential schools, and some require that the applicant be a resident of the United Kingdom or another European country.

Pennsylvania State University

Bachelor's and master's degrees online from a major U.S. university

Department of Distance Education
207 Mitchell Building
University Park, PA 16802-3601

WEBSITE www.worldcampus.psu.edu
EMAIL psuwd@psu.edu
TELEPHONE (814) 865-5403 • (800) 252-3592
FAX (814) 865-3290
YEAR ESTABLISHED 1855
OWNERSHIP STATUS State
RESIDENCY None
COST Average
DEGREE LEVEL Bachelor's, master's

FIELDS OF STUDY OR SPECIAL INTEREST Adult education, business administration (iM.B.A.), letters, arts, and sciences (B.A.), organizational leadership (B.A.)

OTHER INFORMATION The letters, arts, and sciences B.A.–completion program (123 credits) includes 45 credits of general education courses and 18 credits of elective courses. The program offers an option for location-bound students who are looking for a multidisciplinary liberal arts degree. Penn State does not offer credit for life experience but does offer credit by examination for some courses.

Penn State's thirty-three-credit master's degree in adult education, offered by the College of Education, is designed to increase the knowledge and competence of those who work with adult learners. Possible career opportunities are adult basic education-adult literacy; ABE and GED; English as a second language (ESL); and work in social agencies, government, corrections, school systems, and corporations.

Developed as an intercollege effort, the iM.B.A. program draws on the expertise of Penn State Erie, The Behrend College; Penn State Great Valley School of Graduate Professional Studies; Penn State Harrisburg; and the Smeal College of Business Administration at University Park.

The iM.B.A. curriculum is developed to serve primarily the interests of nonbusiness undergraduates. The curriculum provides an innovative integration of four core business areas and six business themes. The core business areas are domestic and global economic environments, human behavior in organizations, creation and distribution of goods and services, financial reporting, analysis, and markets. The business themes are leadership, strategic planning, customer and market, information and analysis, human resources, and process management.

The iM.B.A. program spans eight continuous terms and is composed of twenty-two online courses, totaling forty-eight credits. Program completion takes twenty-four months. Two one-week on-campus experiences enhance the integrative focus of the curriculum.

Courses are taught using a blend of Web technology, print, and other media to provide an effective balance of flexibility and interaction.

Prescott College

Low-residency bachelor's and master's programs in many fields through individualized, mentored study

220 Grove Avenue
Prescott, AZ 86301

WEBSITE www.prescott.edu
EMAIL adpadmissions@prescott.edu
TELEPHONE (928) 778-2090 • (800) 628-6364
FAX (928) 776-5242
YEAR ESTABLISHED 1966
OWNERSHIP STATUS Nonprofit, independent
RESIDENCY Occasional weekends
COST High average
DEGREE LEVEL Bachelor's, master's

FIELDS OF STUDY OR SPECIAL INTEREST Adventure education, counseling and psychology, education, environmental studies, human services, humanities, liberal arts, management

OTHER INFORMATION Prescott College's external undergraduate program offers a student-centered, independent study format, using instructors from the student's home community. Students normally take two courses every three months, meeting weekly with local mentors (which Prescott helps locate) wherever they live.

Students must come to the college for a three-day weekend orientation at the beginning of their program and for an additional liberal arts seminar, also held over a three-day weekend. The B.A. is available in counseling, human services, liberal arts, management, and teacher education. Entering students normally have at least thirty semester hours (or forty-five quarter hours) of prior college work. Credit for life experience can be awarded through the writing of a life-experience portfolio; credit can also be earned through CLEP exams.

Student-directed master's programs are offered in adventure education, counseling and psychology, education, environmental studies, and humanities. Two weekend residencies are required each term, providing students with the opportunity to meet with advisers and faculty members, present works in progress, and attend workshops.

The school's Center for Indian Bilingual Teacher Education serves the needs of Native American students.

Queens University

Bachelor of Arts in quite a few fields through a major Canadian university, based entirely on correspondence and online study

68 University Avenue
F100 Mackintosh-Corry Hall
Kingston, ON K7L 3N6
Canada

WEBSITE www.queensu.ca/cds
EMAIL cds@post.queensu.ca
TELEPHONE (613) 533-2470
FAX (613) 533-6805
YEAR ESTABLISHED 1841
OWNERSHIP STATUS Nonprofit, state
RESIDENCY None
COST Low average
DEGREE LEVEL Bachelor's

FIELDS OF STUDY OR SPECIAL INTEREST Art history, biochemistry, biology, business German, chemistry, classical studies, computing and information sciences, developmental studies, drama, economics, English, film studies, French studies, geography, geological sciences, German, Greek, health studies, history, human services counseling, Italian, Jewish studies, Latin, life sciences, mathematics, music, philosophy, physics, political studies, psychology, religious studies, sociology, Spanish, statistics, women's studies

OTHER INFORMATION Queens University is one of the most respected Canadian universities. The school offers students in Canada and other countries an opportunity to complete a program leading to a bachelor's degree by taking spring, summer, correspondence, online, and evening courses exclusively.

In each academic session, a wide selection of correspondence courses is offered. By enrolling in a combination of correspondence, online, and on-campus courses, it is possible to complete the requirements for a degree. You may also take courses either on campus or via correspondence from another university for credit toward your Queens degree. Contact the school for details.

Regent University

Master's and doctorate programs through online study and short residencies

Distance Education Program
1000 Regent University Drive
Virginia Beach, VA 23464-9800

WEBSITE www.regent.edu
EMAIL admissions@regent.edu
TELEPHONE (757) 226-4127 • (800) 373-5504
FAX (757) 226-4381
YEAR ESTABLISHED 1977
OWNERSHIP STATUS Nonprofit, independent
RESIDENCY Short or none
COST High average
DEGREE LEVEL Master's, doctorate, law

FIELDS OF STUDY OR SPECIAL INTEREST Business administration, communication, computer-mediated communication, education, educational leadership and Christian schools, journalism, management, organizational leadership, political management, public administration, public policy

OTHER INFORMATION Founded by the Reverend Pat Robertson as CBN (Christian Broadcasting Network) University in 1977, Regent University offers an array of low-residency graduate programs conducted almost entirely through online study. The university integrates traditional Judeo-Christian ethical principles in the teaching of each course. Student support services available to nontraditional students include academic advising, career counseling, financial aid, tutoring, and job placement assistance.

Regent School of Business offers an M.B.A. and an M.A. in management, largely through online study, with a two-and-a-half-day residency required at the beginning of each term.

Regent's School of Government offers M.S. programs in public policy, political management, and public administration, conducted largely online and supplemented by annual two-week residencies.

M.A. programs in communication studies (with optional emphasis on computer-mediated communication), journalism, and organizational leadership can be completed entirely through online study with no required annual residency sessions. M.A. programs in biblical studies and practical theology begin with a nine-day colloquium, and the remaining work takes place online.

M.Ed. programs are also available in Christian school administration and educational leadership. Students complete requirements online during the school year, then attend Regent for annual summer residency sessions.

Ph.D. programs in communication and organizational leadership are conducted largely online, supplemented by annual two- to four-week summer residencies.

Regis University

Several bachelor's and master's programs entirely through online study, including an M.S. in computer information systems that was designed in consultation with Sun Microsystems, offered at this Jesuit school

3333 Regis Boulevard
Denver, CO 80221-1099

WEBSITE www.regis.edu
EMAIL online_ed@regis.edu
TELEPHONE (303) 458-4900 • (800) 944-7667
YEAR ESTABLISHED 1877
OWNERSHIP STATUS Nonprofit, church
RESIDENCY None
COST High average
DEGREE LEVEL Bachelor's, master's

FIELDS OF STUDY OR SPECIAL INTEREST Business administration, computer information systems, insurance, nonprofit management

OTHER INFORMATION Regis University's School for Professional Studies is a nationally acclaimed adult learning program that serves more than eleven thousand students. The Regis M.B.A., probably the most well known of its distance-learning programs, can be completed entirely online.

The Regis B.S. completion program in business management (with emphasis on insurance) is designed for students who have already completed a substantial amount of college work; all degree requirements can be completed through online study.

The M.S. in computer information systems, designed in consultation with Sun Microsystems, addresses cutting-edge issues relevant to the information technology industry. Students may choose to specialize in databases, networking, or object-oriented technologies. The program is completed entirely through online study.

The Master of Nonprofit Management is tailored specifically to those who work for, within, or on behalf of nonprofit organizations. The program may be completed by online study or, if the student prefers, through video-based coursework.

Rensselaer Polytechnic Institute

Master's and certificate programs in many business, engineering, and technology fields, available online and through video-based study

Professional and Distance Education
CII Suite 4011
110 Eighth Street
Troy, NY 12180-3590

WEBSITE www.rsvp.rpi.edu
EMAIL rsvp@rpi.edu
TELEPHONE (518) 276-8351
FAX (518) 276-8026
YEAR ESTABLISHED 1824
OWNERSHIP STATUS Nonprofit, independent
RESIDENCY None
COST High average
DEGREE LEVEL Master's

FIELDS OF STUDY OR SPECIAL INTEREST Business, engineering, technology

OTHER INFORMATION Rensselaer Polytechnic Institute offers a number of degree programs and certificates by distance learning through the RSVP program. Students may complete degree requirements online, through video courses on an individual basis, or through two-way streaming video at corporate sites.

Master's degrees are available in business administration (M.B.A.), computer science, computer and systems engineering, electrical engineering (with emphasis on microelectronics), electric power engineering, management of technology, manufacturing systems engineering, microelectronics manufacturing engineering, industrial and management engineering (with emphasis on quality engineering or service systems), information technology, management, mechanical engineering, and technical communication. Each master's program involves three to five years of part-time study.

Graduate-level certificate programs are available in bioinformatics, computer graphics and data visualization, computer networks, computer science, database systems design, electric power engineering, graphical user interfaces, human-computer interaction, management and technology, manufacturing systems engineering, mechanical engineering, microelectronics manufacturing engineering, microelectronics technology and design, quality and reliability, service systems, software engineering, and technical program management for commercial business. Each certificate program involves four courses; an average student can complete such a program in two years of part-time study.

Rochester Institute of Technology

Nonresident bachelor's, master's, and certificate programs in professional, technical, and health-related fields from a 172-year-old school

91 Lomb Memorial Drive
Rochester, NY 14623-5603

WEBSITE online.rit.edu
EMAIL online@rit.edu
TELEPHONE (585) 475-5089 • (800) 225-5748
FAX (585) 475-5077
YEAR ESTABLISHED 1829
OWNERSHIP STATUS Nonprofit, independent
RESIDENCY None or short
COST High average
DEGREE LEVEL Bachelor's, master's

FIELDS OF STUDY OR SPECIAL INTEREST *See* Other Information

OTHER INFORMATION The Rochester Institute of Technology offers more than thirty bachelor's, master's, and certificate programs through online study. Two degree programs among the many described here require short laboratory residencies, but the rest can be completed with no residency at all.

The B.S. in applied arts and sciences is designed primarily for students who already hold an associate's degree or the equivalent number of credits. Credit can be awarded for military and other noncollegiate training and for a number of standardized proficiency examinations. Students choose a specialization from the following list: applied computing, digital imaging and publishing, disaster and emergency management, e-business, environmental management and technology, health systems administration, management, manufacturing management technology, mechanical technology, organizational change, quality management, safety and health technology, structural design, technical communication, or telecommunications.

Other B.S. programs are available in electrical and mechanical engineering technology (requiring some short on-campus laboratory residencies), environmental management and technology, safety technology, and telecommunications engineering technology.

M.S. programs are available in applied statistics, cross-disciplinary professional studies (individualized program), environmental health and safety management (requiring short on-campus laboratory sessions), health systems administration, imaging science, information technology, microelectronics manufacturing engineering, and software development and management. Up to twelve semester hours may be transferred into a Rochester Institute of Technology graduate program.

Undergraduate and graduate certificates are available in many of the same fields.

Applications for admission can be processed online. Financial aid is available at the graduate level; standard state and federal programs, as well as a number of payment options, are open to undergraduates.

International students are welcome, although demonstrated proficiency in English (minimum TOEFL score of 550) is required.

Saint Joseph's College of Maine

Associate's, bachelor's, and master's degrees in a wide range of fields through a distance program; most programs require participation in a two-week summer program on campus

Graduate and Professional Studies
278 Whites Bridge Road
Standish, ME 04084-5263

WEBSITE www.sjcme.edu/gps
EMAIL admiss@sjcme.edu
TELEPHONE (800) 752-4723 (U.S. and Canada) • (207) 892-7841 (International)
FAX (800) 752-4723
YEAR ESTABLISHED 1912
OWNERSHIP STATUS Nonprofit, church
RESIDENCY Two weeks for most degree programs
COST Average
DEGREE LEVEL Associate's, bachelor's, master's

FIELDS OF STUDY OR SPECIAL INTEREST Business, criminal justice, education, health care, health service administration, human services, information technology management, liberal studies, long-term care administration, management, nursing, pastoral studies

OTHER INFORMATION Saint Joseph's offers the following programs: A.S.'s in business, criminal justice, education, general studies, human services, management, and psychology; B.S.'s in business, criminal justice, general studies, health care administration, long-term care administration, and nursing; B.A. in liberal studies; a Master of Health Service Administration (with specializations in international health care, long-term care, and practice management); an M.A. (with specializations in pastoral ministry, pastoral studies, and pastoral theology); and M.S.'s in education (with specializations for corporate/school educators and health care educators) and nursing (with specializations in nursing administration, nursing education, and parish nursing).

All programs are offered through faculty-directed independent study and are available online and in print. Most students in degree programs must attend a two-week summer program at some point during their course of study. (Active military personnel are exempt from all on-site requirements.) The average undergraduate degree takes two to five years, and the average graduate program takes three to five. The average Saint Joseph's undergraduate distance-education student is in his or her forties. Foreign students are welcome in both graduate and undergraduate programs, provided they can show proof of English-language proficiency as evidenced by TOEFL scores.

Saint Mary-of-the-Woods College

For women only, low-residency bachelor's degrees in twenty-four fields; for students of both sexes, innovative master's programs in art therapy, earth literacy, music therapy, and pastoral theology

Saint Mary-of-the-Woods, IN 47876

WEBSITE www.smwc.edu
EMAIL smwcadms@smwc.edu
TELEPHONE (812) 535-5106 • (800) 926-7692
FAX (812) 535-4900
YEAR ESTABLISHED 1840
OWNERSHIP STATUS Nonprofit
RESIDENCY Short
COST Low average
DEGREE LEVEL Bachelor's, master's

FIELDS OF STUDY OR SPECIAL INTEREST *See* Other Information

OTHER INFORMATION Saint Mary-of-the-Woods offers bachelor's degrees for women, with majors available in the following fields: accounting, business administration, computer information systems, digital media communication, e-commerce, English, gerontology, history/prelaw, human resource management, human services, humanities, journalism, kindergarten-elementary education, marketing, mathematics, not-for-profit, paralegal studies, preschool–grade 3 education, professional writing, psychology, secondary education (with emphasis on English, math, special education, or social studies), social science/history, and theology. Education majors must live within two hundred miles of the campus.

The undergraduate must attend a two-and-a-half-day seminar at the beginning of the program and a half-day seminar at the start of each semester. All other work is done by independent study; faculty guidance is provided via mail, email, and phone. Course assignments are usually submitted online or by mail.

Prior learning credit is awarded to those with college-level knowledge acquired by means other than classroom instruction. This knowledge is evaluated through proficiency examinations and portfolio assessment. Up to 95 of the 125 semester hours required for the bachelor's degree may be transferred in, but at least half of the courses in the student's major must be taken through the college.

Students of both sexes are eligible for M.A. programs in art therapy, earth literacy, music therapy, and pastoral theology. Students must attend an on-campus workshop at the beginning of each semester. A limited number of transfer credits are accepted for these programs, as assessed on a student-by-student basis.

Salve Regina University

Bachelor's and master's degrees, almost entirely by distance learning, with only five days required on campus

100 Ochre Point Avenue
Newport, RI 02840-4192

WEBSITE www.salve.edu
EMAIL sruadmis@salve.edu
TELEPHONE (401) 847-6650 • (800) 637-0002
FAX (401) 341-2938
YEAR ESTABLISHED 1934
OWNERSHIP STATUS Nonprofit, independent
RESIDENCY Five days
COST High
DEGREE LEVEL Bachelor's, master's

FIELDS OF STUDY OR SPECIAL INTEREST Business, human development, international relations, liberal studies, management, nursing

OTHER INFORMATION Salve Regina University offers bachelor's degrees in business, liberal studies, and nursing, as well as master's degrees in business administration, human development, international relations, and management. Certificates are available in correctional administration, management, and information systems science.

All students must attend an intensive five-day session in early June at some point during the program. All work must be completed within five years of enrollment, but most students take less time to finish.

Instruction is by online classes, correspondence courses, and guided independent study, supported by regular mail, email, and telephone contact with faculty. There is no thesis, but all students must complete a brief "exit review" paper that details what they have achieved in the program.

The bachelor's is a degree-completion program. An entering student must have at least 45 accredited credits already under the belt. Students then complete at least 15 four-credit courses through Salve Regina for a total of 120 required credits.

At the master's level, graduates of U.S. military colleges may transfer in a maximum of eighteen earned credits toward a degree; CPCUs may transfer twelve earned credits toward the management degree. Other students may transfer up to six of the thirty-six required credits into the program from prior collegiate schooling or ACE military recommendations.

Salve Regina boasts students from almost a dozen countries; all foreign students must take the TOEFL and submit a statement of finances.

Saybrook Graduate School

Master's and doctorate degrees in human science, organizational systems inquiry, and psychology through distance learning, with two weeks per year in San Francisco

450 Pacific, Third Floor
San Francisco, CA 94133

WEBSITE www.saybrook.edu
EMAIL saybrook@saybrook.edu
TELEPHONE (415) 433-9200 • (800) 825-4480
FAX (415) 433-9271
YEAR ESTABLISHED 1971
OWNERSHIP STATUS Nonprofit, independent
RESIDENCY Short yearly residencies
COST High
DEGREE LEVEL Master's, doctorate

FIELDS OF STUDY OR SPECIAL INTEREST Human science, organizational systems inquiry, psychology

OTHER INFORMATION Founded in 1971, Saybrook is an accredited graduate school and research center designed to focus on the study of psychology and human science with a distinctive emphasis on humanistic values. Saybrook offers its academic programs through a distance-learning format that allows midcareer professionals and others who may have difficulty attending classes in traditional settings to pursue their careers while earning a master's or doctorate degree.

Students are mentored through a rigorous program of disciplined, independent academic study. Relationships with faculty tend to be highly personalized and interactive.

M.A. and Ph.D. programs are available in human science, organizational systems inquiry, and psychology. Students must attend two residential conferences in the San Francisco Bay Area each academic year.

Students may begin the program in September or March. A financial aid application must be completed at least three months before the proposed enrollment date if a student wishes to receive aid.

Skidmore College

Individualized bachelor's and master's degrees offered through the University without Walls (nonresident) program, founded in 1971; almost entirely by home study

University without Walls
815 North Broadway
Saratoga Springs, NY 12866-1632

WEBSITE www.skidmore.edu
EMAIL uww@skidmore.edu
TELEPHONE (518) 580-5450 • (866) 310-6444
FAX (518) 580-5449
YEAR ESTABLISHED 1911
OWNERSHIP STATUS Nonprofit, independent
RESIDENCY Three days for the bachelor's, eight days for the master's
COST Low average
DEGREE LEVEL Bachelor's, master's

FIELDS OF STUDY OR SPECIAL INTEREST Individualized major, liberal studies

OTHER INFORMATION Skidmore is one of the pioneers of the nontraditional movement, having offered a University without Walls (nonresident) program since 1971. It is possible to earn its B.A. or B.S. with a total of three days on campus: one for an admissions interview, a second for advising and planning, and a third to present a degree plan to a faculty committee. In addition to fulfilling all other requirements in the degree plan, each student completes a final project demonstrating competence in his or her field.

The B.A. and B.S. are based on a student-defined, faculty-approved plan of study. Preapproved majors are available in American studies, anthropology, art history, arts management, Asian studies, biology, business, chemistry, classics, communications, computer science, dance, economics, English, environmental studies, French, geology, German, government, history, human behavior, Latin American studies, mathematics, music, organizational behavior, philosophy, physics, political science, psychology, religion, sociology, Spanish, studio art, theater, and women's studies.

In 1992, Skidmore launched a Master of Arts in liberal studies, modeled on its highly successful undergraduate program. It is possible to earn this degree with a total of eight days on campus: one day for an admissions interview, six days for an entrance seminar, and one day to present an academic plan to a faculty committee. Coursework consists of the three-credit entrance seminar, twenty-four credit hours of integrative study, and a three-credit written final project/thesis. Students work with two faculty advisers to develop a highly individualized course of study that may draw on many local resources and life experiences.

Southwestern Adventist University

Bachelor's degrees in twenty different fields, with only six days required on campus

Adult Degree Program
100 Hillcrest Drive
Keene, TX 76059

WEBSITE www.swau.edu
EMAIL adp@swau.edu
TELEPHONE (817) 645-3921 • (800) 433-2240
FAX (817) 556-4742
YEAR ESTABLISHED 1893
OWNERSHIP STATUS Nonprofit, church
RESIDENCY Six days at the beginning of the program
COST Average
DEGREE LEVEL Bachelor's

FIELDS OF STUDY OR SPECIAL INTEREST Accounting, broadcasting, business administration, computer information systems, computer science, corporate communication, criminal justice, elementary education, English, history, international affairs, journalism, management, mathematics, office administration, office technology, psychology, religion, secondary education, social science

OTHER INFORMATION Southwestern Adventist offers bachelor's degrees in the previously noted fields through its Adult Degree Program (ADP).

Students must attend a six-day admissions seminar (in March, June, or October); following this seminar, virtually all of the degree work can be completed at a distance through independent study. Coursework options may include Web-based classes, audio- and videocassettes, phone and mail instruction, independent study projects, study guides, and supervised fieldwork.

Credit can be transferred from prior approved schooling and is also awarded for proficiency exams (CLEP, DANTES, and other approved examination standards), as well as for military or other nonacademic learning. A maximum of 96 of the 128 semester hours required for this degree may come from these sources.

ADP students pay 20 percent less than on-campus students do. The average ADP student takes four to seven years to complete the program. Student services available include help with federal financial aid programs, academic counseling, and career advice.

Foreign students are welcome; those from non-English-speaking countries must score at least 550 on the TOEFL.

Although the Seventh-Day Adventist Church operates this school, it is open to all qualified applicants. Applicants must be at least twenty-two years old, and preference is given to those who have at least some college experience.

Stanford University

An online master's degree in electrical engineering from one of the most prominent research universities in the United States

Stanford Center for Professional Development
496 Lomita Mall, Durand Building, Room 401
Stanford, CA 94305-4036

WEBSITE www.stanford-online.stanford.edu
EMAIL sitn-registration@stanford.edu
TELEPHONE (650) 725-3016
FAX (650) 725-2868
YEAR ESTABLISHED 1885
OWNERSHIP STATUS Nonprofit, independent
RESIDENCY None
COST High average
DEGREE LEVEL Master's

FIELDS OF STUDY OR SPECIAL INTEREST Electrical engineering with emphasis on telecommunications, for individuals; computer science, for corporate subscribers

OTHER INFORMATION In fall 1998, Stanford became the first major U.S. research university to offer a master's degree entirely through Internet study: an M.S. in electrical engineering with emphasis on telecommunications. A variety of nondegree graduate courses can also be completed online and transferred into a participating degree program at another school.

The program involves fifteen courses (forty-five semester hours) in fields such as analog integrated circuit design, Fourier optics, wireless communications, computer systems, fiber optics, digital filtering, VLSI, and logic design. The program takes approximately three to five years to complete through part-time study.

An M.S. in computer science is also available to corporate and government subscribers through on-site delivery methods such as two-way video, supplemented when appropriate by Stanford's many available online courses in the field.

Stephens College

Bachelor's and master's degrees, with six to seven days required on campus

School of Graduate and Continuing Education
Campus Box 2083
Columbia, MO 65215

WEBSITE www.stephens.edu
EMAIL sce@wc.stephens.edu
TELEPHONE (573) 876-7125 • (800) 388-7579
FAX (573) 876-7248
YEAR ESTABLISHED 1833
OWNERSHIP STATUS Nonprofit, independent
RESIDENCY Six to seven days
COST High average
DEGREE LEVEL Bachelor's, master's

FIELDS OF STUDY OR SPECIAL INTEREST Business administration, education, English, health information administration, law/philosophy/rhetoric, psychology

OTHER INFORMATION Stephens offers bachelor's degrees in the previously mentioned fields, or students may choose to design an individualized program with faculty approval. Dual majors are also available. Students with a bachelor's degree may work toward a certificate in health information management or early-childhood and elementary education. The curriculum emphasizes issues of particular concern to women and minorities.

Stephens also offers an M.B.A. as an Internet-based program.

All students are required to attend and satisfactorily pass (with a grade of C or better) an on-campus introductory course, held in a seven-day or double-weekend (three weeks apart) format.

Degree requirements can be met through independent study and Internet courses, working individually with Stephens College faculty. For those within driving distance of campus, weekend courses may supplement independent study. Students communicate with instructors by mail, telephone, and, when possible, email. Students may also earn credits through approved courses taken locally, standardized exams (CLEP, DANTES, College Board AP tests, and departmental exams), and portfolio assessment for military and other prior college-level learning gained outside the classroom. Thirty-six semester hours of credit must be taken with Stephens College faculty.

Stephens is open to women and men twenty-three years of age and older. Foreign students able to attend the on-campus introductory course may be accepted, provided they can demonstrate a TOEFL score of 550 or better.

Syracuse University

Associate's, bachelor's, and master's degrees with as little as three weeks per year on campus

Independent Study Degree Programs
700 University Avenue
Syracuse, NY 13244-2530

WEBSITE www.yesu.syr.edu
EMAIL parttime@uc.syr.edu
TELEPHONE (315) 443-9378 • (800) 442-0501
FAX (315) 443-4174
YEAR ESTABLISHED 1870
OWNERSHIP STATUS Nonprofit, independent
RESIDENCY Short
COST High
DEGREE LEVEL Associate's, bachelor's, master's

FIELDS OF STUDY OR SPECIAL INTEREST Advertising design, business administration, communications management, engineering management, information resources management, liberal studies, library science, nursing, social science, telecommunications and network management

OTHER INFORMATION The Independent Study Degree Program of this well-known university offers an A.A. and a B.A. in liberal studies; an M.A. in advertising design or illustration; an M.B.A.; an M.L.S.; a Master of Social Science; and M.S.'s in communications management, engineering management, information resources management, nursing, and telecommunications and network management. All require a short residency on campus. During the home study phase, students communicate with professors by mail, fax, email, Internet, or telephone.

Master's degrees are designed for completion in two or three years. For the bachelor's degree, a minimum of thirty credits must be earned through Syracuse. No standardized tests are required for the B.A. in liberal studies, the Master of Social Science, or the M.A. in illustration or advertising design. The GMAT is required for the M.B.A.; the GRE is required for the M.L.S. and the M.S. programs. The M.A. degrees and the communications management degree require a portfolio review.

Foreign students are admitted to all programs, provided they have a satisfactory TOEFL score.

Texas Tech University

A nonresident bachelor's degree in general studies and several nonresident master's degrees in technical fields

Outreach and Extended Studies
6901 Quaker Avenue
Lubbock, TX 79413

WEBSITE www.ttu.edu
EMAIL distlearn@ttu.edu
TELEPHONE (806) 742-7200 • (800) 692-6877
FAX (806) 742-7222
YEAR ESTABLISHED 1923
OWNERSHIP STATUS Nonprofit, state
RESIDENCY None
COST Average
DEGREE LEVEL Bachelor's, master's

FIELDS OF STUDY OR SPECIAL INTEREST Engineering (five fields), general studies, technical communication

OTHER INFORMATION Texas Tech University (TTU) offers six distance-learning programs designed primarily for adult learners.

The Bachelor of General Studies is a nontraditional program offered through the Department of Continuing Education (www.dce.ttu.edu) and designed primarily for students who have earned thirty semester hours or more of credit at another institution (although TTU does offer the necessary courses to fulfill these basic requirements). Students choose three "concentration areas," each involving six courses (or eighteen semester hours of credit), from the following list: behavioral sciences, communication, English, general business, history, humanities and fine arts, psychology, and restaurant/hotel/institution management. Course requirements can be fulfilled through a variety of nontraditional means, including online study, correspondence coursework, and credit by examination.

The online M.A. in technical communication offered through the Department of English (www.english.ttu.edu) involves twelve courses (thirty-six semester hours of coursework); a thesis is optional and may be taken in lieu of two courses. Nonthesis students must pass a comprehensive written examination. The Website stresses that the online M.A. is patterned after the on-campus M.A., and requirements for the two degrees are identical.

The College of Engineering's distance-learning initiative (aln.coe.ttu.edu) offers four master's programs nonresidentially: the general M.Eng. and M.S. programs in petroleum engineering, software engineering, and systems and engineering management. Lectures are delivered via CD, videocassette, or Internet streaming video; all other interaction occurs over the Internet.

Thomas Edison State College

Associate's and bachelor's degrees in 118 fields, entirely through distance learning; an M.S. in management that requires only a brief residency

101 West State Street
Trenton, NJ 08608-1176

WEBSITE www.tesc.edu
EMAIL info@tesc.edu
TELEPHONE (609) 984-1150 • (888) 442-8372
FAX (609) 984-8447
YEAR ESTABLISHED 1972
OWNERSHIP STATUS Nonprofit, state
RESIDENCY None for bachelor's, brief for master's
COST Low for associate's and bachelor's, average for master's
DEGREE LEVEL Associate's, bachelor's, master's

FIELDS OF STUDY OR SPECIAL INTEREST Accounting, administration of justice, administrative office management, advertising management, air traffic control, anthropology, architectural design, art, aviation flight technology, aviation maintenance technology, banking, biology, biomedical electronics, chemistry, child development services, civil and construction engineering technology, civil engineering technology, clinical laboratory science, communications, community services, computer information systems, computer science, computer science technology, construction, dietetic sciences, dental assisting sciences, dental hygiene, economics, electrical technology, electronic engineering technology, emergency disaster management, engineering graphics, English, environmental sciences, environmental studies, finance, fire protection science, foreign language, forestry, general management, gerontology, health and nutrition counseling, health professions education, health services, health services administration, health services education, health services management, history, horticulture, hospital health care administration, hotel/motel/restaurant management, human resource management, humanities, imaging science, insurance, international business, journalism, labor studies, laboratory animal science, legal services, liberal studies, logistics, manufacturing engineering technology, marine engineering technology, marketing, mathematics, mechanical engineering technology, medical imaging, mental health and rehabilitative services, music, natural sciences and mathematics, nondestructive testing technology, nuclear engineering technology, nuclear medicine technology, nursing, operations management, organizational management, perfusion technology, philosophy, photography, physics, political science, procurement, psychology, public administration, purchasing and materials management, radiation protection, radiation therapy, radiologic technology, real estate, recreation services, religion, respiratory care, respiratory care sciences (advanced), retailing management, small business management and entrepreneurship, social sciences and history, social services, social services administration, social services for special populations, sociology, surveying, theater arts, transportation and distribution management

OTHER INFORMATION This long-recognized leader in non-traditional education offers associate's and bachelor's degrees in all of the previously mentioned fields; no residency is required. A low-residency M.S. in management is also available, and an M.A. in professional studies is under development.

Unlimited credit can be earned through portfolio assessment; Thomas Edison's own exams in dozens of subjects; guided study (distance-learning courses using texts and videocassettes); the "On-Line Computer Classroom" (many courses available through Edison's innovative Computer Assisted Lifelong Learning [CALL] system); equivalency exams; military, business, and industry courses and training programs; telecourses (centered on, for example, PBS's *The Civil War*); licenses and certificates; and transfer credits from accredited colleges. Unique academic advising is available to enrolled students on an 800 number. Foreign students are welcome, with certain restrictions.

Touro University International

The first 100 percent online Ph.D. programs to achieve U.S. regional accreditation, offered through Touro University International, a branch campus of Touro College, New York

5665 Plaza Drive, Third Floor
Cypress, CA 90630

WEBSITE www.tourou.edu
EMAIL registration@tourou.edu
TELEPHONE (714) 816-0366
FAX (714) 827-7407
YEAR ESTABLISHED 1998
OWNERSHIP STATUS Nonprofit, independent
RESIDENCY None
COST High
DEGREE LEVEL Bachelor's, master's, doctorate

FIELDS OF STUDY OR SPECIAL INTEREST business administration, computer science, education, health sciences, information technology management

OTHER INFORMATION Touro University International (TUI), located in southern California, is a branch campus of Touro College, New York, which is fully accredited by the Commission on Higher Education of the Middle States Association of Colleges and Schools. TUI's business degree programs are also accredited by the International Assembly for Collegiate Business Education. TUI is authorized to award its degrees by the state of California.

TUI offers B.S.'s in business administration, computer science, health sciences, and information technology management; an M.B.A.; an M.A. in education; M.S.'s in health sciences and information technology management; and Ph.D.'s in business administration, educational leadership, and health sciences.

Touro University International operates four sessions per year, with each session lasting twelve weeks. Sessions begin in September, December, March, and June.

All courses are four semester credits.

Each course includes a session-long project.

A full-time load is considered to be two courses per session (eight credits).

Troy State University Montgomery

Associate's and bachelor's degrees in a range of fields, with no on-campus requirement

Rosa Parks Library and Museum
252 Montgomery Street, Room 310
Post Office Drawer 4419
Montgomery, AL 36103-4419

WEBSITE www.tsum.edu
EMAIL edp@tsum.edu
TELEPHONE (334) 241-9553 • (888) 357-8843
FAX (334) 241-5465
YEAR ESTABLISHED 1965
OWNERSHIP STATUS Nonprofit, state
RESIDENCY None
COST Low
DEGREE LEVEL Associate's, bachelor's

FIELDS OF STUDY OR SPECIAL INTEREST Business, child care, English, general education, history, professional studies, political science, psychology, social science

OTHER INFORMATION TSUM offers associate's and bachelor's degrees in the previously mentioned fields. Degrees are earned through a combination of learning contracts (independent study/correspondence); online/Internet courses; television/live-into-cable courses; transfer credits from other regionally accredited colleges and universities; CLEP, DANTES, and Excelsior exams; and assessment of prior learning.

Upon request, the school will provide guidelines for exam preparation and presentation of prior learning. Other student services include academic and career counseling, tutoring, and job placement assistance.

Study in the program is totally external. Orientation is provided through an online/Internet welcome package to all students at the beginning of their study. A senior project defense may be completed in person or via telephone conference, depending on the student's location.

Union Institute and University

Individualized bachelor's and doctorate degrees through guided independent study, with short seminar residencies; also a Ph.D. in professional psychology

440 East McMillan Street
Cincinnati, OH 45206-1925

WEBSITE www.tui.edu
EMAIL www.tui.edu/contactus
TELEPHONE (513) 861-6400 • (800) 486-3116
FAX (513) 861-0779
YEAR ESTABLISHED 1964
OWNERSHIP STATUS Nonprofit, independent
RESIDENCY Short, varying by program
COST High
DEGREE LEVEL Bachelor's, doctorate

FIELDS OF STUDY OR SPECIAL INTEREST Addiction counseling, business management, criminal justice, human resources, maternal child health, psychology, social work; individualized courses of study by arrangement

OTHER INFORMATION The Union Institute originated in 1964 as a consortium of liberal arts colleges. In 1969, the consortium became known as The Union for Experimenting Colleges and Universities (UECU) and began functioning as a degree-granting institution. It was responsible for the development and implementation of alternative educational systems, including the nonresident models that are still in operation at many universities. The consortium later dissolved, but the organization remained, eventually known as Union Institute and University.

The college's Center for Distance Learning offers bachelor's degree programs to individuals throughout the United States, using telecommunications and computer technology in its educational delivery systems. Students participate in a four-day residential seminar each term, held in a number of locations across the country. Students may receive credit for prior learning, transcripted and otherwise. The typical student has had some prior college experience (the average age for students in this program is thirty-eight) and completes the program after five semesters of full-time enrollment. Part-time enrollment is also an option. Each program culminates with a senior project based on writing and research.

The Graduate College offers interdisciplinary study and research programs leading to the Ph.D. Students choose their doctoral committee members: two from the Union Institute's faculty as well as two adjunct (external) faculty advisers. Consistent with the Institute's policy of self-directed education, the student chairs the doctoral committee. Each doctorate program culminates in a Project Demonstrating Excellence (PDE), a significant capstone project. The PDE may take the form of a tradi-

tional dissertation or may be a creative work or social action project. Students must attend a ten-day entry colloquium (held at Union's established sites) and three five-day seminars (to be chosen from those held monthly at various locations worldwide). The program is not based on credit hours; a minimum of twenty-four months of full-time enrollment is required for graduation, and the typical program is completed in thirty-six months. International students are accepted.

University of Alabama

Bachelor's in interdisciplinary studies, with only three days of residency

Tuscaloosa, AL 35487-0001

WEBSITE www.exd.ua.edu
EMAIL info@exd.ccs.ua.edu
TELEPHONE (205) 348-3019
YEAR ESTABLISHED 1831
OWNERSHIP STATUS Nonprofit, state
RESIDENCY Three days at beginning
COST Low average to average
DEGREE LEVEL Bachelor's

FIELDS OF STUDY OR SPECIAL INTEREST Interdisciplinary studies with seven specializations; *see* Other Information

OTHER INFORMATION The University of Alabama External Degree Program awards a B.A. or B.S. in interdisciplinary studies almost entirely through nonresidential independent study. The only residency requirement is an on-campus degree-planning seminar that takes three days at the start of the program. Fields of study for the B.A. are communication, humanities, human services, and social sciences. Fields of study for the B.S. are administrative sciences, applied sciences, and natural sciences. These fields cover a wide range of individualized interdisciplinary programs, allowing students to focus on a particular field of interest.

A minimum of 120 semester hours is required for graduation. Up to 90 hours can be transferred in; at least 30 hours of work must be completed after admission. This can be through out-of-class contract learning, correspondence courses, television courses, weekend college, prior-learning evaluation, or on-campus courses at the university. Credit is awarded for military and other noncollegiate PONSI-approved training and for CLEP, DANTES, and departmental challenge exams. A twelve-semester-hour senior project is required of all students. Academic advising and planning can be done by telephone.

Foreign students are not admitted.

University of Bradford

Research Master of Philosophy (M.Phil.) and doctorate programs in twenty-six fields, with as little as two weeks per year of residency

Student Registry, Postgraduate
Richmond Road
Bradford BD7 1DP
United Kingdom

WEBSITE www.brad.ac.uk
EMAIL enquiries@bradford.ac.uk
TELEPHONE 44 (1274) 232-323
FAX 44 (1274) 235-810
YEAR ESTABLISHED 1957
OWNERSHIP STATUS Nonprofit, state
RESIDENCY Variable
COST Average to high average
DEGREE LEVEL Master's, doctorate

FIELDS OF STUDY OR SPECIAL INTEREST *See* Other Information

OTHER INFORMATION The University of Bradford offers research-based M.Phil. and Ph.D. programs to students worldwide, and its policies express a willingness to work with qualified international students who wish to undertake a low-residency format. Residency varies from program to program, depending on a variety of factors, including the student's "home base" facilities; access to necessary resources and, where applicable, appropriate academic or industry research supervision; the specific degree being sought; the field; the dissertation topic; the student's ability to conduct self-directed research; and other extenuating circumstances, including the openness of individual faculty members to negotiating long-distance research arrangements.

It's worth noting, and noting again, that successful applications for nonresidential research arrangements at schools such as Bradford must generally begin with a solid idea for a research topic. Bradford does not offer a special catalog and application form for distance-learning doctorates. Students who undertake a nonresident British research doctorate are seldom described as pursuing distance-learning doctorates; they are just pursuing traditional credentials and happen to be doing all of the work off campus.

That said, Bradford offers research programs in an exceptionally broad range of fields, including applied social sciences, archaeological sciences, biomedical sciences, cancer research, chemical engineering, chemistry, civil and environmental engineering, computing, cybernetics, development and project planning, education, electronic and electrical engineering, electronic imaging and media communications, environmental science, European studies, gender and women's studies, health studies, industrial

technology, interdisciplinary human studies, management, mathematics, mechanical and medical engineering, modern languages, optometry, peace studies, pharmacy, polymer engineering, and social and economic studies. Research Ph.D. programs generally take four to six years to complete through part-time study, whereas research M.Phil. programs can generally be completed in two to three years part-time. British research programs involve no courses; each qualified student immediately pursues a thesis topic without formal doctorate-level coursework.

University of Denver

Online master's degrees from a prestigious private university

University College
2211 South Josephine
Denver, CO 80208

WEBSITE www.learning.du.edu
TELEPHONE (303) 871-3354
FAX (303) 871-3305
YEAR ESTABLISHED 1884
OWNERSHIP STATUS Private
RESIDENCY None
COST Average
DEGREE LEVEL Master's

FIELDS OF STUDY OR SPECIAL INTEREST Environmental policy and management, geographic information systems, liberal studies, technology management, telecommunications

OTHER INFORMATION The University of Denver (UD), the oldest independent university in the Rocky Mountain region, enrolls 9,271 students in its undergraduate, graduate, and professional programs. UD's University College program offers online master's degrees, certificates, and individual courses.

UD's ten-week courses, offered quarterly throughout the year, are characterized by a wide array of learning techniques to help develop knowledge, understanding, and problem-solving skills; lively discussion boards and chat rooms that promote the exchange of ideas and build academic community; personal and extensive communication with faculty over the Internet; an emphasis on creative interaction in the technological era; and collaborative and active learning strategies, with plenty of projects to maximize hands-on learning.

The Master of Technology Management degree requires fifty-four quarter hours of study in five years or less. Typically, it can be completed in two years.

The liberal studies program supplements technical skills and professional experience with a critical awareness of the world at large.

The master's degree requires fifty-six quarter hours of study in five years or less.

University of Idaho

Master's degrees in ten fields, almost entirely through home study

Engineering Outreach Program
Post Office Box 441014
Moscow, ID 83844-1014

WEBSITE www.uidaho.edu/eo
EMAIL outreach@uidaho.edu
TELEPHONE (208) 885-6373 • (800) 824-2889
FAX (208) 885-9249
YEAR ESTABLISHED 1889
OWNERSHIP STATUS Nonprofit, state
RESIDENCY None or brief, depending on program
COST Average
DEGREE LEVEL Master's

FIELDS OF STUDY OR SPECIAL INTEREST Biological and agricultural engineering with an emphasis on water management, civil engineering, computer engineering, computer science, electrical engineering, engineering management, environmental science with an emphasis on water science, mechanical engineering, psychology with an emphasis on human factors, teaching mathematics

OTHER INFORMATION Idaho's Engineering Outreach Program allows students to earn graduate degrees almost entirely through distance learning. Engineering Outreach students are expected to complete all course requirements during the semester in which the course is offered. Courses are taught by on-campus faculty and simultaneously videotaped in specially equipped studio classrooms. Videotapes, plus all related class handouts, are sent by mail to the student. Students and instructors maintain contact using the toll-free number, by fax, and through email and interactive video conferencing. Examinations are sent to an examination proctor recommended by the student and approved by Engineering Outreach. The proctor is responsible for supervising the examination process and returning the exam to Engineering Outreach. At the end of the program, students may need to travel to the Idaho campus for two days, either to present a thesis (for M.S. programs) or to take a comprehensive examination (for M.Eng. programs).

Each program has distinct entrance requirements. No credit is awarded for equivalency exams or noncollegiate learning of any kind. Up to twelve of the thirty to thirty-six credits required for the degree can be transferred in from an accredited college or university. Students have up to eight years to complete their degree requirements. International students are accepted; those whose native language is not English must present a minimum TOEFL score of 550.

University of Illinois at Urbana-Champaign

Master's programs in a variety of fields over the Internet, from one of the most respected public universities in the United States

Urbana, IL 61801

WEBSITE www.uiuc.edu
EMAIL graduate@admissions.uiuc.edu
TELEPHONE (217) 333-1000
FAX (217) 333-9758
YEAR ESTABLISHED 1867
OWNERSHIP STATUS Nonprofit, state
RESIDENCY None
COST High average
DEGREE LEVEL Master's

FIELDS OF STUDY OR SPECIAL INTEREST Computer science, education, engineering, library and information science

OTHER INFORMATION The University of Illinois at Urbana-Champaign offers a variety of master's programs online.

The Master of Computer Science is a professional degree designed for practicing information technologies (IT) industry specialists. Students are required to take nine courses at a rate of one or two per semester and can finish the program in three to five years. No thesis or final project is required.

The M.Ed. is available in curriculum, technology, and education reform or in vocational and technical education (with specialization in human resource education). Each program requires eight online courses and can be completed in about three years.

M.S. programs are available in electrical engineering and in library and information science.

Professional development sequences are available in community college teaching, financial engineering and risk management, French translation studies, and math education. Each sequence involves six graduate-level courses, which may be taken online; a sequence can be completed in two years.

University of Iowa

Interdisciplinary Bachelor of Liberal Studies earned entirely through home study

Division of Continuing Education
116 International Center
Iowa City, IA 52242-1802

WEBSITE www.uiowa.edu
EMAIL credit-programs@uiowa.edu
TELEPHONE (319) 335-2575 • (800) 272-6430
FAX (319) 335-2740
YEAR ESTABLISHED 1847
OWNERSHIP STATUS Nonprofit, state
RESIDENCY None
COST High average
DEGREE LEVEL Bachelor's

FIELDS OF STUDY OR SPECIAL INTEREST Liberal studies

OTHER INFORMATION Iowa offers an interdisciplinary Bachelor of Liberal Studies (B.L.S.) through what is essentially a degree-completion program. Applicants must have already completed at least sixty-two credits elsewhere or hold an associate's degree. An additional thirty credits may be transferred into the program; thirty-two more must be taken from the University of Iowa itself. All of the work can, however, be done nonresidentially.

The degree does not have a major in the traditional sense; rather, students concentrate in three of five broad subject areas: communication and arts, humanities, natural science and math, professional fields, and social sciences. Credit is awarded for ACE military or vocational training recommendations, as well as for CLEP, DANTES, and College Board AP exams. No credit is given for life experience.

Within the program, distance-learning options include courses taken through other schools (either on a local campus or by correspondence), Iowa's own correspondence courses, and Iowa Communications Network (interactive television) courses that allow classes to be held at remote sites throughout Iowa. Iowa offers more than 160 distance-learning courses, and all requirements for the B.L.S. can be fulfilled through this method.

Foreign students are not admitted, but U.S. citizens living overseas may enroll.

In addition, readers may be interested in LionHawk, the Pennsylvania State University and University of Iowa Joint External Degree Program, which allows students to earn an Extended Letters, Arts, and Sciences Associate Degree (E.L.A.S.) from Penn State, then transfer directly to the University of Iowa to pursue the B.L.S. degree. Students who earn the E.L.A.S. degree through Penn State are guaranteed admission to Iowa's B.L.S. program.

University of Kent at Canterbury

Master of Philosophy, LL.M., and Ph.D. programs in sixty-five fields through external research arrangements, with six weeks or less on campus each year

The Registry
Canterbury, Kent CT2 7NZ
United Kingdom

WEBSITE www.ukc.ac.uk
EMAIL graduate-office@ukc.ac.uk
TELEPHONE 44 (1227) 824-040
FAX 44 (1227) 452-196
YEAR ESTABLISHED 1965
OWNERSHIP STATUS Nonprofit, state
RESIDENCY Variable
COST Average to high average
DEGREE LEVEL Master's, doctorate, law

FIELDS OF STUDY OR SPECIAL INTEREST *See* Other Information

OTHER INFORMATION The University of Kent at Canterbury offers research-based LL.M., M.Phil., and Ph.D. programs to students worldwide. Each student works through an approved university in a chosen area. Students pursuing the LL.M. program must generally hold the J.D. (LL.B.) or equivalent, students pursuing the M.Phil. should hold at least a bachelor's, and students pursuing the Ph.D. should have a master's and significant documented research work (a master's thesis, published work, or other equivalent material). Students generally spend six weeks per year on campus.

The LL.M. is available in general law, feminist law, and sociolegal studies. M.Phil. and Ph.D. programs are available in the following fields: accounting, actuarial science, American studies, applied language studies in computing, applied linguistics, applied mathematics, biochemistry, biodiversity management, biotechnology, cartoons and caricature, chemistry, classical archaeology, classical studies, communication and image studies, comparative literary studies, computer science, drama, economics, electronic engineering, English, environmental anthropology, environmental law and conservation, environmental social science, European studies, film studies, forensic psychology, German, health psychology, history, history and cultural studies of science, history and theory of art, industrial relations, international conflict analysis, international relations, Italian, law and philosophy, learning disability, management, management science, medicine and health sciences, medieval and Tudor studies, mental health, microbiology, operations research, personal social services, philosophy, physics, politics and government, postcolonial studies, psychology, psychotherapy, pure mathematics, social anthropology, social policy, social psychology, social work, sociology, Spanish, statistics, theology and religious studies, urban studies, and women's studies.

British research Ph.D. programs involve no courses; a student, once accepted, immediately pursues a thesis topic without formal doctorate-level coursework.

University of Leicester

Nonresidential master's degrees in nineteen fields from an eighty-year-old British school

University Road
Leicester LE1 7RH
United Kingdom

WEBSITE www.leicester.ac.uk
EMAIL graduateoffice@le.ac.uk
TELEPHONE 44 (116) 252-2298
FAX 44 (116) 252-2200
YEAR ESTABLISHED 1921
OWNERSHIP STATUS Nonprofit, state
RESIDENCY None
COST Average
DEGREE LEVEL Master's

FIELDS OF STUDY OR SPECIAL INTEREST *See* Other Information

OTHER INFORMATION Leicester offers master's degrees in nineteen fields through correspondence and online study; each program consists of four to six modules and a capstone dissertation (master's thesis).

Of particular interest to U.S. students might be the M.S. in training and human resource management, offered through Leicester's Centre for Labour Market Studies. The Centre has made a special outreach to the North American and Asian Pacific market, with specially prepared course materials and regular faculty visits for optional meetings with students. Although Leicester is a royally chartered university in its own right, the Centre for Labour Market Studies has achieved additional voluntary accreditation through DETC in the United States.

Other master's programs are offered in applied linguistics, archaeology, business administration, criminal justice, European Union law, finance, forensic and legal psychology, human resources, law and employment relations, marketing, mass communications, museum studies, organizational development, primary education, public order studies, risk and crisis management, security and crime risk management, and sport sociology.

People without an accredited bachelor's degree who possess certain professional qualifications and several years of practical experience may be considered for some programs.

University of London

Nonresident bachelor's, master's, and law degrees in a variety of fields, from the school that invented the whole concept of external study

The External Programme
Senate House, Malet Street
London WC1E 7HU
United Kingdom

WEBSITE www.londonexternal.ac.uk
EMAIL enquiries@external.lon.ac.uk
TELEPHONE 44 (20) 7862-8360
FAX 44 (20) 7862-8358
YEAR ESTABLISHED 1836
OWNERSHIP STATUS Nonprofit, state
RESIDENCY None
DEGREE LEVEL Bachelor's, master's, doctorate, law

FIELDS OF STUDY OR SPECIAL INTEREST *See* Other Information

OTHER INFORMATION The University of London was the first university in the world to offer its degree through external study. With more than twenty-six thousand students registered, it is still one of the most popular.

The university offers B.A. degrees in English, French, geography, German, Italian, Jewish history, philosophy, and Spanish and Latin American studies. Dual-language degrees (German and Italian, French and German, Spanish and French, etc.) are also available. B.S. degrees are available in accounting and finance, banking and finance, computing and information systems, computing and statistics, economics (with optional emphasis on geography, sociology, or politics and international relations), information systems and management, law and management, management, mathematics and computing, and mathematics and statistics. Also available are the Bachelor of Laws and Bachelor of Divinity.

Master's degrees are available in agricultural development, agricultural economics, applied environmental economics, business administration, clinical dentistry (for practicing dentists), community dental practice, dental public health, dental radiology, developmental finance, distance education, drug and alcohol policy and intervention, environment and development, environmental management, epidemiology, financial economics, financial management, food industry management and marketing, geography, health systems management, infectious diseases, law, livestock health and production, managing rural change, materials science and engineering, occupational psychology, organizational behavior, public policy and management, and sustainable agriculture and rural development.

Self-paced programs can be completed in three to eight years for undergraduate programs or two to five years for master's programs. Assessment is mainly by examination.

The university provides subject guides and past examination papers, along with an academic handbook and resource guide, but students are responsible for organizing their own program of study. Several independent correspondence schools offer noncredit, nondegree preparation courses for London's exams.

University of Louisville

Master's degrees in education-related fields and public administration, from a respected public institution

Division of Distance and Continuing Education
University of Louisville
Louisville, KY 40292

WEBSITE www.ddce.louisville.edu
EMAIL training@louisville.edu
TELEPHONE (502) 852-6456
FAX (502) 852-8573
YEAR ESTABLISHED 1798
OWNERSHIP STATUS State
RESIDENCY Some; varies by program
COST Average
DEGREE LEVEL Master's

FIELDS OF STUDY OR SPECIAL INTEREST Administration of justice, higher education, human resource education, public administration, special education

OTHER INFORMATION The University of Louisville is a state-supported metropolitan research university located in Kentucky's largest urban area.

The distance-learning programs offered by the University of Louisville vary in their required credits, residency, admissions criteria, transfer credits, and course technology. Check the Website for details.

The M.A. in higher education requires a minimum of thirty-one to thirty-three credit hours of graduate-level coursework. Required courses include Introduction to Research Methods and Statistics, the American College and University, Philosophy of Higher Education, Principles of Educational Leadership, Planning, Legal Issues in Postsecondary Education, Organization and Administration of Higher Educational Institutions, and Educational Resource Management in Postsecondary Education. Students also choose six credit hours of elective coursework approved by a graduate adviser. For the final course requirements, students may choose either to do an internship in postsecondary education or to write a thesis or professional paper.

The Department of Leadership, Foundations and Human Resource Education offers the M.Ed. program (changing soon to an M.S.). Program graduates are able to assess performance problems in organizations, design and deliver appropriate interventions, and evaluate change and the impact of interventions. Professionals in health care, industry, business, military, and public and private service agencies have completed the program.

The program requires a minimum of thirty credits for completion, with a core curriculum of twenty-seven credits.

The Department of Urban and Public Affairs offers an Internet-based Master of Public Administration degree in cooperation with the Department of Political Science. The program focuses on general administration, public management, policy analysis, applied research, government, and organizational theory. The first students in the program were enrolled during the spring 2001 semester. The program requires a minimum of forty-two credits for completion: a core curriculum of twenty-seven credits, including six credits of practicum or internship or six credits of thesis, and fifteen credits of electives. The core curriculum encompasses studies in public administration, budgeting, statistics, policy analysis, human resource management, and public policy. Students are permitted to pursue core and elective courses simultaneously. The online M.P.A. program offers electives in administrative law, strategic management, advanced organization behavior, and other topics.

University of Maryland

The University of Maryland's University College offers fifteen bachelor's programs, eighteen master's programs, and dozens of certificate programs, entirely through online study

University College
3501 University Boulevard East
Adelphi, MD 20783

WEBSITE www.umuc.edu
EMAIL umucinfo@umuc.edu
TELEPHONE (301) 985-7000 • (800) 888-8682
FAX (301) 454-0399
YEAR ESTABLISHED 1856
OWNERSHIP STATUS Nonprofit, state
RESIDENCY None
COST Average
DEGREE LEVEL Bachelor's, master's

FIELDS OF STUDY OR SPECIAL INTEREST *See* Other Information

OTHER INFORMATION University College, the continuing education campus of the University of Maryland system, offers bachelor's and master's degrees entirely through online study, with no required on-campus residency.

Bachelor's degrees are available in accounting, behavioral and social sciences, business and management, communication studies, computer and information science, computer studies, English, environmental management, fire science, history, humanities, information systems management, management studies, paralegal studies, and psychology.

Online master's degrees are available in biotechnology studies, business administration, computer systems management (with four specializations), distance education, education, electronic commerce, environmental management, information technology, international management (with three specializations), management (with nine specializations), software engineering, teaching, technology management (with three specializations), and telecommunications management.

Undergraduate certificates are available in the areas of business and management, computing and technology, and workplace Spanish. Graduate certificates are available in distance education, general management, information technology systems, international management, and technology and environmental management.

University of New England

Degrees at all levels in an impressive array of fields, from Australia's oldest distance-education provider

Armidale
New South Wales 2351
Australia

WEBSITE www.une.edu.au
EMAIL ioadmin@pobox.une.edu.au
TELEPHONE 61 (2) 6773-3333
FAX 61 (2) 6773-3122
YEAR ESTABLISHED 1938
OWNERSHIP STATUS Nonprofit, state
RESIDENCY None for most programs; varies for research doctorates
COST Low average
DEGREE LEVEL Bachelor's, master's, doctorate, law

FIELDS OF STUDY OR SPECIAL INTEREST *See* Other Information

OTHER INFORMATION The University of New England is Australia's oldest distance-education provider and has thousands of students enrolled in external programs. Learning takes place via printed correspondence texts, audio- and videotapes, radio and television broadcasts, and the Internet.

Bachelor's degrees are available in aboriginal studies, agriculture, ancient history, archaeology, Asian societies, Asian studies, biomedical science, biosystematics, Chinese, classical studies, commerce, communication studies, composition, computer science, ecology, economic history, economics, English, environmental science, ethnomusicology, European cultures, financial administration, French, general science, geography and planning, German, Greek, health studies, history, horticultural science, Indonesian, international relations, Italian, Japanese, Latin, law, linguistics, mathematics, modern Greek, molecular biology, musicology, natural resources, paleoanthropology, philosophy, political science, psychology, rural science, social science, sociology, studies in religion, technology, theater studies, urban and regional planning, and women's and gender studies.

Master's degrees are available in American studies, ancient history, archaeological heritage, Asian societies, Asian studies, biology, business administration (with eight concentrations), Chinese, classics, communication studies, computer science, computer studies, defense studies, development studies, economic studies (with six concentrations), education, English, ethnomusicology, European cultures, French, German, geography and planning, Greek, history, Indonesian, international relations, Islamic studies, Italian, Japanese, Latin, law, linguistics, mathematics, molecular and cellular biology, musicology, philosophy, peace studies, political science, public policy, sociology, statistics, studies in religion, theater studies, women's and gender studies, and zoology.

Research Master of Philosophy and Ph.D. programs are available in a variety of specializations, including arts, biological sciences, business, classics, communication, computer science, cultures, economics, education, engineering, English, health, history, human and environmental studies, languages, law, linguistics, mathematics, music, physical sciences, professional studies, religion, and theater.

University of Northern Iowa

Bachelor's and master's programs in a broad range of fields

1227 West Twenty-Seventh Street
Cedar Falls, IA 50614

WEBSITE www.uni.edu/contined/cp/distance.shtml
EMAIL contined@uni.edu
TELEPHONE (319) 273-2121 • (800) 772-1746
FAX (319) 273-2885
YEAR ESTABLISHED 1847
OWNERSHIP STATUS Nonprofit, state
RESIDENCY At least one semester on campus for most graduate programs
COST Average
DEGREE LEVEL Bachelor's, master's

FIELDS OF STUDY OR SPECIAL INTEREST Education (with many specializations), liberal studies, library science

OTHER INFORMATION Northern Iowa offers an undergraduate degree-completion program, the Bachelor of Liberal Studies (B.L.S.). The B.L.S. is interdisciplinary, with students concentrating coursework in three of five broad subject areas: communication and arts, humanities, professional fields, science and math, and social sciences. Credit is earned primarily through guided independent study courses, but other options include on-campus evening and weekend courses, televised courses, off-campus course sites throughout Iowa, courses from other regionally accredited four-year colleges (both on campus and through correspondence), and online courses. To qualify for admission, a student must live in the United States and have completed sixty-two transferable units or have an associate's degree.

Courses for graduate programs are delivered primarily via a statewide interactive television network (the Iowa Communications Network). In addition to interactive television courses, some programs incorporate Web delivery and/or on-campus coursework. M.A. programs are offered in communication education, education (specializing in educational leadership, literacy, middle-school education, or special education), educational technology, TESOL/ ESL, library science, and middle school mathematics. A master's in music education is also available.

University of Oklahoma

Bachelor's and master's degrees in liberal studies, with a negotiable amount of time on campus

College of Liberal Studies
1700 Asp Avenue, Suite 226
Norman, OK 73072-6400

WEBSITE www.ou.edu/cls
EMAIL cls@ou.edu
TELEPHONE (405) 325-1061 • (800) 522-4389
FAX (405) 325-7132
YEAR ESTABLISHED 1890
OWNERSHIP STATUS Nonprofit, state
RESIDENCY Two to four weeks
COST Low average
DEGREE LEVEL Bachelor's, master's

FIELDS OF STUDY OR SPECIAL INTEREST Liberal studies

OTHER INFORMATION Oklahoma offers the Bachelor and Master of Liberal Studies through directed independent study.

Bachelor's students begin the program by attending an introductory seminar held over two consecutive weekends and continue by completing independent study assignments and attending two to four ten-day seminars on campus, depending on the number of credit hours they transfer into the program. There are no majors; students work in three general areas: humanities, natural sciences, and mathematics. Some on-campus residencies may be waived based on prior study. Credit is available for ACE-evaluated training programs and military recommendations, as well as for equivalency examinations.

Master's students are allowed to self-design a degree program incorporating interdisciplinary perspectives or may choose from the following career-oriented program tracks: administrative leadership, health and human services, interdisciplinary education, or museum emphasis. Master of Liberal Studies students complete the program by attending a total of three ten-day seminars on campus and by finishing several directed independent reading assignments. It may be possible to negotiate alternatives for some of these residency requirements. The college does not allow transfer credit hours in the master's program.

University of Phoenix

Bachelor's and master's degrees entirely through online study, from the largest private university in the United States

4615 East Elwood Street
Phoenix, AZ 85040

WEBSITE www.phoenix.edu
TELEPHONE (480) 966-9577 • (800) 742-4742
FAX (480) 829-9030
YEAR ESTABLISHED 1976
OWNERSHIP STATUS Proprietary
RESIDENCY None for bachelor's and master's; brief for doctorate
COST High
DEGREE LEVEL Bachelor's, master's, doctorate

FIELDS OF STUDY OR SPECIAL INTEREST Business (*see* Other Information), education, information technology, nursing

OTHER INFORMATION The University of Phoenix established its online campus in 1989. The following programs are currently available entirely over the Internet: bachelor's degrees in business (specializing in accounting, administration, information systems, management, or marketing), e-business, information technology, and nursing; and master's degrees in business administration (specializing in accounting, e-business, global management, or technology), computer information systems, education, nursing, and organizational management. A low-residency Doctor of Management in organizational leadership is also available.

All of the degrees are designed for midcareer professionals. Students get their assignments, have group discussions, and ask questions of their professors online, from wherever they and their computers happen to be. Each class meeting is spread out over an entire week, allowing busy students to complete their work at the most convenient time for them. Software instruction and technical orientation are provided for enrolled students.

The University of Phoenix also offers bachelor's and master's programs in business through evening and weekend study at fifty-two locations throughout the country.

University of South Africa

Nonresidential bachelor's, master's, doctorate, and law degrees in many fields, from one of the largest distance-education universities in the English-speaking world

Post Office Box 392
Unisa 0003
South Africa

WEBSITE www.unisa.ac.za
EMAIL study-info@alpha.unisa.ac.za
TELEPHONE 27 (12) 429-3111
FAX 27 (12) 429-3221
YEAR ESTABLISHED 1873
OWNERSHIP STATUS Nonprofit, state
RESIDENCY None
COST Low
DEGREE LEVEL Bachelor's, master's, doctorate, law

FIELDS OF STUDY OR SPECIAL INTEREST *See* Other Information

OTHER INFORMATION The University of South Africa offers a vast number of courses, degrees, and diplomas at all levels, and nearly all of them are available entirely through distance learning (usually via guided research or correspondence, although UNISA has recently begun to offer online courses as well). Examinations may be taken at South African embassies and consulates worldwide. At one time, UNISA offered the least-expensive nonresidential credentials in the world; this was because, until recently, UNISA subsidized students worldwide. This practice is being phased out at press time, although UNISA's unsubsidized rates are still extremely low by U.S. standards.

Bachelor's degrees are available in the following fields: accounting, African languages (with nine specializations), African politics, Afrikaans, ancient history, anthropology, applied mathematics, Arabic, art history, astronomy, auditing, biblical studies, business management, chemistry, church history, classics, commerce, communication, computer science, criminology, development administration, economics, education, educational management, English, French, gender studies, geography, German, gifted-child education, Greek, guidance and counseling, history, industrial psychology, information science, information systems, international politics, Islamic studies, Italian, Judaica, Latin, law, linguistics, mathematics, missiology, modern Hebrew, musicology, New Testament, Old Testament, operations research, penology, philosophy, physics, police science, politics, Portuguese, practical theology, preprimary education, primary education, psychology, public administration, quantitative management, religious studies, Romance languages, Russian, secondary education, Semitic languages, social science (with five specializations),

Spanish, statistics, systematic theology, theological ethics, theory of literature, and transport economics.

Master's degrees are available in nearly all of the same fields, as well as the following: ancient languages and cultures, archaeology, banking law, business leadership, Christian spirituality, clinical psychology, commercial law, comparative education, corporate law, counseling psychology, criminal law and criminal procedure, didactics, educational management, environmental education, history of education, insurance law, intellectual property law, international communication, international economic law, labor law, mathematics education, mental health, natural science education, nursing science (with five specializations), pastoral therapy, philosophy of education, philosophy of law, psychology of education, socioeducation, sociolinguistics, urban ministry, and visual arts.

Doctorates are available in virtually all of the fields listed previously and awarded as follows: the D.Litt. and D.Phil. for degrees in the arts; the Ph.D. for degrees awarded in the natural and social sciences; the Ed.D. for degrees awarded in education; the Th.D. for degrees awarded in theology; and the LL.D. for degrees awarded in law. As is true in the case of British programs, South African doctorate programs are based entirely around the student's dissertation research and do not involve preparatory courses as such (although students are frequently assigned preliminary reading lists upon undertaking a doctorate program).

U.S. students interested in UNISA should contact UNISA's U.S. agent, the American International Higher Education Corporation (AIHEC), by telephone at (512) 343-2031, by fax at (512) 343-8644, by email at jcraparo@aihec.com, or on the Web at www.aihec.com.

University of South Australia

Nonresidential degrees at all levels through correspondence, online coursework, and guided research

G.P.O. Box 2471
Adelaide, SA 5001
Australia

WEBSITE www.unisa.edu.au
EMAIL international.office@unisa.edu.au
TELEPHONE 61 (8) 8302-0114
FAX 61 (8) 8302-0233
YEAR ESTABLISHED 1991
OWNERSHIP STATUS Nonprofit, state
RESIDENCY None for most programs; variable for research doctorates
COST Average to high average
DEGREE LEVEL Bachelor's, master's, doctorate

FIELDS OF STUDY OR SPECIAL INTEREST Primarily business and education; *see* Other Information

OTHER INFORMATION The University of South Australia has made its distance-learning programs available to students worldwide through a variety of nontraditional learning methods.

Bachelor's degrees are available in accountancy, business administration, business banking and finance, communication and media management, computer and information science, early-childhood studies, nursing (for licensed or registered nurses), and pharmacy; master's degrees are available in business administration, manufacturing management, project management, and social science (with a specialization in counseling).

At the doctorate level, students can complete a D.B.A. or an Ed.D. through a mix of correspondence coursework and guided research. External research Ph.D.'s are also available in business and management and in education (with specializations in art education, curriculum leadership, distance education, early childhood studies, religious education, and women in education).

University of Southern Queensland

Many, many online and correspondence-based bachelor's, master's, and doctorate programs through an Australian University of the Year

International Office
Toowoomba
Queensland 4350
Australia

WEBSITE www.usqonline.com.au or www.usq.edu.au
EMAIL international@usq.edu.au
TELEPHONE 61 (74) 631-2362
FAX 61 (74) 636-2211
YEAR ESTABLISHED 1967
OWNERSHIP STATUS Nonprofit, state
RESIDENCY None
COST Average
DEGREE LEVEL Bachelor's, master's, doctorate

FIELDS OF STUDY OR SPECIAL INTEREST *See* Other Information

OTHER INFORMATION Voted joint University of the Year 2000–2001 (alongside the prestigious University of Wollongong) by the *Australian Good Universities Guide,* the University of Southern Queensland is generally regarded as one of the most energetic universities in Australia when it comes to global online education. Although most programs still require some correspondence coursework, many can now be completed entirely by online study.

Bachelor's programs are available in accounting, administrative management, anthropology, applied economics and resource management, applied finance, applied mathematics, Asian studies, banking, business administration, communication and media studies, computer software development, computing, education, engineering (with ten specializations), engineering technology (with five specializations), English literature, finance, further education and training, general studies, geographic information systems, human resource management practices, Indonesian language, information technology (with six specializations), information technology management, international relations, journalism, logistics and operations management, marketing, mathematics, nursing, psychological studies, psychology, public relations, statistics, strategic human resource management, and surveying. Double majors are generally also available.

Master's programs are available in accounting, applied finance, applied linguistics, arts management, business administration, business information technology, business law, commercial law, e-business, editing and publishing, education (with twelve specializations, including children's literature), educational technology, engineering (with six specializations), engineering technology (with six speciali-

zations), environmental management, finance, geomatics, health communication systems, human resource management, information systems, information technology, international business, leadership, management, marketing, midwifery, nursing, occupational health and safety, occupational health and safety nursing, online education, open and distance learning, professional accounting, professional communication, project management, and rural and remote health.

At the doctorate level, students may choose the D.B.A. or the Ed.D. in professional leadership. Negotiation of a research Master of Philosophy or Ph.D. may also be possible on a case-by-case basis.

University of Texas

Several online master's degrees (including an M.B.A.) from one of the largest state-funded university systems in the United States

UT TeleCampus
The University of Texas System
210 West Sixth Street
CTJ—Suite 2.100
Austin, TX 78701-2980

WEBSITE www.telecampus.utsystem.edu
EMAIL telecampus@utsystem.edu
TELEPHONE (512) 499-4323 • (888) TEXAS-16
FAX (512) 499-4715
YEAR ESTABLISHED 1973
OWNERSHIP STATUS Nonprofit, state
RESIDENCY None
COST Average for in-state students; high average for out-of-state students
DEGREE LEVEL Master's

FIELDS OF STUDY OR SPECIAL INTEREST Business administration, computer science, educational technology, electrical engineering, kinesiology, reading

OTHER INFORMATION The University of Texas (UT) TeleCampus pools the distance-learning offerings of the fifteen-campus University of Texas system. Work is completed through the Telecampus, and the relevant specific branch of the University of Texas awards the degree.

The UT TeleCampus Online M.B.A. in general business administration involves forty-eight semester hours of coursework and takes two to six years to complete. Each student must apply to a home campus at the beginning of the program (Arlington, Brownsville, Dallas, El Paso, Pan American, Permian Basin, San Antonio, or Tyler). Entrance requirements and curricula vary depending on the home campus chosen.

The University of Texas at Brownsville awards the online M.Ed. in educational technology. The program involves thirty-six semester hours of coursework and generally takes two to three years to complete. Thesis and nonthesis tracks are available. Up to one-third of the program may consist of approved elective coursework, allowing wide berth for student-defined specialization.

Other master's degrees offered through online study are the M.Ed. in health and kinesiology (awarded by Tyler), the M.Ed. in reading (with emphasis on English as a second language, or ESL; Arlington), the M.S. in computer science (Arlington and Dallas), the M.S. in computer science and engineering (Arlington), the M.S. in electrical engineering (Arlington and Dallas), and the M.S. in kinesiology (El Paso, Permian Basin, and Pan American). Online graduate-level certificates are available in ESL (Arlington) and telecommunications (Arlington and Dallas).

University of Wales—Lampeter

Nonresidential correspondence-based master's degrees and research-based doctorates from a 179-year-old Welsh university

Ceredigion, Wales SA48 7ED
United Kingdom

WEBSITE www.lamp.ac.uk
EMAIL pg-office@lampeter.ac.uk
TELEPHONE 44 (1570) 424-748
FAX 44 (1570) 423-530
YEAR ESTABLISHED 1822
OWNERSHIP STATUS Nonprofit, state
RESIDENCY None for taught master's programs; varies for research programs
COST Low average to average
DEGREE LEVEL Master's, doctorate

FIELDS OF STUDY OR SPECIAL INTEREST Mostly history, philosophy, and/or religion related; *see* Other Information

OTHER INFORMATION Lampeter offers correspondence-based master's programs in some highly specialized humanities-oriented fields.

The M.A. in death and immortality is a good example of Lampeter's unique programs. Students study such topics as the Self in Indian thought, Christian concepts of death, bereavement counseling, reincarnation, life-death ethical issues, and death in popular culture. The program involves an extensive reading list. Similar M.A. programs are available in death studies (focusing more on anthropology and history than on philosophy and religion) and ethics of life and death (focusing primarily on medical ethics, the ethics of war, capital punishment, etc.).

Other correspondence-based M.A. programs are available in British Empire and Commonwealth studies, Celtic Christianity, feminist theology, religion/politics/international relations (addressing religion's influence on war and international politics), religious experience, study of religion, and visual representations of history. A Master of Theology in church history is also available.

Research-based M.Phil. and Ph.D. programs are available in anthropology, archaeology, classics, English, geography, history, Islamic studies, philosophy, religious studies, and theology. Residency is negotiated on a case-by-case basis.

University of Waterloo

Nonresident bachelor's degrees for people in Canada and the United States and a nonresident master's degree in technology management for students worldwide

Distance Education
Waterloo, ON N2L 3G1
Canada

WEBSITE www.dce.uwaterloo.ca
EMAIL distance@uwaterloo.ca
TELEPHONE (519) 888-4050
FAX (519) 746-4607
YEAR ESTABLISHED 1957
OWNERSHIP STATUS Nonprofit, state
RESIDENCY None
COST Low for Canadians; average to high average for non-Canadians
DEGREE LEVEL Bachelor's, master's

FIELDS OF STUDY OR SPECIAL INTEREST *See* Other Information

OTHER INFORMATION The University of Waterloo's bachelor's degrees, which can be earned entirely through distance education, include a non-major B.A. or B.S.; a B.A. with a major in Canadian studies, classical studies, economics, English, environmental studies, French, geography, history, medieval studies, philosophy, psychology, religious studies, social development studies, or sociology; and a Bachelor of Environmental Studies in geography.

The undergraduate distance courses are normally available to people residing in Canada and the United States. Others may be eligible to enroll in some undergraduate distance courses if they can meet criteria related to communication and assignment due dates and if they are willing to assume extra charges related to the delivery of materials and the proctoring of examinations. Non-Canadians pay three times as much tuition for undergraduate courses as Canadian citizens do.

Upon approval and evaluation, students may obtain credit for prior academic experience, but not for experiential learning.

The University of Waterloo's undergraduate distance-learning courses are offered on a time schedule; papers and exams must be completed by specific times within one of three terms available each academic year. Both online and correspondence-based classes are available.

The Master of Applied Science in management of technology is designed for engineers and scientists who need to deal with technology management in their jobs. This part-time program is available to students worldwide and may be completed through a mix of online and correspondence courses.

University of Wisconsin—Superior

An individualized Bachelor of Science degree completed through off-campus study assignments with occasional student-faculty meetings

Distance Learning Center
Erlanson 105, Belknap & Catlin
Post Office Box 2000
Superior, WI 54880

WEBSITE http://edp.uwsuper.edu
EMAIL extdegree@uwsuper.edu
TELEPHONE (715) 394-8487
FAX (715) 394-8139
YEAR ESTABLISHED 1893
OWNERSHIP STATUS Nonprofit, state
RESIDENCY Negotiable
COST Average
DEGREE LEVEL Bachelor's

FIELDS OF STUDY OR SPECIAL INTEREST Individualized

OTHER INFORMATION In Superior's Extended Degree Program, the student can design a B.S. program in any field of academic or professional interest, provided that the faculty is willing and able to accommodate the intended program of study. The student earns credit by following predesigned study plans or by negotiating new learning contracts for faculty review. Work is organized around negotiable meetings between the student and faculty member. During these meetings, the student and faculty member review prior work and plan the next phase of independent study.

A considerable amount of credit is available for prior learning through transfer credit, credit by examination, and life-experience assessment.

Upper Iowa University

Associate's, bachelor's, and master's degrees in business-related and other fields, entirely through home study

External Degree Office
Post Office Box 1861
Fayette, IA 52142

WEBSITE www.uiu.edu
EMAIL extdegree@uiu.edu
TELEPHONE (563) 425-5252 • (888) 877-3742
FAX (563) 425-5353
YEAR ESTABLISHED 1857
OWNERSHIP STATUS Nonprofit, independent
RESIDENCY None
COST High average
DEGREE LEVEL Associate's, bachelor's, master's

FIELDS OF STUDY OR SPECIAL INTEREST Accounting, business, business leadership, human resource management, human services, management, marketing, public administration, social science

OTHER INFORMATION Upper Iowa's External Degree Program offers the opportunity to earn a B.S. in accounting, business, human resource management, human services, management, marketing, public administration, or social science. An A.A. with a liberal arts or general business concentration is also available. The program is based on directed independent study. Frequent interaction with the faculty by phone, mail, or email is encouraged. Enrollment is open to anyone, and applicants with a high school diploma or a GED are almost always admitted. Students are admitted throughout the year and can enroll in courses at any time. Optional one-week summer sessions are offered on the Fayette campus, allowing students to complete up to six semester hours of credit in a small amount of time. Credits may be awarded for previous college work (including online or correspondence courses from other institutions), job and military training, other noncollegiate educational experiences, life experience, and equivalency exams. Up to 90 of the 120 semester credits required for the degree can be transferred into the program. Students must complete a minimum of 30 semester hours with Upper Iowa University.

Upper Iowa University also offers an online M.A. in business leadership with three areas of emphasis: human resource management, organizational development, and quality management.

International students are admitted. Those interested should contact the school for application details.

Vermont College

Mentor-based degrees from one of the oldest nontraditional programs in North America

36 College Street
Montpelier, VT 05602

WEBSITE www.tui.edu/vermont college/index.htm
EMAIL vcadmis@tui.edu
TELEPHONE (802) 828-8500 • (800) 336-6794
FAX (802) 828-8855
YEAR ESTABLISHED 1834
OWNERSHIP STATUS Nonprofit, independent
RESIDENCY Short
COST High average
DEGREE LEVEL Bachelor's, master's

FIELDS OF STUDY OR SPECIAL INTEREST Art, education, environmental studies, history, human development, humanities, individualized major, interdisciplinary studies, liberal studies, management, psychology, social sciences, writing

OTHER INFORMATION Students seeking a Bachelor of Arts degree may choose between two residency programs: The first option meets from Friday evening to Sunday afternoon once every month; the second option meets for nine days once every six months. Students may choose from a wide variety of liberal arts majors, or create their own, including a general or specialized major in education. Students may also opt for another program that offers a B.A. in liberal studies, in which the student attends a two-week residency at the beginning of each semester, and a five-day residency at the end; in this program students are required to have a computer, and are offered the option to lease a laptop computer from the school, which they can then buy at half its fair market value upon graduation. This program is designed for students who wish to incorporate life experience, travel, and work experience into their curriculum.

The M.A. program has a similar flexibility in allowing the student to create an individualized major, and has several residency options, including the following: The first option allows the student to attend a single introductory colloquium upon enrollment, and otherwise conduct his studies through the Internet; the second option includes a colloquium to be attended at some point before graduation, and regular, regional seminars that occur at selected sites throughout the United States. In the third option, students come to the campus for a one-day weekend seminar every month; and finally, students may opt to work more closely with the experts in their field of study by attending two four-day colloquia each semester, which are preceded and followed by meetings with their professors and fellow students for further discussion. Program sched-

uling is flexible, and students can obtain their M.A. in as little as eighteen months.

Those seeking a Master of Education can earn their degree largely online, attending two residencies per year: a two-week residency in July, and a one-week residency in February. The M.F.A. in visual arts requires two ten-day residencies each year, one in August and one in February. The M.F.A. in writing has four eleven-day residencies throughout the year.

Formerly Vermont College of Norwich University; now owned by Union Institute & University.

Walden University

Master's and doctorate degrees in many fields by guided independent study

155 Fifth Avenue South
Minneapolis, MN 55401

WEBSITE www.waldenu.edu
EMAIL info@waldenu.edu
TELEPHONE (612) 338-7224 • (800) 925-3368
FAX (612) 338-5092
YEAR ESTABLISHED 1970
OWNERSHIP STATUS Independent
RESIDENCY None for master's programs; some for doctorates
COST High average
DEGREE LEVEL Master's, doctorate

FIELDS OF STUDY OR SPECIAL INTEREST Applied management and decision sciences, education, educational technology, health services, human services, psychology

OTHER INFORMATION Walden is a pioneer in offering graduate-level education by distance learning. Its degrees are earned through a combination of independent study, intensive weekend sessions held regionally (optional except for doctorate students), personal interaction with faculty, and a summer session held at Indiana University (also optional except for doctorate students). Indiana and Walden collaborate to give students online access to the Indiana University library and reference services.

Online master's degrees are available in educational technology and psychology and typically take eighteen months to complete.

The doctorate programs in applied management and decision sciences, education, health services, human services, and psychology allow students to complete an individualized study plan within a curriculum developed by Walden faculty. In the final phase of doctorate study, students design and carry out a research project written up as a dissertation, which must be orally defended. Most students complete their doctorate within three years of enrolling, but each student determines his or her own pace.

Walden students are mostly midcareer professionals. They engage in self-directed research in consultation with faculty mentors and by interacting with other students, both during residential periods and by use of the Internet.

Washington State University

Bachelor's and master's programs available to students everywhere by distance learning

Extended Degree Programs
Van Doren Hall 204
Post Office Box 645220
Pullman, WA 99164-5220

WEBSITE www.distance.wsu.edu
EMAIL ddpsvcs@wsu.edu
TELEPHONE (509) 335-3557 • (800) 222-4978
FAX (509) 335-4850
YEAR ESTABLISHED 1890
OWNERSHIP STATUS Nonprofit, state
RESIDENCY None (except for Doctor of Pharmacy)
COST Average
DEGREE LEVEL Bachelor's, master's, doctorate

FIELDS OF STUDY OR SPECIAL INTEREST Agriculture, business administration, criminal justice, education, engineering management, human development, manufacturing engineering, pharmacy, social sciences

OTHER INFORMATION Washington State University's (WSU's) office of Extended Degree Programs currently offers five degrees to students nationally and internationally. Courses are delivered through a variety of distance-learning technologies, primarily Internet and videotape delivery.

The B.A. in social sciences is a broad-based, interdisciplinary liberal arts degree. Working with an academic adviser, each student develops a program of study that best meets his or her educational goals. The B.A. in business administration leads students through a broad range of business disciplines. The B.A. in criminal justice offers a policy-focused curriculum based on a twenty-four-credit major and twenty-four credits of electives in psychology and sociology. The B.A. in human development involves a supervised internship in the student's local community setting. The B.S. in agriculture is offered by the Tri-State Agricultural Distance Delivery Alliance (TADDA), a cooperative distance delivery program developed jointly with the University of Idaho and Oregon State University.

Applicants to WSU's bachelor's programs must have already completed at least twenty-seven semester credits of coursework. Credit may be awarded by examination. Instruction takes place through a mix of online, correspondence, and video-based courses. The university offers more than 150 distance courses.

An M.S. in agriculture is also available.

Washington residents are also eligible for the following low-residency programs: a B.A. in education (with a teaching certificate), a B.S. in manufacturing engineering, a Master of Engineering Management, and a Doctor of Pharmacy.

Foreign students are admitted if they can provide an email address.

Western Illinois University

An individualized, student-centered Bachelor of Arts with no required on-campus residency

Non-Traditional Programs
5 Horrabin Hall
1 University Circle
Macomb, IL 61455

WEBSITE www.wiu.edu/users/mintp
EMAIL np-bot@wiu.edu
TELEPHONE (309) 298-1929
FAX (309) 298-2226
YEAR ESTABLISHED 1899
OWNERSHIP STATUS Nonprofit, state
RESIDENCY None
COST Low average
DEGREE LEVEL Bachelor's

FIELDS OF STUDY OR SPECIAL INTEREST Individualized major

OTHER INFORMATION Western Illinois University offers The Board of Trustees Bachelor of Arts through a nontraditional program designed to allow working adults with family and other responsibilities the chance to complete their degree requirements off campus. No major need be declared.

Of the 120 credits required for the B.A., at least 30 must be earned through WIU. Remaining credit can be awarded based on prior schooling at other regionally accredited colleges or universities, military and job-related training, examination (including CLEP, DANTES, and ECE), departmental exams, and other documentation of college-level learning. The university stresses that skills and knowledge acquired by nonacademic means can be evaluated for academic credit. Western Illinois provides a helpful guide to the preparation of a prior-learning portfolio.

Students who have not graduated from an Illinois high school must pass an exam on the United States and Illinois state constitutions or take an equivalent course in political science. All students must pass a university writing exam.

The time to complete the B.A. depends on the amount of transferable prior credit and the level of academic activity after admission.

The total cost of the program depends on the number and type of courses taken.

Appendix A

Law Degrees

There are two ways to become a lawyer in the United States without going to a traditional law school. One is to earn a law degree from a correspondence law school whose graduates can take the Bar exam. The other is to qualify for the Bar exam through apprenticeship study, the way Abraham Lincoln, four or five other U.S. presidents, and thousands of others have done. (Study by firelight is not required.)

Law Degrees by Mail

Many states used to permit people who studied law by correspondence to sit for their Bar exams. Now only California has this policy. People who pass the California Bar can apply to be licensed in a limited number of other states, typically after practicing law for three to five years in California. Earning a law degree by correspondence requires either three or four years of study, but only the four-year programs qualify for taking the California Bar. The four-year degree is earned by studying at home for 864 hours a year (an average of about seventeen hours per week) for four years. There are no shortcuts; you must take the full four calendar years, even if you have time for more study. At the end of the first year, correspondence students must take the First Year Law Students' Qualifying Exam, known as the Baby Bar, which the California Bar requires as an indication of whether a student is being well trained. Only about 20 percent of students pass the Baby Bar at any given sitting. In case of failure, the exam can be retaken an unlimited number of times. After completion of the Baby Bar, three more years of study follow and then the regular Bar exam—the same one taken by students at Stanford, Berkeley, and all the state's traditional law schools.

California's correspondence law schools are not approved by the American Bar Association (ABA), but they are accredited by the California Bar, thus qualifying students to take the regular Bar exam. Pass rates for individual schools vary widely, ranging from 0 to more than 75 percent (Oak Brook College).

Following is a list of all Bar-exam-qualifying correspondence law schools.

Bar-Exam–Qualifying Correspondence Law Schools

At the time of writing, graduates of the following schools qualified to take the California Bar exam. Because the rules change from time to time, it would be appropriate to confirm the status with the California Committee of Bar Examiners (180 Howard Street, San Francisco, CA 94105-1639; [415] 538-2303; email info@calbar.org; Website www.calbar.org) before embarking on any program. In the past, even when a school was disqualified, graduates were given a generous time period (typically seven years) in which to pass the Bar. But as any lawyer would caution, that is no guarantee of future behavior.

Abraham Lincoln University
3000 South Robertson Boulevard, Fourth Floor
Los Angeles, CA 90034
Phone: (310) 204-0222
Fax: (310) 204-7025
Email: info@alu.edu
Website: www.alu.edu/law/law.html

British-American University School of Law

2026 Summer Wind
Santa Ana, CA 92704
Phone: (714) 850-1027 • (888) 264-3261
Fax: (714) 850-4621
Email: info@lawprogram.com
Website: www.british-american.edu

Concord University School of Law

1133 Westwood Boulevard, Suite 2000
Los Angeles, CA 90024
Phone: (310) 824-6980 • (800) 439-4794
Fax: (888) 564-6745
Email: info@concordlawschool.com
Website: www.concord.kaplan.edu

The very large Kaplan test preparation company, which is itself a part of the very much larger *Washington Post* company, owns and operates this university.

Newport University School of Law

20101 Southwest Birch Street, Suite 120
Newport Beach, CA 92660
Phone: (949) 757-1155
Fax: (949) 757-1156
Email: info@newport.edu
Website: www.newport.edu

Northwestern California University School of Law

3620 American River Drive, Suite 115
Sacramento, CA 95864
Phone: (916) 480-9470
Fax: (916) 487-5681
Email: inquiry@nwculaw.edu
Website: www.nwculaw.edu

This university divides its law studies into four parts. Students who complete the first two parts earn a Bachelor of Science in law. Those who complete three parts earn the J.D. degree but do not yet qualify to take the Bar exam. Completion of four parts qualifies students to take the California Bar.

Oak Brook College of Law and Government Policy

Post Office Box 26870
Fresno, CA 93729
Phone: (559) 650-7755 • (888) 335-3425
Fax: (559) 650-7750
Email: info@obcl.edu
Website: www.obcl.edu

This evangelical Christian school has achieved impressive results on both the Baby Bar and the main Bar.

Saratoga University
780 Blairwood Court
San Jose, CA 95120
Phone: (408) 927-6760 • (800) 870-4246
Email: mhn@saratogau.edu
Website: www.saratogau.edu

Southern California University for Professional Studies
1840 East Seventeenth Street
Santa Ana, CA 92705-8605
Phone: (714) 480-0800 • (800) 477-2254
Fax: (714) 480-0834
Email: info@scups.edu
Website: www.scups.edu

University of London
The Information Centre, Malet Street
London, WC1E 7HU United Kingdom
Phone: 44 (20) 7862-8360
Fax: 44 (20) 7862-8358
Email: enquiries@external.lon.ac.uk
Website: www.londonexternal.ac.uk

William Howard Taft University
201 East Sandpointe Avenue, #400
Santa Ana, CA 92707-5703
Phone: (714) 850-4800 • (800) 882-4555
Fax: (714) 708-2082
Email: admissions@taftu.edu
Website: www.taftu.edu

In addition to the Bar-qualifying J.D. program, William Howard Taft offers an LL.M. in taxation.

The Apprenticeship Approach

It is possible to qualify for the Bar exam in a few states by studying law privately under the supervision of either a lawyer or a judge. Although setting up an apprenticeship program on one's own is not easy, it can be—and has been—done.

All of the states where apprenticeship is possible—Alaska, California, Maine, New York, Vermont, Virginia, Washington, and Wyoming—require evidence of four continuous years of law study. Some of those—Alaska, Maine, New York, and Wyoming—require that one of those years be at an ABA–approved law school. California also requires one year at a law school, but it doesn't have to be ABA-approved. (These are general guidelines; be sure to contact the individual state's Bar for specific requirements.)

For those aspiring to become a lawyer by apprenticeship, one interesting resource is the Law School Apprenticeship Program (2565 I-Road, Grand Junction, CO 81501; [800] 529-9383; Website www.lawprogram.com), operated by Roger Agajanian, who also runs the British-American University School of Law (see listing under Law Degrees by Mail). Its library of more than two hundred video lectures (available over the Web, on CD-ROM, or on tape) is designed to supplement the study of apprentice law students.

The Parlay Approach

Some California correspondence law schools have written about a "parlay" approach, in which their graduates would go on to do a Master of Law (LL.M.) degree—a higher degree than the J.D.!—at an ABA-accredited law school. The claim is that the student would be permitted to take the Bar in most states of the United States following this one-year residential program. While the idea is creative, no one has yet actually done it, and we would urge the exercising of caution before becoming involved in such a parlay approach.

Appendix B

For More Information on Schools in This Book

If you have questions about one of the schools described in this book, don't hesitate to write to us. We'll do our best to help. Following are the ground rules.

What to do before writing to us:

1. Point your Web browser to www.degree.net/updates/mailandinternet. At this site, we will post updates and corrections to the school listings in this book.

2. Check out the excellent news forum at www.degreeinfo.com, where more than fifty thousand messages have been posted, asking questions about distance-learning programs and providing answers from quite a few experts, including the authors of this book. The site has a good search engine, making it easy to check out schools.

3. Do your own homework. Check first with your local library, the relevant state education department, or the Better Business Bureau, as well as the Internet. Any major search engine should locate a school's Website. There is, for instance, a complete university list in the "universities" section of www.yahoo.com.

4. If a letter comes back as undeliverable, call directory assistance (information) in the school's city and see if a number is listed. You can get a new street address from directory assistance as well. Schools do move, and the post office will only forward mail for a short while.

5. If you can't reach a school by phone, write to it, or try directory assistance to see if there has been a change. Schools do change phone numbers, and the telephone company only notifies you of the new number for a short while.

Communicating with us

If you cannot reach a school by phone or mail or on the Internet, or if you have questions or problems, please write to us. We may be able to help. Also share any new information you think we should know.

- If you want a response, enclose a self-addressed, stamped envelope. If you are outside the United States, enclose two international postal reply coupons, available at your post office.

- If you want extensive advice or opinions on your personal situation, use the Degree Consulting Service that John established (although he no longer runs it). This service is described in appendix D.

- Keep in mind that we do our best to respond, but we get overwhelmed sometimes, and we travel a lot, so unfortunately not every question gets answered.

- Please don't telephone.

- Write to us at: Bears' Guide
  Ten Speed Press
  Post Office Box 7123
  Berkeley, CA 94707 USA

- Or email us at johnandmariah@degree.net.

Again, do let us know of any mistakes or outdated information you find in this book; we will post corrections at www.degree.net/updates/mailandinternet.

Appendix C

For Information on Schools Not in This Book

There are four reasons why a school in which you might be interested is not described in this book.

1. It might be relevant, but it simply was not one of the 101 schools we chose to include in this edition.

2. It is not relevant for this book because it does not offer degrees entirely or mostly by distance learning.

3. It's new, and we hadn't heard about it before this book went to press. (If so, write and tell us about it.)

4. It does not have recognized accreditation.

If you have questions about a school that is not described in this book, here is what we suggest, in the following order:

1. Check *Bears' Guide to Earning Degrees by Distance Learning,* a complete source for all distance-learning programs published by Ten Speed Press. In it we list more than twenty-five hundred schools that offer degrees by home study—good, bad, and otherwise. For more information, write to the address in the next list, or visit our Website at www.degree.net.

2. Check the excellent news forum at www.degreeinfo.com, where more than fifty thousand messages have been posted, asking and answering questions. It is free and easy to use, and if you post a question, you are almost certain to get a whole bunch of responses.

3. Look it up in one of the standard school directories that you can find in any public library or bookstore: Lovejoy's, Barron's, Peterson's, Patterson's, ARCO, and half a dozen others. These books describe virtually every traditional college and university in the United States and Canada.

4. Ask for the help of a reference librarian. Your tax dollars pay his or her salary.

5. If you know the location of the school—even just the state—check with the relevant state education agency.

If none of the above approaches produces any useful information, then write to us or email us, and we will do what we can to help.

- If you write, enclose a self-addressed, stamped envelope.

- If you want extensive advice or opinions on your personal situation, use the Degree Consulting Service described in appendix D.

- Don't get too annoyed if we don't respond promptly. We do our best, but we get overwhelmed sometimes, and we travel a lot.

- Please don't telephone.

- Write to us at: Bears' Guide
Ten Speed Press
Post Office Box 7123
Berkeley, CA 94707

- Or email us at johnandmariah@degree.net.

Appendix D

For Personal Advice on Your Own Situation

If you would like advice and recommendations on your own specific situation, a personal counseling service offers this information, by mail only. John started this service in 1977 at the request of many readers. Although he still remains a consultant, the actual consulting and personal evaluations have been done since 1981 by two colleagues of his, leading experts in the field of nontraditional education.

For a modest consulting fee, you get these things:

1. A long personal letter evaluating your situation, recommending the best degree programs for you (including part-time programs in your area, if relevant), and estimating how long it will take and what it will cost you to complete your degree(s).

2. Answers to any specific questions you may have with regard to programs you may now be considering, institutions you have already dealt with, or other relevant matters.

3. Detailed, up-to-the-minute information on institutions and degree programs, equivalency exams, sources of the correspondence courses you may need, career opportunities, resumé writing, sources of financial aid, and other topics in the form of extensive prepared notes.

4. Unlimited follow-up counseling by telephone, to keep you updated on new programs and other changes and to otherwise serve as your personal information resource.

If you are interested in this personal counseling, please write or call to receive descriptive literature and a counseling questionnaire, without cost or obligation.

If after you have these materials you do want counseling, simply fill out the questionnaire and return it, with a letter and a resumé if you like, along with the fee. Your personal reply and counseling materials will be airmailed to you as quickly as possible.

For free information about this service, write, telephone, or email to

Degree Consulting Services
Post Office Box 3533
Santa Rosa, CA 95402
Phone: (707) 539-6466
Fax: (707) 538-3577
Email: degrees@sonic.net
Website: www.degreeconsult.com

Appendix E

Higher-Education Agencies

The following agencies license, regulate, or are otherwise concerned with higher education in their state, province, or country. If you have any concerns about the legality of an institution, or its right to award degrees, these are the places to ask. This information changes on almost a daily basis. If you discover errors or changes, please let us know at johnandmariah@degree.net. Thank you.

United States: State Agencies

Alabama
Commission on Higher Education
100 North Union Street
Montgomery, AL 36130
Phone: (334) 242-1998
Fax: (334) 242-0268
Website: www.ache.state.al.us

Alaska
Alaska Commission on Postsecondary
Education
3030 Vintage Boulevard
Juneau, AK 99801
Phone: (907) 465-2962
Fax: (907) 465-5316
Website: www.state.ak.us/acpe

Arizona
Arizona Commission for Postsecondary
Education
2020 North Central Avenue, Suite 275
Phoenix, AZ 85004
Phone: (602) 229-2591
Fax: (602) 229-2599
Website: www.acpe.asu.edu

Arkansas
Arkansas Department of Higher
Education
114 East Capitol Avenue
Little Rock, AR 72201
Phone: (501) 371-2000
Fax: (501) 371-2003

California
Bureau for Private, Postsecondary and
Vocational Education
1027 Tenth Street, Fourth Floor
Sacramento, CA 95814

Phone: (916) 445-3427
Fax: (916) 323-6571
Website: www.dca.ca.gov/bppve

Colorado
Colorado Commission on Higher
Education
1300 Broadway, Second Floor
Denver, CO 80203
Phone: (303) 866-2723
Fax: (303) 860-9750

Connecticut
Board of Governors for Higher
Education
61 Woodland Street
Hartford, CT 06105
Phone: (860) 947-1801
Fax: (860) 947-1310
Website: www.ctdhe.commnet.edu

Delaware
Delaware Higher Education
Commission
Carvel State Office Building
820 North French Street
Wilmington, DE 19801
Phone: (302) 577-3240
Fax: (302) 577-6765
Website: www.doe.state.de.us

District of Columbia
Office of Postsecondary Education
Research and Assistance
2100 Martin Luther King, Jr. Avenue SE
Suite 401
Washington, DC 20020
Phone: (202) 727-3688
Fax: (202) 727-2739

Florida
Florida Postsecondary Education
Planning Commission
Turlington Building
Tallahassee, FL 32399
Phone: (904) 488-7894
Fax: (904) 922-5388

Georgia
Board of Regents
270 Washington Street SW
Atlanta, GA 30334
Phone: (404) 656-2202
Fax: (404) 657-6979
Website: www.usg.edu

Hawaii
State Postsecondary Education
Commission
2444 Dole Street, Room 209
Honolulu, HI 96822
Phone: (808) 956-8207
Fax: (808) 956-5286

Idaho
Idaho Board of Education
Post Office Box 83720
Boise, ID 83720-0027
Phone: (208) 334-2270
Fax: (208) 334-2632
Website: www.sde.state.id.us/Dept

Illinois
Board of Higher Education
431 East Adams, Second Floor
Springfield, IL 62701
Phone: (217) 782-2551
Fax: (217) 782-8548
Website: www.ibhe.state.il.us

Indiana
Indiana Commission for Higher
Education
101 West Ohio Street, Suite 550
Indianapolis, IN 46204
Phone: (317) 464-4400
Fax: (317) 464-4410
Website: www.che.state.in.us

Iowa
Board of Regents
100 Court Avenue, Suite 203
Des Moines, IA 50319
Phone: (515) 281-3934
Fax: (515) 281-6420
Website: www2.state.ia.us/regents

Kansas
Kansas Board of Regents
700 Southwest Harrison, Suite 1410
Topeka, KS 66603
Phone: (913) 296-3421
Fax: (913) 296-0983
Website: www.kansasregents.org

Kentucky
Kentucky Council on Postsecondary
Education
1024 Capital Center Drive, Suite 320
Frankfort, KY 40601
Phone: (502) 573-1555
Fax: (502) 573-1535
Website: www.cpe.state.ky.us

Louisiana
Board of Regents
150 Third Street, Suite 129
Baton Rouge, LA 70801
Phone: (504) 342-4253
Fax: (504) 342-9318
Website: www.regents.state.la.us

Maine
Department of Education Office of
Higher Education
23 State House Station
Augusta, ME 04333
Phone: (207) 287-5323
Fax: (207) 287-1344
Website:
www.janus.state.me.us/education

Maryland
Maryland Higher Education
Commission
16 Francis Street
Annapolis, MD 21401
Phone: (410) 974-2971
Fax: (410) 974-3513
Website: www.mhec.state.md.us

Massachusetts

Massachusetts Board of Higher
Education
1 Ashburton Place, Room 1401
Boston, MA 02108
Phone: (617) 727-7785
Fax: (617) 727-6397
Website: www.mass.edu

Michigan

Michigan Department of Career
Development
Office of Postsecondary Services
Post Office Box 30714
Lansing, MI 48909
Phone: (517) 373-3820
Fax: (517) 373-2759
Website: www.state.mi.us/career

Minnesota

Minnesota Higher Education Services
Office
1450 Energy Park Drive, Suite 350
Saint Paul, MN 55108-5227
Phone: (651) 642-0533
Fax: (651) 642-0672
Website: www.mheso.state.mn.us

Mississippi

Board of Trustees of State Institutions of
Higher Learning
3825 Ridgewood Road
Jackson, MS 39211
Phone: (601) 982-6623
Fax: (601) 987-4172
Website: www.ihl.state.ms.us

Missouri

Coordinating Board for Higher
Education
3515 Amazonas Drive
Jefferson City, MO 65109
Phone: (573) 751-2361
Fax: (573) 751-6635
Website: www.mocbhe.gov

Montana

Office of the Commissioner of Higher
Education
Montana University System
2500 Broadway
Helena, MT 59620

Phone: (406) 444-6570
Fax: (406) 444-1469
Website: www.montana.edu/wwwoche

Nebraska

Coordinating Commission for
Postsecondary Education
Post Office Box 95005
Lincoln, NE 68509
Phone: (402) 471-2847
Fax: (402) 471-2886
Website: www.ccpe.state.ne.us

Nevada

University and Community College
System of Nevada
2601 Enterprise Road
Reno, NV 89512
Phone: (775) 784-4905
Fax: (775) 784-1127
Website: www.nevada.edu

New Hampshire

New Hampshire Postsecondary
Education Commission
2 Industrial Park Drive
Concord, NH 03301
Phone: (603) 271-2555
Fax: (603) 271-2696
Website: www.state.nh.us/postsecondary

New Jersey

Commission on Higher Education
20 West State Street
Post Office Box 542
Trenton, NJ 08625
Phone: (609) 292-4310
Fax: (609) 292-7225
Website: www.state.nj.us/highereducation

New Mexico

Commission on Higher Education
1068 Cerrillos Road
Santa Fe, NM 87501
Phone: (505) 827-7383
Fax: (505) 827-7392
Website: www.nmche.org

New York

New York State Education Department
89 Washington Avenue
Albany, NY 12234

Phone: (518) 474-5844
Fax: (518) 473-4909
Website: www.nysed.gov

North Carolina
Commission on Higher Education
Facilities
UNC General Administration
910 Raleigh Road, Post Office Box 2688
Chapel Hill, NC 27515
Phone: (919) 962-4611
Fax: (919) 962-0008

North Dakota
North Dakota University System
Tenth Floor, State Capitol
600 East Boulevard Avenue, Department
215
Bismarck, ND 58505
Phone: (701) 328-2960
Fax: (701) 328-2961
Website: www.ndus.nodak.edu

Ohio
Ohio Board of Regents
30 East Broad Street, Thirty-Sixth Floor
Columbus, OH 43266
Phone: (614) 466-6000
Fax: (614) 466-5866
Website: www.bor.state.oh.us

Oklahoma
Oklahoma State Regents for Higher
Education
500 Education Building
State Capitol Complex
Oklahoma City, OK 73105
Phone: (405) 524-9100
Fax: (405) 524-9230
Website: www.okhighered.org

Oregon
Governor's Office of Education and
Workforce Policy
Office of Degree Authorization
255 Capitol Street NE, Suite 126
Salem, OR 97310
Phone: (503) 378-3921
Fax: (503) 378-4789
Website: www.ode.state.or.us

Pennsylvania
Pennsylvania Department of Education
Postsecondary and Higher Education
333 Market Street, Twelfth Floor
Harrisburg, PA 17126
Phone: (717) 787-5041
Fax: (717) 783-0583
Website: www.pde.psu.edu

Rhode Island
Office of Higher Education
301 Promenade Street
Providence, RI 02908
Phone: (401) 222-6560
Fax: (401) 222-6111
Website: www.uri.edu/ribog

South Carolina
South Carolina Commission on Higher
Education
1333 Main Street, Suite 200
Columbia, SC 29201
Phone: (803) 737-2260
Fax: (803) 737-2297
Website: www.che400.state.sc.us

South Dakota
South Dakota Board of Regents
306 East Capital Avenue
Pierre, SD 57501
Phone: (605) 773-3455
Fax: (605) 773-5320
Website: www.ris.sdbor.edu

Tennessee
Tennessee Higher Education
Commission
Parkway Towers, Suite 1900
404 James Robertson Parkway
Nashville, TN 37243
Phone: (615) 741-3605
Fax: (615) 741-6230
Website: www.state.tn.us/thec

Texas
Texas Higher Education Coordinating
Board
Post Office Box 12788
Austin, TX 78711
Phone: (512) 427-6101
Fax: (512) 483-6127
Website: www.thecb.state.tx.us

Utah
Utah State Board of Regents
3 Triad Center, Suite 550
Salt Lake City, UT 84180
Phone: (801) 321-7101
Fax: (801) 321-7199
Website: www.utahsbr.edu

Vermont
State Department of Education
Career and Lifelong Learning
120 State Street
Montpelier, VT 05620
Phone: (802) 828-3147
Fax: (802) 828-3140
Website: www.cit.state.vt.us/educ

Virginia
State Council of Higher Education
for Virginia
James Monroe Building, Ninth Floor
101 North Fourteenth Street
Richmond, VA 23219
Phone: (804) 225-2600
Fax: (804) 371-7911
Website: www.schev.edu

Washington
Higher Education Coordinating Board
917 Lakeridge Way
Post Office Box 43430
Olympia, WA 98504
Phone: (360) 753-7800
Fax: (360) 753-7808
Website: www.hecb.wa.gov

West Virginia
West Virginia Higher Education Policy
Commission
1018 Kanawha Boulevard East, Suite 700
Charleston, WV 25301
Phone: (304) 558-2101
Fax: (304) 558-5719
Website: www.hepc.wvnet.edu

Wisconsin
Higher Educational Aids Board
131 West Wilson Street, Room 902
Madison, WI 53703
Phone: (608) 267-2206
Fax: (608) 267-2808
Website: www.heab.state.wi.us

Wyoming
Wyoming Community College
Commission
2020 Carey Avenue, Eighth Floor
Cheyenne, WY 82002
Phone: (307) 777-7763
Fax: (307) 777-6567
Website: www.commission.wcc.edu

American Samoa
Board of Higher Education
American Samoa Community College
Post Office Box 2609
Pago Pago, AS 96799
Phone: (684) 699-9155

Puerto Rico
Puerto Rico Council on Higher
Education
Post Office Box 19900
San Juan, PR 00910
Phone: (787) 724-7100
Fax: (787) 725-1275

Canada

Alberta
Alberta Learning
Seventh Floor, Commerce Place
10155–102 Street
Edmonton, AB T5J IX4
Phone: (780) 427-7219
Fax: (780) 422-1263

British Columbia
Private Postsecondary Education
Commission
960 Quayside Drive, Suite 405
New Westminster, BC V3M 6G2
Phone: (604) 660-4400
Fax: (604) 660-3312

Manitoba
Department of Education and Training
Second floor, 800 Portage Avenue
Winnipeg, MB R3C 0N4
Phone: (204) 945-2211
Fax: (204) 945-8692
Website: www.gov.mb.ca/educate

New Brunswick
Department of Training and
Employment Development
Post Office Box 6000
470 York Street
Frederickton, NB E3B 5H1
Phone: (506) 453-2597
Fax: (506) 453-3038

Newfoundland
Newfoundland and Labrador Council on
Higher Education
Third Floor, West Block, Confederation
Building
Post Office Box 8700
Saint John's, NL A1B 4J6
Phone: (709) 729-2083
Fax: (709) 729-3669
Website: www.gov.nf.ca/edu

Nova Scotia
Department of Education
Post Office Box 578
2021 Brunswick Street, Suite 402
Halifax, NS B3J 2S9
Phone: (902) 424-5168
Fax: (902) 424-0511
Website: www.ednet.ns.ca

Ontario
Ministry of Education
Fourteenth Floor, Mowat Block
900 Bay Street
Toronto, ON M7A 1L2
Phone: (416) 325-2929
Fax: (416) 325-2934
Website: www.edu.gov.on.ca

Prince Edward Island
Department of Education
Second Floor, Sullivan Building
Sixteen Fitzroy Street, Post Office Box
2000
Charlottetown, PE C1A 7N8
Phone: (902) 368-4600
Fax: (902) 368-4663
Website: www.gov.pe.ca

Quebec
Ministère de l'Éducation
1035, rue De La Chevrotière
Édifice Marie-Guyart, 28e étage
Québec, QC G1R 5A5
Phone: (418) 643-7095
Website: www.meq.gouv.qc.ca

Saskatchewan
Saskatchewan Education
2220 College Avenue
Regina, SK S4P 3V7
Phone: (306) 787-6030
Fax: (306) 787-7392
Website: www.sasked.gov.sk.ca

Agencies Outside the United States and Canada

Australia
Australian Qualifications Framework
Advisory Board Secretariat
Post Office Box 609, Carlton South 3053
Victoria
Phone: 61 (3) 9639-1606
Fax: 61 (3) 9639-1315
Email: aqfab@curriculum.edu.au
Website: www.aqf.edu.au/

Belgium
Ministry of National Education
Centre Arts Lux, Fourth and Fifth
Floors
58 Avenue des Arts, BP5
1040 Brussels
Phone: 32 (2) 512-66-60

Brazil
Ministry of Education and Culture
Esplanada dos Ministerios, Bloco L
74.047 Brasilia, DF
Phone: 55 (61) 214-8432

Bulgaria
Ministry of Education and Science
Boulevard A, Stamboliski 18
Sofia 1000

Cuba
Ministry of Higher Education
Calle 23y F, Vedado
Havana

Denmark
The Danish Ministry of Education
Frederiksholms Kanal 21
DK-1220 Copenhagen
Phone: 45-3392-5000
Fax: 45-3392-5547
Website: www.uvm.dk/eng

Egypt
Ministry of Education
12 El Falaki Street, Cairo
Phone: 20 (2) 516-9744
Fax: 20 (2) 516-9560

Finland
Ministry of Education
Post Office Box 293
FIN-00171 Helsinki
Phone: 358 (9) 1341-71
Fax: 358 (9) 135-9335
Website: www.minedu.fi

France
Ministry of National Education
110 Rue de Grenelle
75700 Paris
Phone: 33 (1) 45-50-10-10

Germany
Ministry of Education and Science
Heinemannstr. 2
5300 Bonn 2

Greece
Ministry of Education and Science
Odo Mihalakopoulou 80, Athens
Phone: 30 (1) 21-3230461

Hungary
Ministry of Education
Szalay u. 10-14
1055 Budapest
Phone: 36 (1) 302-0600
Fax: 36 (1) 302-3002
Website: www.om.hu

India
Department of Education
Ministry of Human Resource
Development
Government of India
Shastri Bhawan, New Delhi-110001
Phone: 91 (11) 3387342
Fax: 91 (11) 3381355
Website: www.education.nic.in

Indonesia
Ministry of National Education
Jalan Jenderal Sudirman
Senayan, Jakarta Pusat
Website: www.pdk.go.id

Ireland
Department of Education and Science
Marlborough Street
Dublin 1
Phone: 353 (1) 8734700, ext. 2162
Fax: 353 (1) 8786712
Website: www.irlgov.ie/educ

Israel
Council for Higher Education
Post Office Box 4037
Jerusalem 91040
Phone: 972 (2) 5679911
Fax: 972 (2) 5660625
Website: www.israel-mfa.gov.il

Italy
Ministry of Public Education
Viale Trastevere 76/A
00153 Rome
Phone: 39 (6) 58-49-1
Website: www.istruzione.it

Japan
Ministry of Education, Science, Sports
and Culture
Website: www.monbu.go.jp

Mexico
Secretaria de Education Publica
Website: www.sep.gob.mx

Netherlands
Ministry of Education, Culture and
Science
Department of Foreign Information
Post Office Box 25000
2700 LZ Zoetermeer
Phone: 31 (79) 3232323
Fax: 31 (79) 3232320
Website: www.minocw.nl

New Zealand
Ministry of Eduation
National Office
45-47 Pipitea Street
Post Office Box 1666
Thorndon, Wellington
Phone: 64 (4) 473-5544
Fax: 64 (4) 499-1327

Norway
Ministry of Education, Research and
Church Affairs
Akersgt. 44, Post Office Box 8119
Dep. 0032 Oslo
Phone: 47 (22) 24-77-01
Fax: 47 (22) 24-27-33
Website: www.odin.dep.no/kuf/engelsk

Philippines
Department of Education, Culture and
Sports
DECS Complex, Meralco Avenue
Pasig City
Phone: 63 (2) 633-7228
Fax: 63 (2) 632-0805
Website: www.decs.gov.ph

Portugal
Ministry of Education
Av. 5 de Outubro 107
Lisbon
Phone: 351 (1) 21-793-16-03
Fax: 351 (1) 21-796-41-19
Website: www.min-edu.pt

South Africa
Department of Education
Private Bag X895
Pretoria 0001
Phone: 27 (12) 312-5911
Fax: 27 (12) 325-6260
Website: www.education.pwv.gov.za

South Korea
Ministry of Education
77, Sejong-ro, Chongro-ku
Seoul 110-760
Phone: 82 (2) 739-3345
Fax: 82 (2) 723-7691
Website: www.moe.go.kr/english

Spain
Ministry of Education and Culture
Website: www.mec.es

Sweden
Ministry of Education and Cultural
Affairs
Mynttorget 1
Stockholm 103 33
Phone: 46 (8) 736-10 00

Turkey
Ministry of Education, Youth, and
Sports
Milli Egitum, Genclik ve Spor
Bakanligi, Anakara

United Kingdom
Department of Education and Science
Elizabeth House, York Road
London SEI 7PH
Phone: 44 (171) 928-9222

Appendix F

State Laws in Transition

Laws are rarely carved in stone: Both the laws themselves and their interpretations can change. This is certainly true in the areas of school recognition and degree acceptance. Often, the laws are quite imprecise. For instance, a school-licensing law may say, "The State Department of Education shall establish standards and procedures for licensing degree-granting schools, and implement them by [such and such a date]." It is then up to the appropriate state officials to make the policies. And even then, laws are always subject to challenge by people who don't like them (or are arrested for violation of them).

Many nontraditional schools and most unaccredited schools have addresses in one of a small number of U.S. states, either because those states have laws that encourage or permit such schools (California, Florida, Hawaii) or because they have such weak laws that almost anyone can do almost anything (Alabama, Mississippi, Montana, Wyoming). The situation in these states changes with some regularity because of new laws, new interpretations, or both. And it is not uncommon for any given school to move (or, more likely, simply to change its mailing address) from one place to another, as the laws change. California used to be the haven for many nonwonderful schools. When California laws got tougher, many schools moved to Arizona, then to Louisiana (which finally got some tough school laws in 2002), then to Hawaii (which had more than two hundred "universities" in 2000, all but a few run from mailbox services—but thanks to zealous enforcement by the state consumer agency, very few bad ones remain) and South Dakota (which moved very quickly to toughen its laws after a good many bad schools started renting mailboxes there). Now the nonwonderfuls operate mostly from Alabama, Mississippi, Montana, and Wyoming and, increasingly, from offshore addresses, ranging from the Caribbean (Saint Kitts, Barbados, the Virgin Islands) to Liberia.

Here is the situation in some of the important states, and worldwide.

Alabama

For many years, Alabama has had a school licensing law. It doesn't have much power. There is no evaluation; no visit by the state is required. The "campus" can be a post office box or secretarial service. Indeed, some Alabama universities are, in fact, run from Louisiana, Rhode Island, California, and other locations. The situation has been, for years, complicated by the fact that four universities operated by Dr. Lloyd Clayton from Birmingham (Chadwick, American Institute of Computer Science, and two health and nutrition schools) did not even have the most minimal state license, yet they clearly operated with the knowledge and, it seemed, permission of the state. They did not, however, accept students living in the state of Alabama. The schools' position was that not taking Alabama students was simply their policy. It took us nearly five years of writing letters, sending faxes, and making telephone calls before we finally learned the truth. It seems that in the 1980s, the then-attorney general of Alabama issued a ruling that schools that did not do business in the state of Alabama did not need to be licensed by the state.

In 1996, however, this all changed. In response to a request from the Department of Education, the current attorney general ruled that all institutions based in the state *must* be licensed by the state, regardless of their policy for accepting in-state students. Nearly two years later, Chadwick and the others finally got their license to operate, and one of Dr. Clayton's schools, the American Institute of Computer Science, even went on to get recognized accreditation.

But in 2003, the state still does not evaluate the schools that it allows to call themselves "state approved." Some may be quite good; others have a "campus" that is a mailbox rental store. The state doesn't care.

Arizona

Arizona went from being one of the worst states to one of the toughest, following publication of a four-day series called *"Diploma Mills: a festering sore on the state of Arizona"* in the Phoenix newspaper in the 1980s. But Arizona law does allow new degree-granting universities to be established, as long as it is done on a small scale: fewer than 100 students unless and until the school gains recognized accreditation.

California

Well, at least California is unfailingly interesting. For many years, until the late 1980s, California was the laughingstock of U.S. education. California authorization required little more than a short disclosure form and evidence of $50,000 in assets. Shady operators were declaring that their homes were their universities, or buying a bundle of obsolete textbooks and declaring that they were worth $100 each. At the time diploma-mill operator Ernest Sinclair went to federal prison for mail fraud (selling degrees), his California Pacifica University was still a state-authorized institution.

For a few years, the state had a three-tiered system: authorized (the $50,000 rule) for entire schools, state approved (for specific programs within schools), or accredited. The authorized category was dropped, and approval was extended to entire schools, resulting in the current two-tier system. At that time, dozens of schools closed down, and some of the big ones opened offices in other states: Kennedy-Western in Idaho (later Hawaii and Wyoming), Century in New Mexico, Pacific Western in Louisiana (later Hawaii), Kensington in Hawaii (later Montana), etc.

State approval used to be granted by the Department of Education, through the Council on Private Postsecondary and Vocational Education. Then things got really silly.

In the early '90s, California's Superintendent of Public Instruction was indicted and convicted of several counts of felony conflict of interest and removed from office. For three years, the state had no superintendent, and things went somewhat adrift. In 1996, the Council's fate got caught up in political bickering, with the end result that by 1998 it was replaced by the Bureau of Private Postsecondary and Vocational Education, which fell under the jurisdiction not of the Department of Education but rather the Department of Consumer Affairs. And thus it came to pass that California has become the only state in the country, perhaps the only government in the world, in which school licensing and regulation does not take place in the Department of Education.

The Bureau (like the Council before it) is underfunded and understaffed, and still seems unable to deal with the common situation of schools that are run from California but claim their legitimacy from licensing in an easier state: Kennedy-Western (run from California, license from Wyoming), Kensington (California/Montana), Pacific Western (California/Hawaii), Century (California/New Mexico), and so on.

Another confusion in California is that the state senate decreed that holders of approved degrees should be permitted to take relevant state licensing exams, such as those in marriage, family, and child counseling. But the state board of professional licensing refused to go along with this automatic permission, saying that the standards for approval and the standards for certain exams were not at all the same. They now permit degree-holders from some schools, but not others, to take the exams. And almost no other state will accept California-approved degrees for state licensing purposes. Be sure to check on these matters if state licensing is part of your goal.

Florida

Florida is a classic case of what can happen when legislation gets out of hand. A 1988 Florida statute (Sections 817.566 and .567, Florida Statutes, 1988 Supplement) made it a crime to use an unaccredited degree in any way in that state, even if it is from a school approved or licensed in another state. It was a "misdemeanor of the first degree" [*sic*] for a person with, say, a California-approved or a Minnesota-approved degree, to reveal, within the boundaries of Florida, that he or she has that degree.

This rather extraordinary statute was challenged in court, and in 1995, the state supreme court found it to be unconstitutional. However, the judges strongly suggested that if the legislature were to rewrite the law a bit more carefully, it could achieve the same intent and be within the bounds of the constitution. So at the present time, it would appear that holders of legitimate degrees from other states can use them in Florida, but it is clear the situation is far from over. Indeed the legislature is once again considering a strong school licensing law.

Hawaii

Hawaii went from being one of the worst states to one of the best, almost overnight, due almost entirely to the efforts of one man. Jeffrey E. Brunton, an attorney with the state Office of Consumer Protection, is the marvelous and sadly rare thing—a true believer who sets out to make a difference. And make a difference he did. Brunton has been tremendously successful in getting judgments—sizeable cash judgments—against more than a dozen phony schools that operated with Hawaii addresses, and is working on a bunch more cases as we speak. If only every state had a Jeffrey Brunton! (Every state could. Where are the reformers out there?)

What was the situation he was working with? Glad you asked. Until 1999, Hawaii did not regulate any institutions of higher education at all. In 1990, a law was passed requiring the state Department of Consumer Affairs to register all unaccredited schools in the state, but it was minimally enforced. As you'd expect, Hawaii a few years ago had more unaccredited and highly questionable "universities" than the other 49 states combined. An article in the *Pacific Business News* in 2000 listed more than 200 unaccredited colleges and universities with Hawaii addresses, along with the dozen or so properly accredited ones.

When Edward Reddeck, one of America's most notorious degree mill operators, moved his fake schools to the state of Hawaii, neither the state's attorney general nor the Department of Consumer Affairs showed any interest, nor did the education editor of Honolulu's major newspaper (who declined to run a story on this situation, stating, "Our job is to *report* news, not *make* news"). Fortunately, in this instance, federal authorities did care, and those phony schools were closed by the action of postal inspectors. *Then* the newspaper ran a big page-one story!

In the late 1990s, the tide began to turn, with the state's Department of Consumer Affairs exercising its muscle, with lawsuits for violation of the disclosure law against American State University, Pacific Western University, Cambridge State University, Monticello University, and others.

Finally, in 1999, the legislature passed a law calling for the regulation of unaccredited schools and requiring that any unaccredited schools claiming to operate from Hawaii must have at least one employee living in Hawaii, and at least 25 full-time students in the state of Hawaii.

Iowa

Iowa is another state in transition. Until 1995, it not only had a somewhat misleading school licensing law, but it also seemed extremely lax in enforcing what little law they had. Registration with the state was virtually automatic, but only gave schools permission to offer classes in Iowa. It did not authorize them to award degrees or to claim they were an Iowa-licensed school. Nonetheless, at least half a dozen schools did just that.

In 1995, the legislature attempted to address this situation by requiring all unaccredited schools to be on an approved "accreditation track," or leave the state: the so called "up or out" provision. But three years later, nothing seemed to have changed, with some of Iowa's wonders still operating without benefit of accreditation or any motion toward it.

We finally learned, thanks to a persistent reader of this book, that the Department of Education felt that it was too much to expect a school to get on an accreditation track quickly, and so they quietly gave the Iowa unaccredited schools three years to get on track. At least three of the many various unaccredited Iowa schools announced they would be applying for accreditation from the Distance Education and Training Council. But none of them seems actually to have done so, yet this may have bought more time from the state. Other schools with Iowa addresses have moved to more hospitable states like Alabama and Wyoming.

Louisiana

For many years, Louisiana has been the victim of what one highly placed state regulator privately calls the "Woody Jenkins law." Jenkins is the prominent Republican politician who is so opposed to the state regulation of almost *anything* that even though he graduated from law school with highest honors, he has refused to take the bar exam, believing that the state has no right to require such of lawyers.

Under Jenkins's influence, the legislature required that Louisiana's Board of Regents register any school that filled out a short form, with no evaluation whatsoever. This permitted some completely phony schools to advertise that they were "Appropriately registered with the Board of Regents," or even (improperly) that they were "Recognized by the Board of Regents."

In 1991, Louisiana passed a new law, which gave the Board of Regents power to regulate proprietary (privately owned) schools, although nonprofit schools were still exempt. In 1992, the Board of Regents decided that only proprietary schools with an actual physical presence in the state could be registered. Since dozens of "Louisiana" schools operate either from mail forwarding services or "executive suite" office-rental-by-the-hour establishments, quite a few schools using Louisiana addresses moved their addresses elsewhere, mostly to Iowa, Hawaii, or South Dakota. More than 20 closed down.

Following Jenkins's defeat in his try for the U.S. Senate, Louisiana legislators saw their chance, and in 1999 passed a law regulating not-for-profit schools that ostensibly operate from within Louisiana but, in fact, have nothing more than a convenience address and telephone answering service there. It took effect in early 2000 and, like the laws in Arizona and Iowa, requires unaccredited schools to be on an approved accreditation path. Unlike the other states, Louisiana inaugurated clear and specific requirements.

Louisiana unaccredited schools must now be accepted as an accreditation applicant by the Distance Education and Training Council (DETC), a recognized national accreditor. Schools rejected by DETC (as happened to Fairfax University, one of the first through the gate) either lose their Louisiana license or (as happened with Fairfax) can choose the one loophole in the new law: dropping all but purely religious degrees.

Schools whose applications are accepted by DETC must then pursue accreditation with all deliberate speed. If they get it, they remained licensed; if not, they lose their license to operate (and presumably look toward Montana, Wyoming, the Caribbean, or oblivion).

The Louisiana religious loophole is now a tiny one, but it was not always this way. Previously, religious schools were exempt from licensing, but there was no requirement that they offer purely religious degrees. LaSalle University, which operated for years under the religious exemption, used to claim that even their Ph.D.'s in physics, psychology, and political science were religious, because God created everything, including atoms, minds, and politicians. No matter what you study, they argued, you are studying the work of God. Thankfully, the loophole has been redefined; religious schools can offer only religious degrees: divinity, theology, and so on.

New Mexico

For some years, New Mexico had only one visible unaccredited school, Century University. But after the number reached two, then three, then four, with other schools looking in that direction and writing to the state agency in Santa Fe for information, New Mexico's Commission on Higher Education issued "Rule 730," a 21-page set of rules and guidelines for proprietary schools that either operate within the state, or recruit citizens of New Mexico from outside the state. Now, after the influx had begun, a tough new law has been passed. Unfortunately, it appears that Century has been grandfathered in.

Oregon

Hands down, Oregon has the strictest school laws of any state in the nation. In Oregon, it is *illegal* to use a degree from an institution not accredited by an accrediting agency recognized by the U.S. Department of Education or approved by Oregon's Office of Degree Authorization (ODA). In *Bears' Guide* terms, that roughly translates to any school.

Oregon takes the additional strong step of publishing, at www.osac.state.or.us/oda, a list of the most recently reported schools whose degrees are illegal in Oregon. They also note that these 141 schools, listed below, do not constitute a comprehensive listing of institutions whose degrees cannot be used in Oregon. It is a list of those most recently reported.

Academy for Contemporary Research
Academy of Healing Arts
Academy of Natural Therapies (Hawaii)
Academy of Religious & Spiritual Studies
Accelerated Degree Programs
Adam Smith University (Liberia, Saipan)
Addison State University (Ottawa, Canada)
Advanced Education Trust
Advanced Learning Network (Vermont)
Albert University (Delaware?)
Alexandria University (U.S. online, not Egyptian)
Almeda College (Florida?)
American Coastline University (Hawaii)
American Columbus University (California)
American Independent International University
American International University of Management and Technology (Hawaii)
American Pacific University (Hawaii)
American State University (Hawaii)
American World University (Mississippi)
Anacrusis Institute (Greece)
Anglo American University (Hawaii)
Ashington University (British Virgin Islands; Louisiana)

Atlantic International University (Hawaii)
Azaliah (New Mexico)
Barrington University (Alabama)
Benjamin Franklin Institute of Global Education
Berne University (New Hampshire; St. Kitts)
Bircham International University (U.K.; Bahamas; etc.)
Brantridge University (Hawaii)
Brighton University (Missouri; Hawaii)
British American Business Institute
California Coast University (California)
California Pacific University (California)
Cambridge State University (Hawaii)
Canyon College (Idaho)
Central Pacific University (Hawaii)
Central States Consortium of Colleges and Schools
Century University (New Mexico)
Clayton College of Natural Health (Alabama)
Clermont College of Business (Montana)
Colorado University of Naturopathic Medicine
Columbia Commonwealth University (Montana; Malawi, Africa)
Columbia Pacific U. (now Col. Commonwealth) (California)
Columbia State University (Louisiana)
Columbus University (New Orleans)
Commonwealth Open University (Virgin Islands)
Cornerstone University
Cranston University (online; Singapore; Nevada?)
Crown Church College & University
Earlscroft University (Great Britain, Commonwealth; Seychelles)
East Point Unversity
Edison University
Expressive Psychology Association
Fairfax University (Louisiana; Montana; S. Dakota; U.K.)
Frederick Taylor International University (Hawaii; California)
Glencullen University (U.K.)
Golden State University (Hawaii)
Greenleaf University (Missouri)
Greenwich University (Norfolk Island)
Hamilton University (Wyoming)
Hampton College (U.S. online; not Hampton U. of Virginia)
Harrington University (Great Britain)
Hawaii American University (Hawaii)
Holos (Missouri)
Holos University (Norfolk Island; South Dakota)
Honolulu University (Hawaii)
Illawarra College (New Hampshire; Virginia; Australia)
Institute for Creative Process
Institute for Human Dynamics
Institute for Science in Mind
Institute of New Media & Technology
John Thomas (Missouri)

Kennedy-Western University (Wyoming; formerly California and Idaho)
Kensington University (Hawaii; California)
Kingdom College of Natural Health (Louisiana; Russia)
LaSalle University (Louisiana)
Laureate University
Leibniz (New Mexico; Italy)
Lexington University (online; Nevada?)
Lincoln (New Mexico; Italy)
Lincoln International University, Inc. (Hawaii)
Madison University (Mississippi)
Marlborough University (Hawaii)
Midwestern U (Springfield, Missouri)
Monterrey Institute for Graduate Studies
Monticello University/Thomas Jefferson University (Kansas; Hawaii)
Newport University (Hawaii)
Northwestern International University, Ltd. (Cyprus; Denmark)
Oxford International University (Great Britain)
Pacific Southern University (Hawaii)
Pacific Western University (Hawaii; California)
Personal Therapy Institute
Pickering University (Hawaii)
Prescott College of Business and Leadership Studies (Hawaii)
Preston University (Wyoming)
Robert F. Kennedy University (Switzerland)
Romano (Minnesota)
Rushmore University (South Dakota)
Shelbourne University (Pennsylvania)
South Pacific University (Hawaii)
Southwest International University (Bayside, NY)
Southwest University (Louisiana)
St. George University International (St. Kitts)
St. John's University College of Medicine (Montserrat)
St. Mary's College of Medicine (Hawaii)
St. Regis University (Dominica)
Stanton University (Hawaii)
Stefan International University, Inc. (Hawaii)
Synergystics (Rochester, NY)
Tecana International Universita (South America)
Templeton University (online; Singapore; Nevada?)
The Dream Institute
The Thornwood University (probably U.K.; Netherlands)
Trident University of Technology
Trinity College and University (South Dakota)
United Pacific University (Hawaii)
University of Advanced Research (Hawaii)
University of Devonshire (U.K.)
University of Ecoforum for Peace (Hawaii)
University of Health Science (Hawaii)
University of Honolulu USA (Hawaii)
University of Metaphysics (California; possibly Nevada)

University of Northern Washington (Hawaii)
University of Palmers Green (U.K.)
University of San Moritz (Great Britain; Cyprus)
University of Santa Barbara (California)
University of Santa Monica (California)
Vancouver University Worldwide (British Columbia)
Verity (Michigan)
Verity College (Illinois; Michigan)
Vernell University
Warnborough College
Washington Institute for Graduate Studies (Utah)
Washington International University (Pennsylvania)
Washington School of Law (Utah)
Westbrook University (New Mexico; New York; California)
Wilson State University, Inc. (Hawaii)
Wittfield University (Hawaii)
YUIN/American University (Hawaii)
Zenith University (Hawaii)

South Dakota

South Dakota is an inspiring example of a state that was on the road to educational ruin and acted quickly to forestall that outcome. By 2000, as laws and the enforcement thereof showed signs of getting tougher in former havens such as Hawaii, Louisiana, and Iowa, the dreadful schools suddenly began to advertise from addresses in South Dakota, typically in malls and business centers just across the border from some of the larger towns in Iowa. Clearly it had simply never occurred to the good folks who run South Dakota that they needed a bunch of rules on the books to deal with a sudden influx of universities. And so there were virtually none. In the year 2000, one could take out a business license, rent a mailbox in a Mail Boxes Etc. store, hire a telephone answering service, and in little more than 24 hours, this new legal "state-licensed" (i.e. that business license) university can place its first ads in *The Economist* and *USA Today*.

To their credit, the South Dakotans took notice of the situation much more rapidly than most other states have. The newspapers, radio and television stations, and the Better Business Bureau all chimed in and, in 2001, SB160 was passed, requiring all institutions offering post-secondary education credit or degrees in South Dakota to hold accreditation from a regional accrediting agency recognized by the U.S. Department of Education or to participate in federal financial assistance programs. Good on ya South Dakota!

Wyoming

Wyoming may be the only state that not only does not regulate "religious" schools but also does not question the fact that a school says it is religious. Thus it is the last refuge of that strategy that says, "Let's start a religious school with a non-religious name, not tell the public that we are religious, and off we go." This has led, for example, to a truly dreadful place called Hamilton University operating without benefit of any scrutiny or regulation. Because Hamilton advertises extensively, and doubtless people are regularly calling the Department of Education to ask about them, this has led to the piteous situation in which Hamilton is the *only* school mentioned on the official state education Web site:

Question: Does the State of Wyoming exempt any postsecondary school from licensing?

Answer: ... The following types of schools are ... exempt: any parochial, church or religious school under the control of a local church, or religious congregation or a denomination, such as Hamilton University ...

Read it and weep at www.k12.wy.us/higher_ed/faq.html.

The Rest of the United States

Often, legislation arises in response to behavior. If legislators don't like the behavior, they pass laws against it. Commonly, it is only after unaccredited schools (good, bad, or in-between) become so numerous or so visible they cannot be ignored that states consider and even pass legislation to restrict or regulate them (see New Mexico and South Dakota, above).

Unless and until there is more international cooperation, it may be that schools will continue to be run like puppets: Operators in one country pulling the strings that make the school work in another country. As an example, there are at least six well-advertised universities actually run from England, but claiming their degree-granting authority from their registration in the U.S., Ireland, or a Caribbean nation. England apparently looks on them as "American" or "Irish" (etc.) schools and doesn't try to regulate them. And the U.S., Ireland, etc., may consider them to be British schools, since it is from there that things are run.

The Rest of the World

This is an evolving section, which may, one day, include both the laws and the actual practices of school licensing in countries worldwide. This is no simple matter, in part because of the difficulty of getting information, and in part because some smaller countries are just not prepared to deal with the matter of newly appearing universities in their territory. A few years ago, no one would have predicted, for instance, that the tiny island nation of St. Kitts and Nevis, with no degree-granting institutions of its own, would be home to five or more international universities (which happen to be run from the U.S., England, and Australia). Surely not the Minister of Youth, Education, and Community Affairs, who issues Certificates of Accreditation with, it seems, little semblance of a traditional evaluation process. For instance, the totally fraudulent Eastern Caribbean University, run from Smithville, Texas, was duly accredited by St. Kitts a few years ago, although they subsequently went out of business.

The United Nations and other agencies have attempted to address this issue, with varying degrees of success. It would be wonderful if there were one source that made the process of determining the legitimacy of schools relatively straightforward, at least as far as many registrars, admissions officers, and other evaluators are concerned. For a time, we (and most others) believed that the *International Handbook of Universities*, published regularly by UNESCO, was such a book and, indeed, it is the generally accepted arbiter in many places. However, they have been slow to react to the phenomenon of sketchy schools setting up operations in Caribbean (and perhaps other) nations, hence damaging this still quite authoritative work's credibility.

Other prime sources include the *World Education Series* published by PIER (Projects in International Education Research); the annual directory of the Association of Commonwealth Universities; and the *Countries Series* published by Australia's National Office on Overseas Skills Recognition. If a university in Singapore or Senegal, Barbados or Bangladesh, appears in any of these books, then it is still probably safe to assume that it meets the standards of GAAP, Generally Accepted Accreditation Principles (see the section on "Accreditation"). If it is not in those books, it still might be OK, but more due diligence is suggested. If it is in those books but anything, anything at all causes you concern, dig deeper. Search and/or post queries on degreeinfo.com and do some additional Internet research. It's your career and your money. You really can't be too careful.

What about the notion of an international accrediting agency? One that was thorough and well-respected and internationally accepted in the academic, government, and business worlds would be a wonderful thing to have. The waters have been well-muddied by dozens of such agencies that have arisen in recent years, ranging, in our opinion, from dreadful to extremely dreadful. One bright light on the horizon is GATE, the Global Association for Transnational Education, funded by Glenn Jones, the same entrepreneur who founded the now-regionally-accredited Jones International University. GATE has done good things in the direction of putting on international conferences on many aspects of reconciling the different education systems of 200+ countries, and has, in fact, initiated a "certification" process for schools. Perhaps one day, they will let the other shoe, the one called "international accreditation," drop. GATE's Web site is found at www.edugate.org.

Appendix G

Bending the Rules

One of the most common complaints or admonishments we hear from readers goes something like this: "You said thus-and-so, but when I inquired of the school, they told me such-and-such." Often a school claims that a program we have written about does not exist. Sometimes a student achieves something (such as completing a certain degree entirely by correspondence) that a high official of the school has told us was impossible. One of the open secrets in the world of higher education is that the rules are constantly being bent. But as with the Emperor's new clothes, no one dares to point and say what is really going on, especially in print.

Unfortunately, we cannot provide many specific examples of bent rules, naming names and all. This is for two good reasons.

1. Many situations where students profit from bent rules would disappear in an instant if anyone dared mention the situation publicly. There is, for instance, a major state university that is forbidden by its charter from granting degrees for correspondence study. But some employees there regularly work out special arrangements for students who are carried on the books as residential students even though all work is done by mail. Indeed, some graduates have never set foot on campus. If this ever got out, the board of trustees, the relevant accrediting agency, and all the other universities in that state would probably have conniptions, and the practice would be suspended at once.

2. These kinds of things can change so rapidly, particularly with new personnel or new policies, that a listing of anomalies and curious practices would probably be obsolete before the ink dried.

Consider a few examples of the sort of thing that is going on in higher education every day, whether or not anyone will admit it (except perhaps behind closed doors or after several drinks).

- A friend of John's at a major university was unable to complete one required course for her doctorate before she had to leave for another state. This university does not offer correspondence courses, but she was able to convince a professor to enroll her in a regular course, which she would just happen never to visit in person.

- A man in graduate school needed to be enrolled in nine units of coursework each semester to keep his employer's tuition-assistance plan going. But his job was too demanding one year, and he was unable to do so. The school enrolled him in nine units of "independent study," for which no work was asked or required but for which a "pass" grade was given.

- A woman at a large school needed to get a certain number of units before an inflexible time deadline. When it was clear that she was not going to make it, a kindly professor turned in grades for her and told her she could do the actual coursework later on.

- A major state university offers nonresident degrees for people living in that state only. When a reader wrote to John saying that he, living a thousand miles from that state, was able to complete his degree entirely by correspondence, we asked a contact at that school what was going on. "We will take students from anywhere in our correspondence degree program," she told us. "But for God's sake, don't print that in your book, or we'll be deluged with applicants."

- If we are to believe a book by a member of Dr. Bill Cosby's dissertation committee at the University of Massachusetts (*Education's Smoking Gun*, by Reginald Damerell), the only class attendance on Cosby's transcript was one weekend seminar, and the only dissertation committee meeting was a dinner party with spouses at Cosby's house.

- Partway through John's final doctoral oral exam, a key member of his committee had to leave for an emergency. The committee member scrawled a note and passed it to the dean, who read it, then crumpled it up and threw it away. The grueling exam continued for several hours more. After it was over and the committee had congratulated him and departed, John retrieved the note from the wastebasket. It read, "Please give John my apologies for having to leave and my congratulations for having passed."

- A man applied to a well-known school that had a rigid requirement that all graduate work (thesis or dissertation) must be begun after enrollment. He started to tell an admissions officer about a major piece of independent research he had completed for his employer. "Stop," he was told. "Don't tell me about that. Otherwise, you wouldn't be able to use it for your master's thesis."

- Mariah was denied admission to the University of California at Berkeley because of some "irregularities" on her high school transcript. (It was a nontraditional high school.) The high school's records had been destroyed in a fire. The former principal checked with the university and discovered that the admissions people would be glad to accept her once the computer said it was okay. He typed up a new transcript saying what the computer wanted said. The computer said okay, and three years later, Mariah graduated Phi Beta Kappa. But how many other applicants accepted the initial "no," not realizing that rules can often be bent?

Please use this information prudently. It will probably do no good to pound on a table and say, "What do you mean, I can't do this? John Bear says that rules don't mean anything, anyway." But when faced with a problem, it can surely do no harm to remember that there do exist many situations in which the rules have turned out to be far less rigid than the printed literature of a school would lead you to believe.

Appendix H

Advice for People in Prison

More than a few readers and users of this book are incarcerated or are friends and relatives of those who are incarcerated. We have invited a man who has completed his bachelor's, master's, and Ph.D. (University of South Africa) from prison and who consults often with inmates and others around the country to offer his thoughts and recommendations. Dr. Douglas G. Dean offers some very useful advice for noninstitutionalized people as well.

Arranging Academic Resources for the Institutionalized
by Douglas G. Dean, Ph.D.

One obstacle for any institutionalized person interested in pursuing a degree is limited resources: lack of available community, faculty, library facilities, phone access, and financial aid. To overcome these problems, it helps to streamline the matriculation process. Time spent in preparation prior to admission can help avoid wasted effort and time in a program, thereby reducing operating expenses and cutting down the number of tuition periods. A second obstacle is finding ways to ensure that a quality education can be documented. Because courses are generally not prepackaged, it is your responsibility as a student to identify varied learning settings, use a range of learning methods, find and recruit community-based faculty, provide objective means to appraise what has been learned, and, indeed, design the study plan itself.

Finding a flexible degree program

Most well-established degree programs grant credit for a variety of learning experiences. In terms of cost and arrangements required, equivalency examinations and independent study projects are the most expedient. Credit for life-experience learning is another option sometimes offered. If a degree program does not offer at least two of these options, it is unlikely that the program as a whole will be able to accommodate your needs as an institutionalized student.

Writing a competency-based study plan

The traditional method of acquiring credits is to take narrowly focused courses of two to four credits each. Because the nontraditional student must enlist his or her own instructors, find varied learning methods, and quantify the whole experience, the single-course approach creates much needless duplication of effort.

A better approach is to envision a subject area to be studied for nine to twelve credits (e.g., statistics) and designate a relevant independent study project. Identify what topics are germane to the area (e.g., probability theory, descriptive statistics, inferential statistics); the level of comprehension to be achieved (e.g., introductory through intermediate or advanced); how the topic is to be studied (e.g., directed reading, programmed textbooks); and how the competencies acquired are to be demonstrated (e.g., oral examination, proctored examination including problem solving). A single independent study project can in this way take the place of a series of successive courses in a given area (e.g., Statistics 101, 201, 301).

Designing the curriculum

Every accredited degree program has graduation requirements. These requirements broadly define the breadth of subject areas that make up a liberal arts education and the depth to which they are to be studied. It is the responsibility of the external student not only to identify a curriculum fulfilling these requirements but, in most cases, to design the course content that will make up each study module.

But how do you know what an area of study consists of before you have studied it? The answer lies in meticulous preparation.

Well in advance of formally applying for an off-campus degree program, obtain course catalogs from several colleges and universities. Look at what these schools consider the core curriculum and what is necessary to fulfill the graduation requirements. With this broad outline in mind, begin to form clusters of courses that fulfill each criterion. This approach helps shape the study plan academically.

Next, decide which subjects are of interest within each criterion area. Compare topical areas within each subject as described in the course listings, and commonalities will emerge. From there, it is simply a matter of writing to the various instructors for copies of their course syllabi. These course outlines will provide more detailed information about the subject matter and identify the textbooks currently used at that level of study.

Determining the means of study

Having decided what is to be studied, you must then propose various ways to study it. Equivalency exams (such as CLEP) will enable the student to acquire credits instantly, often in core or required areas of study. This helps reduce overall program costs by eliminating the need for textbooks and tuition fees. More importantly, it helps to reduce the number of special learning arrangements that must otherwise be made.

"Testing out" of correspondence courses (taking the examinations without doing the homework assignments) is another excellent way to acquire credits quickly. This can, however, be an expensive method, because full course fees are still assessed. Nonetheless, if you study on your own in advance according to the course syllabus, and if the instructor can then be convinced to waive prerequisite assignments, it can be an efficient and cost-effective method to use.

Independent study projects should form the balance of any study plan. With the topical areas, learning objectives, and learning materials identified, an independent study project allows you to remain with the same instructor(s) from an introductory through an intermediate or advanced level of study. This eliminates the need for new arrangements to be made every two to four credits. An independent study project can take the form of simple directed reading, tutorial instruction, practicum work, or a combination of these methods, culminating in the final product.

Direct tutorial arrangements, similar to the European don system, commit you to learning under a single instructor until he or she is convinced that you have mastered a given subject at a predetermined level of competency. The tutoring itself may take the form of directed reading from both primary and secondary sources, writing and orally defending assigned topical papers, monitored practica, and/or supervised research projects. The caveat is that the tutor determines when you have satisfied all study requirements, so the study plan should meticulously spell out the breadth and depth of what is to be studied.

You may also be able to use existing classroom courses as a setting in which to have your mastery of a given subject evaluated. Some institutions periodically offer an on-site college or vocational course (e.g., communications skills). Instead of taking such a course for the standard two to three credits, you may also be able to arrange for specific communication skills (composition, rhetoric) to be evaluated at a given level of mastery (beginning to advanced). In this single step, you may be able to earn advanced credit and fulfill all the communication skills core requirements for graduation.

Various professions require practitioners to earn continuing-education credits, usually through seminars and/or home study courses. These courses represent the latest knowledge in a given field, come prepackaged with an evaluation test, and are an excellent source of study material. The breadth and depth of specialization offered in such courses is especially useful to students with graduate or postgraduate aspirations.

Independent study projects require the aid of qualified people to act as community faculty and to oversee personally the progress of the work. It is therefore highly advantageous to line up faculty in advance of entering the degree program. It is equally important to have alternates available in the event that an instructor is unable, for any reason, to fulfill his or her commitment. It is better to anticipate these needs at the preparatory stage than to scramble for a replacement while the tuition clock is running.

Finding multiple treatments of subject matter

The external student is often without benefit of lecture halls, interactions with other students, or readily available academic counseling services. For the institutionalized student, stopping in to see a faculty member (or sometimes even picking up the phone) for help with a study problem is not an option. This is why alternative methods of study are so valuable.

One approach is to use several textbooks covering the same subject matter. If something does not make sense, you can turn to a different treatment of the subject. Programmed textbooks make especially good substitute tutors. A programmed text breaks the subject matter into small segments requiring a response from the reader, with periodic tests to check progress. Such texts are now available in many subject areas but are particularly useful for the sciences. Titles can be obtained from the *Books in Print* subject guide or by writing directly to textbook publishers.

Audiovisual materials can, to some extent, make up for the lack of lectures and classes typical of college life. Audiovisual departments at large universities often have a catalog of materials available for rental. These materials frequently take the form of a comprehensive tape series and may address even the most advanced subject matter. When using such materials, it is best to obtain them through the school or social service department of your institution of residence.

Some large campuses have lecture-note services that employ advanced students to attend class lectures and take copious lecture notes, which are then sold to students. Aside from yielding insights into good note taking, these published notes are an additional treatment of course content and can indicate what topical areas are given special emphasis. Such notes are especially recommended for new students.

Documenting study

The administrators of a degree program must be convinced that what has been learned and what levels of subject mastery have been achieved can be acceptably documented with more than just the student's word. Community faculty members may be asked to provide written or oral examinations, but it does not hurt to make their jobs easier.

It is highly recommended that each study project be evaluated using a number of means (objective tests, essay exams, oral exams) and documented using a variety of methods (student narrative, faculty narrative, test results, final product, grade equivalent, etc.). Self-evaluation, not unlike personal logs or journals, provides an excellent primary source from which to glean what you truly know, how you came to know it, and what new questions the acquired knowledge has given rise to. Any future employer or admissions counselor unfamiliar with nontraditional or off-campus degree programs can gain a fuller appreciation of the process through such narratives.

Likewise, a narrative evaluation written by the instructor provides a description of your competencies that ordinary assessment methods are unable to detect or reflect. Nuances of learning style, ability to converse in the field of study, and scholarly integrity are examples of such insights.

Depending on the subject at hand, a final product may take the form of a research monograph, video presentation, musical manuscript, senior thesis, and so forth—whatever will best prove and record that you have achieved the target level of competency in that field.

Most professions (accounting, psychology, law, medicine, and so forth) require licensing and/or board certification examinations. An industry has built up around this need, providing parallel or actual past examinations to help prepare students. If you agree to take a relevant sample examination under proctored conditions, with cutoff scores negotiated in advance, the community faculty member is relieved of having to design his or her own objective examination for just one student. This approach adds validity to the assessment process and provides a standardized score that has some universal meaning. This is an optional approach but may be worth the effort.

Recruiting community faculty

Just as it is easier for a student to organize a study plan into blocks of subject areas, a competency-based study plan of this sort makes it easier for a prospective instructor to visualize what is being asked of him or her. A typical independent study project defines for the instructor what specific topics are to be studied, what levels of mastery will be expected of the student, what textbooks or other materials will be used, and what is expected of the instructor.

Many traditional academics are unfamiliar with external degree programs. Consequently, they tend to assume that serving as your community faculty member will require greater effort and time on their part than for the average student, who in fact may expect their services in many roles, from academic adviser to tutor. The more you can do up front to define clearly the role and expected duties of the community faculty member, the more successful you will be in enlisting instructors for independent study projects.

Instructors may sometimes be found on the staff of the institution where you are located. They can also be found through a canvass letter sent to the appropriate department heads at area colleges, universities, and technical schools. The same approach can be used to canvass departments within area businesses, museums, art centers, hospitals, libraries, theaters, zoos, banks, and orchestras, to name but a few possibilities. People are often flattered at being asked, provided it is clear to them exactly what they are getting into.

The more you can operate independently and rely on community faculty for little more than assessment purposes, the more likely that you will be successful in recruiting help and thereby broadening your range of study options.

Revealing your institutionalized status

It is generally proper and appropriate to inform potential schools and potential faculty of institutionalized status. (Many institutions now have mailing addresses that do not indicate that they are, in fact, institutions.) Some schools or individuals may be put off by this, but you would not want to deal with them anyway. Others may be especially motivated to help.

A recommended approach is to first make a general inquiry about the prospective school or program. With this information (which is intended for the general student) in hand, you can better tailor inquiries to specific departments or faculty, addressing your specific needs.

Financing the educational process

Unfortunately, there are virtually no generalizations to be made here whatsoever. Each institution seems to have its own policy with regard to the way finances are handled. Some institutionalized people earn decent wages and have access to the funds. Others have little or no ability to pay their own way. Some institutions permit financial gifts from relatives or friends; others do not. Some schools make special concessions or have some scholarship funds available for institutionalized students; many do not. Contact the financial aid office of the prospective school with any such questions.

Again, start with a general inquiry, as would any student; then ask about the applicability of specific programs to your situation. Often a key element is to find someone on campus, perhaps in the financial aid office or in your degree program, who is willing to do the actual legwork, walking your financial aid paperwork to various administrative offices. A financial aid package is of no use to anyone if it cannot be processed.

In conclusion

Institutionalized students must be highly self-directed and honest enough with themselves to recognize if they are not. Because you live where you work, it takes extra effort to set aside daily study time. Not only do you have to get in the right frame of mind, but you have to accommodate institution schedules, too.

It can mean working with a minimum number of books or tapes to comply with property rules. It can mean study periods that begin at eleven o'clock at night, when the cell hall begins to quiet down. It means long periods of delayed gratification in an environment where pursuing education is often suspect. And it is the greatest feeling in the world when it all comes together.

An interesting program for inmates

We are aware of only one U.S. school that makes a significant outreach to prisoners: the University of Southern Colorado. Qualifying inmates can receive financial assistance in the form of grants and scholarships.

> University of Southern Colorado
> Office of Continuing Education (attention Donald Spano)
> 2200 Bonforte Boulevard
> Pueblo, CO 81001
> Phone: (877) 872-9653, option 3
> Email: orspano@rmi.net

Appendix I

Glossary of Important Terms

academic year: The period of formal academic instruction, usually from September or October to May or June. Divided into semesters, quarters, or trimesters.

accreditation: Recognition of a school by an independent private organization. Not a governmental function in the United States. There are more than a hundred accrediting agencies, some recognized by the U.S. Department of Education and/or CHEA, some unrecognized, some phony or fraudulent.

adjunct faculty: Part-time faculty members, often at a nontraditional school, often with a full-time teaching job elsewhere. More and more traditional schools are hiring adjunct faculty because they don't have to pay them as much or provide health care and other benefits.

advanced placement (AP): Admission to a school at a higher level than usual as a result of getting credit for prior learning experience or for passing advanced-placement exams.

alma mater: The school from which one has graduated, as in "My alma mater is Michigan State University."

alternative: Offering an alternate, or different, means of pursuing learning or degrees or both. Often used interchangeably with *external* or *nontraditional*.

alumni: Graduates of a school, as in "This school has some distinguished alumni." Technically for males only; females are alumnae. The singular is alumnus (male) or alumna (female), although neither of these terms is in common use.

alumni association: A confederation of alumni and alumnae who have joined together to support their alma mater in various ways, generally by donating money.

American College Testing (ACT) program: Administrators of aptitude and achievement tests.

American Council on Education (ACE): Publishes the *National Guide to Educational Credit for Training Programs* and *Guide to the Evaluation of Educational Experiences in the Armed Forces*.

approved: In California, a level of state recognition of a school generally regarded as one step below accredited.

arbitration: A means of settling disputes, as between a student and a school, in which one or more independent arbitrators or judges listen to both sides and make a decision. A means of avoiding a courtroom trial. Many learning contracts have an arbitration clause. *See also* binding arbitration.

assistantship: A means of assisting students (usually graduate students) financially by offering them part-time academic employment, usually in the form of a teaching assistantship or a research assistantship.

associate's degree: A degree traditionally awarded by community or junior colleges after two years of residential study or after completion of sixty to sixty-four semester hours.

auditing: Sitting in on a class without earning credit for that class.

authorized: Until recently, a form of state recognition of schools in California. This category was phased out beginning in 1990, and now all schools must be approved or accredited to operate. Many formerly authorized schools are now billing themselves as candidates for approval.

bachelor's degree: A degree awarded in the United States after four years of full-time residential study (two to five years in other countries) or the earning of 120 to 124 semester units by any means.

binding arbitration: Arbitration in which both parties have agreed in advance that they will abide by the decision of one or more independent arbitrators or judges and take no further legal action. *See also* arbitration.

branch campus: A satellite facility, run by officers of the main campus of a college or university, at another location. Can range from a small office to a full-fledged university center.

campus: The main facility of a college or university, usually comprising buildings, grounds, dormitories, cafeterias and dining halls, sports facilities, and so forth. The campus of a nontraditional school may consist solely of offices.

chancellor: Often the highest official of a university. Also a new degree title proposed by some schools to be a higher degree than the doctorate, requiring three to five years of additional study.

coeducation: Education of men and women on the same campus or in the same program. This is the basis of the term *coeds* to refer to female students.

college: In the United States, an institution offering programs leading to the associate's and/or bachelor's degree and sometimes to a higher degree. Often used interchangeably with *university*, although traditionally a university is a collection of colleges. In England and elsewhere, *college* may denote part of a university (Kings College, Cambridge) or a private high school (Eton College).

College-Level Examination Program (CLEP): A series of equivalency examinations that can be taken for college credit.

colloquium: A gathering of scholars to discuss a given topic over a period of a few hours to a few days. ("The university is sponsoring a colloquium on marine biology.")

community college: A two-year traditional school offering programs leading to the associate's degree and, typically, many noncredit courses in arts, crafts, and vocational fields for community members not interested in a degree. Also called *junior college*.

competency: The philosophy and practice of awarding credit or degrees based on learning skills rather than on time spent in courses.

correspondence course: A course offered by mail and completed entirely by home study, often with one or two proctored, or supervised, examinations.

Council for Higher Education Accreditation (CHEA): An agency that recognizes accrediting agencies in the United States.

course: A specific unit of instruction, such as a course in microeconomics or in abnormal psychology. Residential courses last for one or more semesters or quarters; correspondence courses often have no rigid time requirements.

cramming: Intensive preparation for an examination. Most testing agencies now admit that cramming can improve scores on exams.

credit: A unit used to record courses taken. Each credit typically represents the number of hours spent in class each week. Hence a three-credit or three-unit course would commonly be a class that meets three hours each week for one quarter or semester.

curriculum: A program of courses to be taken in pursuit of a degree or other objective.

degree: A title conferred by a school to show that a certain course of study has been completed.

diploma: The certificate that shows that a certain course of study has been completed. Diplomas are awarded for completing degrees or other shorter courses of study.

dissertation: The major research project normally required as part of the work for a doctorate. Dissertations are expected to make a new and creative contribution to the field of study or to demonstrate excellence in the field. *See also* thesis.

Distance Education and Training Council (DETC; formerly the National Home Study Council): The recognized accreditor for schools offering degrees and diplomas largely or entirely through distance learning.

doctorate: The highest degree one can earn (but *see also* chancellor). Includes Doctor of Philosophy (Ph.D.), Doctor of Education (Ed.D.), and many other titles.

dormitory: Student living quarters on residential campuses. May include dining halls and classrooms.

early decision: An earlier-than-usual decision on whether a student will be admitted. Offered by some schools primarily as a service either to students applying to several schools or to those who are especially anxious to know the outcome of their application.

electives: Courses one does not have to take but may choose to take as part of a degree program.

equivalency examination: An examination designed to demonstrate knowledge in a subject where the learning was acquired outside a traditional classroom. A person who learned nursing skills while working in a hospital, for instance, could take an equivalency exam to earn credit in, say, obstetrical nursing.

essay test: An examination in which the student writes narrative sentences as answers to questions instead of the short answers required by a multiple-choice test. Also called a *subjective test*.

external: Away from the main campus or offices. An external degree may be earned by home study or at locations other than on the school's campus.

fees: Money paid to a school for purposes other than academic tuition. Fees might pay for parking, library services, use of the gymnasium, binding of dissertations, and so forth.

fellowship: A study grant, usually awarded to a graduate student and usually requiring no work other than the usual academic assignments (in contrast to an assistantship).

financial aid: A catch-all term that includes scholarships, loans, fellowships, assistantships, tuition reductions, and so forth. Many schools have a financial aid officer, whose job is to deal with all funding questions and problems.

fraternity: A collegiate social organization, usually all male, often identified by Greek letters, such as Zeta Beta Tau. There are also professional and scholastic fraternities open to men and women, such as Beta Alpha Psi, the national fraternity for students of accounting. *See also* sorority.

freshman: The name for the class in its first of four years of traditional study for a bachelor's degree—and its individual members. ("She is a freshman and thus is a member of the freshman class.")

grade-point average (GPA): The average score a student has achieved in all of his or her classes, weighted by the number of credits or units for each class.

grades: Evaluative scores provided for each course and often for individual examinations or papers written for that course. There are letter grades (usually A, B, C, D, F), number grades (usually percentages from 0 to 100), or sometimes grades on a scale of 0 to 3, 0 to 4, or 0 to 5. Some schools use a pass/fail system with no grades.

graduate: One who has earned a degree from a school. Also, the programs offered beyond the bachelor's level. ("He is a graduate of Yale University and is now doing graduate work at Princeton.")

Graduate Record Examination (GRE): The exam required by many traditional schools and a few nontraditional ones for admission to graduate programs.

graduate school: A school or a division of a university offering work at the master's or doctorate degree level.

graduate student: One attending graduate school.

honor societies: Organizations for persons with a high grade-point average or other evidence of outstanding performance. There are local societies on some campuses and several national organizations, the most prestigious of which is called Phi Beta Kappa.

honor system: A system in which students are trusted not to cheat on examinations, and to obey other rules, without proctors or others monitoring their behavior.

honorary doctorate: A nonacademic award given regularly by more than a thousand colleges and universities to honor distinguished scholars, celebrities, and donors of large sums of money. Holders of this award may, and often do, call themselves "Doctor."

junior: The name for the class in its third year of a traditional four-year U.S. bachelor's degree program, or any member of that class. ("She is a junior this year.")

junior college: *See* community college.

language laboratory: A special room in which students can listen to foreign-language tapes over headphones, allowing many students to be learning different languages at different skill levels at the same time.

Law School Admission Test (LSAT): The test required by most U.S. law schools of all applicants.

learning contract: A formal agreement between a student and a school specifying independent work to be done by the student and the amount of credit the school will award on successful completion of the work.

lecture class: A course in which a faculty member lectures to anywhere from a few dozen to many hundreds of students. Often lecture classes are followed by small-group discussion sessions led by student assistants or junior faculty.

liberal arts: A term with many complex meanings but generally referring to the nonscientific curriculum of a university: humanities, arts, social sciences, history, and so forth.

liberal education: Commonly taken to be the opposite of a specialized education—one in which students are required to take courses in a wide range of fields, as well as courses in their major.

licensed: Holding a permit to operate. This can range from a difficult-to-obtain state school license to a simple local business license.

life-experience portfolio: A comprehensive presentation listing and describing all learning experiences in a person's life, with appropriate documentation. The basic document used in assigning academic credit for life-experience learning.

maintenance costs: The expenses incurred—other than tuition and fees—while attending school. Includes room and board (food), clothing, laundry, postage, travel, and so forth.

major: The subject or academic department in which a student takes concentrated coursework leading to a specialty. ("His major is in English literature; she is majoring in chemistry.")

Medical College Admission Test (MCAT): The test required of all applicants by most U.S. medical schools.

mentor: Faculty member assigned to supervise independent study work at a nontraditional school; comparable to adjunct faculty.

minor: The secondary subject or academic department in which a student takes concentrated coursework. ("She has a major in art and a minor in biology.") Optional at most schools.

multiple-choice test: An examination in which the student chooses the best of several alternative answers provided for each question; also called an *objective test*. ("The capital city of England is (a) London, (b) Ostrogotz-Plakatz, (c) Tokyo, or (d) none of the above.")

multiversity: A university system with two or more separate campuses, each a major university in its own right, such as the University of California or the University of Wisconsin.

narrative transcript: A transcript issued by a nontraditional school in which, instead of simply listing the courses completed and grades received, there is a narrative description of the work done and the school's rationale for awarding credit for that work.

nonresident: (1) A means of instruction in which the student does not need to visit the school; all work is done by correspondence, Internet, telephone, or exchange of audiotapes or videotapes; (2) a person who does not meet residency requirements of a given school and, as a result, often has to pay higher tuition or fees.

nontraditional: In education, refers to learning and degrees completed by methods other than spending many hours in classrooms and lecture halls.

objective test: An examination in which questions requiring a very short answer are posed. It can be multiple choice, true/false, fill-in-the-blank, and so forth. The questions are related to facts (thus objective) rather than to opinions (which would be subjective).

on the job: In the United States, experience or training gained through employment that may be converted to academic credit. In England, slang for having sex, which either confuses or amuses English people who read about "credit for on-the-job experience."

open admissions: An admission policy in which everyone who applies is admitted, on the theory that those who are unable to do university work will drop out before long.

out-of-state student: One from a state other than that in which the school is located. Because most state colleges and universities have much higher tuition rates for out-of-state students, many people attempt to establish legal residence in the same state as their school.

parallel instruction: A method in which nonresident students do exactly the same work as resident students, during the same general time period, except that they do it at home.

pass/fail option: An option in which the only grades are either "pass" or "fail." Instead of getting a letter or number grade in a course, the student may elect, at the start of the course, this option. Some schools permit students to elect pass/fail for one or two of their courses each semester.

Phi Beta Kappa: A national honor society that recognizes students with outstanding grades.

plan of study: A detailed description of the program an applicant to a school plans to pursue. Many traditional schools ask for this as part of the admission procedure. The plan of study should be designed to meet the objectives of the statement of purpose.

portfolio: *See* life-experience portfolio.

Preliminary Scholastic Aptitude Test (PSAT): A test given annually to high school juniors.

prerequisites: Courses that must be taken before certain other courses may be taken. For instance, a course in algebra is often a prerequisite for a course in geometry.

private school: A school that is privately owned rather than operated by a governmental department.

proctor: A person who supervises the taking of an examination to be certain there is no cheating and that other rules are followed. Many nontraditional schools permit unproctored examinations.

professional school: A school in which one studies for the various professions, including medicine, dentistry, law, nursing, veterinary, optometry, ministry, and so forth.

public school: In the United States, a school operated by the government of a city, county, district, or state or by the federal government. In the United Kingdom, a privately owned or run school.

quarter: An academic term at a school on the quarter system, in which the calendar year is divided into four equal quarters. New courses begin each quarter.

quarter hour: An amount of credit earned for each classroom hour spent in a given course during a given quarter. A course that meets four hours each week for a quarter would probably be worth four quarter hours, or quarter units.

recognized: A term used by some schools to indicate approval from some other organization or governmental body. The term usually does not have a precise meaning, so it may mean different things in different places.

registrar: The official at most colleges and universities who is responsible for maintaining student records and, in many cases, for verifying and validating applications for admission.

rolling admissions: A year-round admission procedure. Many schools admit students only once or twice a year. A school with rolling admissions considers each application at the time it is received. Many nontraditional schools, especially ones with nonresident programs, have rolling admissions.

scholarship: A study grant, either in cash or in the form of tuition or fee reduction.

Scholastic Aptitude Test (SAT): One of the standard tests given to qualify for admission to colleges and universities.

score: A numerical rating of performance on a test. ("His score on the Graduate Record Exam was not so good.")

semester: A school term, generally four to five months. Schools on the semester system usually have two semesters a year, with a shorter summer session.

semester hour: An amount of credit earned in a course representing one classroom hour per week for a semester. A class that meets three days a week for one hour, or one day a week for three hours, would be worth three semester hours, or semester units.

seminar: A form of instruction combining independent research with meetings of small groups of students and a faculty member, generally to report on reading or research the students have done.

senior: The fourth year of study of a four-year U.S. bachelor's degree program, or a member of that class. ("Linnea is a senior this year and is president of the senior class.")

sophomore: The second year of study in a four-year U.S. bachelor's degree program, or a member of that class.

sorority: A women's social organization, often with its own living quarters on or near a campus. Usually identified with two or three Greek letters, such as Alpha Xi Delta. The male version is called a *fraternity*.

special education: Education of the physically or mentally disabled or, often, of the gifted.

special student: A student who is not studying for a degree because he or she either is ineligible or does not wish the degree.

statement of purpose: A detailed description of the career the applicant intends to pursue after graduation. A statement of purpose is often requested as part of the admission procedure at a university.

subject: An area of study or learning covering a single topic, such as the subject of chemistry or economics or French literature.

subjective test: An examination in which the answers are in the form of narrative sentences or long or short essays, often expressing opinions rather than reporting facts.

syllabus: A detailed description of a course of study, often including books to be read, papers to be written, and examinations to be given.

Test of English as a Foreign Language (TOEFL): Test required by many schools of those for whom English is not their native language.

thesis: The major piece of research that is completed by many master's degree candidates. A thesis is expected to show a detailed knowledge of one's field and the ability to do research and integrate knowledge of the field. *See also* dissertation.

traditional education: Education at a residential school in which the bachelor's degree is completed through four years of classroom study, the master's in one or two years, and the doctorate in three to five years.

transcript: A certified copy of the student's academic record showing courses taken, examinations passed, credits awarded, and grades or scores received.

transfer student: A student who has earned credit in one school and then transfers to another school.

trimester: A term consisting of one-third of an academic year. A school on the trimester system has three equal trimesters each year.

tuition: In the United States, the money charged for formal instruction. In some schools, tuition is the only expense other than postage. In other schools, there may be fees as well as tuition. In the United Kingdom, tuition refers to the instruction or teaching at a school, such as the tuition offered in history.

tuition waiver: A form of financial assistance in which the school charges little or no tuition.

tutor: Hired assistant who helps a student prepare for a given class or examination. *See also* mentor.

undergraduate: Pertaining to the period of study from the end of high school to the earning of a bachelor's degree; also to a person in such a course of study. ("Barry is an undergraduate at Reed College, one of the leading undergraduate schools.")

university: An institution that usually comprises one or more undergraduate colleges, one or more graduate schools, and, often, one or more professional schools.

U. S. Department of Education: The federal agency concerned with all educational matters in the United States that are not handled by the departments of education in the fifty states. In other countries, similar functions are commonly the province of a ministry of education.

Appendix J

Subject Index

For years, our readers have been telling us how nice it would be if this book had a complete index to the subjects offered by the many degree programs described. What lies before you is indeed a comprehensive subject index. For each field of study, we list the offering schools, the degrees offered (B, M, D), and whether or not they are entirely non-resident (NR) or require short residency (SR).

There are three things to say about subject areas:

1. Many subject areas are so broad ("general studies") or all-inclusive ("social science") that a wide range of things can be done in them.

2. There are "side door" approaches to various fields. If a school offers only "history" and a student wishes to study "technology," it may be possible to do a degree in the "history of technology." The field of education is another commonly used side door.

3. There are a great many courses available by distance learning that do not result in a degree, but which may be applied to another school's degree. For instance, although there is no listing here for botanical sciences, there are individual courses available. A student could, for instance, take courses from any of a dozen universities, and apply those courses to the B.S. degree of schools such as Excelsior College, Thomas Edison State College, and Charter Oak State College. How does one find these courses? See the earlier chapter called "Correspondence Courses."

Accounting
Auburn University (M, SR)
Baker College (M, NR)
Caldwell College (B, SR)
Capital University (B, NR)
Charles Sturt University (B-M-D, NR)
City University (B, NR)
Deakin University (M, NR)
Edith Cowan University (B-M, NR)
Empire State College (B, NR)
Excelsior College (B, NR)
Golden Gate University (M, NR)
Nova Southeastern University (M, SR)
Saint Mary-of-the-Woods College (B, SR)
Southwestern Adventist University (B, SR)
Thomas Edison State College (B, NR)
University of Kent at Canterbury (M-D, SR)
University of London (B, NR)
University of Maryland (B, NR)
University of Melbourne (M-D, NR)
University of New England (M, NR)
University of South Africa (B-M-D, NR)
University of South Australia (B, NR)
University of Southern Queensland (B-M, NR)
Upper Iowa University (B, NR)
See also Finance
See also Taxation

Acquisition Management and Procurement
Thomas Edison State College (B, NR)
Addiction Counseling and Intervention
Edith Cowan University (B, NR)
University of London (M, NR)
Adult and Continuing Education
Edith Cowan University (M-D, NR)
Indiana University (M, NR)
Penn State University (M, NR)
Saint Joseph's College (M, SR)
University of Southern Queensland (B-M, NR)
Adventure Education
Prescott College (M, SR)
Advertising Design
Syracuse University (M, SR)
Aerospace Engineering
Auburn University (M, SR)
African Languages and Literature
University of South Africa (B-M-D, NR)
See also Afrikaans Language and Literature
African Politics
University of South Africa (B-M-D, NR)
Afrikaans Language and Literature
University of South Africa (B-M-D, NR)

Agribusiness
See Agriculture and Agriculture Management

Agricultural Engineering
Colorado State University (M, NR)
University of Idaho (M, NR)
University of Southern Queensland (B-M, NR)

Agriculture and Agriculture Management
Charles Sturt University (B-M-D, NR)
Colorado State University (M, NR)
Kansas State University (M, SR)
University of London (M, NR)
Washington State University (B-M, NR)

Agriculture Law
De Montfort University (M, NR)

American Studies
Brigham Young University (B, SR)
Skidmore College (B, SR)
University of Kent at Canterbury (M-D, SR)
University of Melbourne (M-D, NR)
University of New England (M, NR)

Ancient History
University of Melbourne (M-D, NR)
University of New England (B-M, NR)
University of South Africa (B-M-D, NR)

Ancient Languages and Cultures
University of South Africa (M, NR)

Animal Science
See Veterinary Science

Anthropology
Charter Oak State College (B, NR)
Edith Cowan University (B, NR)
Skidmore College (B, SR)
Thomas Edison State College (B, NR)
University of Kent at Canterbury (M-D, SR)
University of Melbourne (M-D, NR)
University of South Africa (B-M-D, NR)
University of Southern Queensland (B, NR)
University of Wales—Lampeter (M-D, NR)

Applied and Professional Studies
Antioch University (D, SR)
Athabasca University (B, NR)
California State University—Dominguez Hills (B, NR)
Murdoch University (B, NR)
Nova Southeastern University (B, SR)
Thomas Edison State College (M, NR)

Applied Economics
University of Southern Queensland (B, NR)
See also Economics

Applied Linguistics
Edith Cowan University (M-D, NR)
University of Kent at Canterbury (M-D, SR)
University of Leicester (M, NR)
University of Melbourne (M-D, NR)
University of Southern Queensland (M, NR)
See also Linguistics

Applied Mathematics
University of Kent at Canterbury (M-D, SR)
University of South Africa (B-M-D, NR)
University of Southern Queensland (B, NR)
See also Mathematics

Applied Science
University of Alabama (B, SR)

Applied Social Studies
See Social Sciences
See Social Work
See Sociology

Aquaculture
Deakin University (M, NR)

Arabic Language and Literature
University of Melbourne (M-D, NR)
University of South Africa (B-M-D, NR)

Archaeology
University of Bradford (M-D, SR)
University of Kent at Canterbury (M-D, SR)
University of Leicester (M, NR)
University of Melbourne (M-D, NR)
University of New England (B-M, NR)
University of South Africa (M, NR)
University of Wales—Lampeter (M-D, NR)

Architecture
University of Melbourne (M-D, NR)
See also Contracting and Building

Art
Burlington College (B, SR)
Caldwell College (B, SR)
California State University—Dominguez Hills (M, NR)
Charter Oak State College (B, NR)
De Montfort University (M-D, SR)
Open University (B-M, NR)
Skidmore College (B, SR)
Thomas Edison State College (B, NR)
University of Kent at Canterbury (M-D, SR)
University of Melbourne (M-D, NR)
University of South Africa (B-M-D, NR)
Vermont College (B-M, SR)
See also Cartooning

Art Education
Edith Cowan University (M-D, NR)

Art History
Charter Oak State College (B, NR)
Skidmore College (B, SR)
University of Kent at Canterbury (M-D, SR)
University of Melbourne (M-D, NR)
University of South Africa (B-M-D, NR)
University of Wales—Lampeter (M, NR)

Art Therapy
Saint Mary-of-the-Woods (M, NR)

Asian Studies
Murdoch University (B-M, NR)
Skidmore College (B, SR)
University of Melbourne (M-D, NR)
University of New England (B-M, NR)
University of Southern Queensland (B, NR)

Asthma Education
Charles Sturt University (M, NR)

Astronomy
University of South Africa (B-M-D, NR)

Audiology
Central Michigan University (D, NR)
University of Melbourne (M-D, NR)

Auditing
    University of South Africa (B, NR)

Australian Studies
    Charles Sturt University (M-D, NR)
    University of Melbourne (M-D, NR)

Banking
    See Finance

Biblical Studies
    Regent University (M, SR)
    University of South Africa (B-M-D, NR)

Biochemistry
    University of Kent at Canterbury (M-D, SR)
    University of Melbourne (M-D, NR)

Bioethics
    University of South Africa (M, NR)
    University of Wales—Lampeter (M, NR)

Biology
    Charter Oak State College (B, NR)
    Excelsior College (B, NR)
    Skidmore College (B, SR)
    Thomas Edison State College (B, NR)
    University of Melbourne (M-D, NR)
    University of New England (B-M-D, NR)

Biophysics
    Georgia Institute of Technology (M, NR)

Biotechnology
    Charles Sturt University (B, NR)
    University of Bradford (M-D, SR)
    University of Maryland (M, NR)

British and Commonwealth Studies
    University of Wales—Lampeter (M, NR)

Building Services
    See Contracting and Building

Business Administration (B.B.A./M.B.A./D.B.A.)
    Argosy University (M-D, SR)

Business and Commerce (General)
    Athabasca University (B, NR)
    California College for Health Sciences (B, NR)
    Charles Sturt University (B-M-D, NR)
    Charter Oak State College (B, NR)
    City University (B, NR)
    De Montfort University (B, NR)
    Deakin University (M, NR)
    Eastern Oregon University (B, NR)
    Edith Cowan University (B-M-D, NR)
    Empire State College (B-M, NR)
    Excelsior College (B, NR)
    Judson College (B, NR)
    Kansas State University (B, NR)
    Open University (B-M-D, NR)
    Saint Joseph's College (B, SR)
    Salve Regina University (B, SR)
    Skidmore College (B, SR)
    Troy State University Montgomery (B, NR)
    University of Maryland (B, NR)
    University of Melbourne (M-D, NR)
    University of New England (B-M, NR)
    University of South Africa (B-M-D, NR)
    University of South Australia (B, NR)

    University of Southern Queensland (B-M, NR)
    Upper Iowa University (B, NR)
    See also Business Administration
    See also Finance
    See also Management
    Athabasca University (M, SR)
    Auburn Univeristy (M, SR)
    Baker College (B-M, NR)
    Bellevue University (M, NR)
    California College for Health Sciences (M, NR)
    California State University—Dominguez Hills (M, NR)
    Capella University (M, SR)
    Charles Sturt University (M-D, NR)
    City University (M, NR)
    Colorado State University (M, NR)
    Edith Cowan University (M, NR)
    Empire State College (M, SR)
    Excelsior College (B-M, NR)
    Golden Gate University (M, NR)
    "Guerilla Marketing" MBA (M, SR)
    Henley Management College (M-D, NR)
    Heriot-Watt University (M, NR)
    Indiana University (M, NR)
    ISIM University (M, NR)
    Jones International University (B-M, NR)
    National Technological University (M, NR)
    Nova Southeastern University (M, SR)
    Ohio University (M, SR)
    Penn State University (M, NR)
    Regent University (M, SR)
    Regis University (M, NR)
    Rensselaer Polytechnic Institute (M, NR)
    Salve Regina University (M, SR)
    Stephens College (M, SR)
    Syracuse University (M, SR)
    Touro University International (M-D, NR)
    University of Leicester (M, NR)
    University of London (M, NR)
    University of Maryland (M, NR)
    University of New England (M, NR)
    University of Phoenix (B-M, NR)
    University of South Australia (B-M-D, NR)
    University of Southern Queensland (B-M-D, NR)
    University of Texas (M, NR)

Business Administration (Other)
    Argosy University (B, SR)
    Athabasca University (B, NR)
    Caldwell College (B, SR)
    Central Michigan University (B-M, NR)
    City University (B, NR)
    Clarkson College (B, NR)
    Columbia Union College (B, NR)
    Judson College (B, NR)
    Saint Mary-of-the-Woods College (B, SR)
    Southwestern Adventist University (B, SR)
    Stephens College (B, SR)
    Touro University International (B, NR)
    University of South Africa (B-M-D, NR)
    University of South Australia (D, NR)
    University of Southern Queensland (B, NR)

Washington State University (B, NR)
See also Business
See also Management

Business Information Systems
Bellevue University (B, NR)
University of Southern Queensland (M, NR)
See also Management Information Systems

Business Law
De Montfort University (M, NR)
University of London (B, NR)
University of South Africa (M, NR)
University of Southern Queensland (M, NR)

Business Management
See Business Administration
See Management

Canadian Studies
University of Waterloo (B, NR)

Cancer Research
See Oncology

Cartooning
University of Kent at Canterbury (M-D, SR)

Catalan Language and Literature
University of Melbourne (M-D, NR)

Celtic Christianity
University of Wales—Lampeter (M, NR)

Chemical Engineering
Auburn University (M, SR)
Excelsior College (B, NR)
Kansas State University (M, NR)
National Technological University (M, NR)
University of Bradford (M-D, NR)
University of Melbourne (M-D, NR)

Chemistry
Charles Sturt University (B, NR)
Charter Oak State College (B, NR)
De Montfort University (M, NR)
Excelsior College (B, NR)
Murdoch University (B, NR)
Skidmore College (B, SR)
Thomas Edison State College (B, NR)
University of Bradford (M-D, NR)
University of Kent at Canterbury (M-D, SR)
University of Melbourne (M-D, NR)
University of South Africa (B-M-D, NR)

Chemistry Education
University of South Africa (M, NR)
See also Science Education

Children's Literature
University of Southern Queensland (M, NR)

Chinese Language and Literature
University of Melbourne (M-D, NR)
University of New England (B-M, NR)

Church History
University of South Africa (B-M-D, NR)
University of Wales—Lampeter (M, NR)

Civil Engineering
Auburn University (M, SR)
Colorado State University (M, NR)

Kansas State University (M, NR)
Thomas Edison State College (B, NR)
University of Bradford (M-D, SR)
University of Idaho (M, NR)
University of Melbourne (M-D, NR)
University of Southern Queensland (B-M, NR)

Classics
Skidmore College (B, SR)
University of Kent at Canterbury (M-D, SR)
University of Melbourne (M-D, NR)
University of New England (B-M-D, NR)
University of South Africa (B-M-D, NR)
University of Wales—Lampeter (M-D, NR)
University of Waterloo (B, NR)
See also Ancient History
See also Greek Language and Literature
See also Latin Language and Literature

Clinical Psychology
Fielding Graduate Institute (D, SR)
Union Institute and University (D, SR)
University of South Africa (M, NR)
See also Counseling
See also Psychology and Behavioral Science

Commerce
See Business and Commerce (General)

Communication
Caldwell College (B, SR)
Capital University (B, NR)
Charles Sturt University (M-D, NR)
Charter Oak State College (B, NR)
Edith Cowan University (B, NR)
Jones International University (B-M, NR)
Murdoch University (B, NR)
Regent University (M-D, NR)
Rensselaer Polytechnic Institute (M, NR)
Skidmore College (B, SR)
Southwestern Adventist University (B, SR)
Texas Tech University (M, NR)
Thomas Edison State College (B, NR)
University of Alabama (B, SR)
University of Bradford (M-D, NR)
University of Kent at Canterbury (M-D, SR)
University of Leicester (M, NR)
University of Louisville (B, NR)
University of Maryland (B, NR)
University of Melbourne (M-D, NR)
University of New England (B-M-D, NR)
University of Northern Iowa (M, NR)
University of Phoenix (B, NR)
University of South Africa (B-M-D, NR)
University of South Australia (B, NR)
University of Southern Queensland (B-M, NR)

Communication Management
University of South Australia (B-M, NR)
See also Information Technology and
    Information Technology Management

Community Studies
Central Michigan University (B, NR)
De Montfort University (M, NR)
Deakin University (M, NR)
Thomas Edison State College (B, NR)

Comparative Literature
California State University—Dominguez Hills (M, NR)
Charter Oak State College (B, NR)
Excelsior College (B, NR)
University of Kent at Canterbury (M-D, SR)
University of South Africa (B-M-D, NR)

Comparative Religion
See Religious Studies

Complementary Health
Charles Sturt University (B, NR)

Computer-Aided Design (CAD)
University of Southern Queensland (B, NR)

Computer Engineering and Computer Engineering Technology
Georgia Institute of Technology (M, NR)
National Technological University (M, NR)
University of Idaho (M, NR)
University of Southern Queensland (B-M, NR)
See also Electrical Engineering
See also Software Engineering
See also Systems Engineering

Computer Information Systems
Athabasca University (B, NR)
Baker College (M, NR)
Caldwell College (B, SR)
Charles Sturt University (B-M-D, NR)
Charter Oak State College (B, NR)
City University (B-M, NR)
Deakin University (M, NR)
Edith Cowan University (B-M, NR)
Excelsior College (B, NR)
ISIM University (M, NR)
National Technological University (M, NR)
New Jersey Institute of Technology (B-M, NR)
Nova Southeastern University (M-D, SR)
Open University (B-M-D, NR)
Regis University (M, NR)
Rensselaer Polytechnic Institute (M, NR)
Rochester Institute of Technology (M, SR)
Saint Mary-of-the-Woods College (B, SR)
Southwestern Adventist University (B, SR)
Thomas Edison State College (B, NR)
University of Bradford (M-D, NR)
University of London (B, NR)
University of Maryland (B-M, NR)
University of Melbourne (M-D, NR)
University of Phoenix (B-M, NR)
University of South Africa (B-M, NR)
University of South Australia (B, NR)
University of Southern Queensland (M, NR)
See also Computer Science

Computer-Mediated Communication
Regent University (M, NR)
Texas Tech University (M, NR)
See also Internet Studies

Computer Networking
City University (B, NR)
University of Southern Queensland (B, NR)
See also Computer-Mediated Communication
See also Information Technology and Information Technology Management

Computer Programming
See Software Engineering

Computer Science
Auburn University (M, SR)
Capital University (B, NR)
Charter Oak State College (B, NR)
Colorado State University (M, NR)
Columbia University (M-S, NR)
Murdoch University (B, NR)
National Technological University (M, NR)
New Jersey Institute of Technology (B-M, NR)
Northwood University (B, SR)
Nova Southeastern University (M-D, SR)
Rensselaer Polytechnic Institute (M, NR)
Skidmore College (B, SR)
Stanford University (M, NR)
Southwestern Adventist University (B, SR)
Texas Tech University (M, NR)
Thomas Edison State College (B, NR)
Touro University International (B, NR)
University of Idaho (M, NR)
University of Illinois at Urbana-Champaign (M, NR)
University of Kent at Canterbury (M-D, SR)
University of Maryland (B, NR)
University of Melbourne (M-D, NR)
University of New England (B-M-D, NR)
University of South Africa (B-M-D, NR)
University of Southern Queensland (B, NR)
University of Texas (M, NR)

Conflict Resolution and Peace Studies
California State University—Dominguez Hills (M, NR)
Nova Southeastern University (M-D, SR)
University of Bradford (M-D, NR)
University of New England (M, NR)

Construction
Thomas Edison State College (B, NR)
University of Melbourne (M-D, NR)
University of Southern Queensland (B, NR)
See also Contracting and Building

Continuing Education
See Adult and Continuing Education

Contracting and Building
University of Southern Queensland (B, NR)
See also Architecture
See also Construction

Copyright Law
See Intellectual Property Law

Counseling
Argosy University (M-D, SR)
Athabasca University (M, NR)
Charles Sturt University (M, NR)
City University (M, NR)
Prescott College (B-M, SR)
University of Melbourne (M-D, NR)
University of South Africa (M, NR)
University of South Australia (M, NR)
University of Southern Queensland (M, NR)
See also Clinical Psychology
See also Pastoral Counseling
See also Psychology and Behavioral Science

Creative Writing
See Writing

Criminal Justice and Law Enforcement
Bellevue University (B, NR)
Caldwell College (B, SR)
Charles Sturt University (B-M-D, NR)
Charter Oak State College (B, NR)
Edith Cowan University (B, NR)
Empire State College (B, NR)
Judson College (B, NR)
Saint Joseph's College (B, SR)
Southwestern Adventist University (B, SR)
University of Leicester (M, NR)
University of Louisville (M, NR)
University of Melbourne (M-D, NR)
University of South Africa (B-M-D, NR)
Upper Iowa University (B, NR)
Washington State University (B, NR)
See also Criminology, Forensic Psychology, and
    Criminal Intelligence

Criminal Law
University of South Africa (M, NR)

**Criminology, Forensic Psychology, and Criminal
Intelligence**
Capital University (B, NR)
Charles Sturt University (M, NR)
University of Kent at Canterbury (M-D, SR)
University of Leicester (M, NR)
University of South Africa (B-M-D, NR)
See also Criminal Justice and Law Enforcement

Crisis Management
Charles Sturt University (B, NR)
Empire State College (B, NR)
Thomas Edison State College (B, NR)
University of Leicester (M, NR)

Cultural Studies
See Anthropology

Curriculum Design
Argosy University (M-D, SR)
City University (M, NR)
Deakin University (M, NR)
Nova Southeastern University (M, SR)
University of Southern Queensland (M, NR)
See also Education

Dance
Skidmore College (B, SR)

Death Studies
University of Wales—Lampeter (M, NR)

Defense Management
University of New England (M, NR)

Dentistry
University of London (M, NR)

Development Studies and Sustainable Agriculture
De Montfort University (M, NR)
Deakin University (B-M, NR)
Murdoch University (B-M, NR)
University of Bradford (M-D, NR)
University of London (M, NR)
University of Melbourne (M-D, NR)

University of New England (B-M, NR)
University of South Africa (B-M-D, NR)
University of Southern Queensland (M, NR)
University of Waterloo (B, NR)
See also Rural Development

Developmental Psychology
Edith Cowan University (B-M-D, NR)
Fielding Graduate Institute (D, SR)
Salve Regina University (M, SR)
Vermont College (B-M, SR)

Diaconology
See Divinity
See Ministry

Dietetics
See Nutrition

Digital Preservation
University of Glasgow (M, NR)

Diplomacy
See Conflict Resolution and Peace Studies
See Intelligence Studies
See International Relations

Direct Marketing
See Marketing

Disability Studies
Edith Cowan University (B, NR)
University of Kent at Canterbury (M-D, SR)

Distance Education
Athabasca University (M, NR)
Deakin University (M, NR)
Jones International University (M, NR)
Nova Southeastern University (M-D, SR)
University of London (M, NR)
University of Maryland (M, NR)
University of Southern Queensland (M, NR)

Divinity
University of London (B, NR)

Drama and Theater Studies
Charles Sturt University (M-D, NR)
Skidmore College (B, SR)
Thomas Edison State College (B, NR)
University of Kent at Canterbury (M-D, SR)
University of Melbourne (M-D, NR)
University of New England (B-M-D, NR)

E-Business
See E-Commerce

E-Commerce
Bellevue University (B, NR)
Capella University (B, NR)
City University (B, NR)
Saint Mary-of-the-Woods (B, SR)
University of Maryland (M, NR)
University of Phoenix (B, NR)
University of Southern Queensland (M, NR)

Economics
Capital University (B, NR)
Charter Oak State College (B, NR)
Deakin University (M, NR)
Eastern Oregon University (B, NR)
Excelsior College (B, NR)

Murdoch University (B, NR)
Skidmore College (B, SR)
Thomas Edison State College (B, NR)
University of Kent at Canterbury (M-D, SR)
University of London (B-M, NR)
University of Melbourne (M-D, NR)
University of New England (B-M-D, NR)
University of South Africa (B-M-D, NR)
University of Waterloo (B, NR)

Editing and Publishing
University of Southern Queensland (M, NR)

Education
Argosy University (M-D, SR)
Capella University (M-D, NR)
Charles Sturt University (B-M-D, NR)
City University (M, NR)
Deakin University (B-M, NR)
Eastern Oregon University (M, SR)
Edith Cowan University (B-M-D, NR)
Goddard College (B-M, NR)
Judson College (B, NR)
Murdoch University (B-M, NR)
Naropa University (M, SR)
Nova Southeastern University (B-M-D, SR)
Open University (B-M-D, NR)
Prescott College (M, SR)
Regent University (M, NR)
Saint Joseph's College (B-M, SR)
Stephens College (B, SR)
Thomas Edison State College (B, NR)
Touro International University (M, NR)
University of Bradford (M-D, NR)
University of Illinois at Urbana-Champaign
   (M, NR)
University of Louisville (B, NR)
University of Maryland (M, NR)
University of Melbourne (M-D, NR)
University of New England (B-M-D, NR)
University of Northern Iowa (M, NR)
University of Phoenix (M, NR)
University of South Africa (B-M-D, NR)
University of South Australia (B-D, NR)
University of Southern Queensland (B-M-D,
   NR)
University of Texas (M, NR)
Vermont College (B-M, SR)
Walden University (M-D, NR)

Educational Leadership and Administration
Argosy University (M-D, SR)
City University (M, NR)
Edith Cowan University (M-D, NR)
Fielding Graduate Institute (D, SR)
Nova Southeastern University (M-D, SR)
Regent University (M, SR)
Touro International University (D, NR)
University of Northern Iowa (M, NR)
University of South Africa (B-M-D, NR)
University of Southern Queensland (M-D, NR)

Educational Psychology
University of South Africa (B-M-D, NR)

Educational Technology
City University (M, NR)
Edith Cowan University (M-D, NR)
George Washington University (M, NR)
Nova Southeastern University (M-D, SR)
University of Northern Iowa (M, NR)
University of Southern Queensland (M, NR)
University of Texas (M, NR)
Walden University (M, NR)

Electrical Engineering
Colorado State University (M-D, SR)
Columbia University (M-S, NR)
Kansas State University (M, NR)
National Technological University (M, NR)
Rensselaer Polytechnic Institute (M, NR)
Rochester Institute of Technology (B, SR)
Stanford University (M, NR)
University of Bradford (M-D, NR)
University of Idaho (M, NR)
University of Illinois at Urbana-Champaign
   (M, NR)
University of Southern Queensland (B-M, NR)
University of Texas (M, NR)
See also Computer Engineering
See also Electronics

Electromechanical Engineering
See Robotics

Electronic Commerce
See E-Commerce

Electronics
Excelsior College (B, NR)
Thomas Edison State College (B, NR)
University of Kent at Canterbury (M-D, SR)
University of New England (B, NR)
University of Southern Queensland (B-M, NR)
See also Electrical Engineering

Elementary Education
See Primary Education

Emergency Management
See Crisis Management

Emergency Medical Services
Charles Sturt University (B, NR)

Engineering (General)
Auburn University (M, SR)
Charter Oak State College (B, NR)
Colorado State University (M, NR)
Kansas State University (M, NR)
Stanford University (M, NR)
Texas Tech University (M, NR)
University of Illinois at Urbana-Champaign
   (M, NR)
University of Melbourne (M-D, NR)
University of Southern Queensland (B-M, NR)

Engineering Management
Columbia University (M, NR)
Kansas State University (M, NR)
National Technological University (M, NR)
New Jersey Institute of Technology (M, NR)
Syracuse University (M, SR)
Texas Tech University (M, NR)
University of Idaho (M, NR)
Washington State University (M, NR)

Engineering Science
Murdoch University (B, NR)
Rensselaer Polytechnic Institute (M, NR)
University of Illinois at Urbana-Champaign
(M, NR)

English Language and Literature
Brigham Young University (B, SR)
Burlington College (B, SR)
Caldwell College (B, SR)
California State University—Dominguez Hills
(M, NR)
Capital University (B, SR)
Charter Oak State College (B, NR)
Excelsior College (B, NR)
Judson College (B, NR)
Murdoch University (B, NR)
Saint Mary-of-the-Woods College (B, SR)
Skidmore College (B, SR)
Stephens College (B, SR)
Southwestern Adventist University (B, SR)
Thomas Edison State College (B, NR)
Troy State University Montgomery (B, NR)
University of Kent at Canterbury (M-D, SR)
University of London (B, NR)
University of Maryland (B, NR)
University of Melbourne (M-D, NR)
University of New England (B-M-D, NR)
University of Northern Iowa (M, NR)
University of South Africa (B-M-D, NR)
University of Southern Queensland (B, NR)
University of Wales—Lampeter (M-D, NR)
University of Waterloo (B, NR)

**Environmental Economics, Engineering,
and Management**
Auburn University (M, SR)
Charles Sturt University (B-M-D, NR)
Colorado State University (M, NR)
De Montfort University (B-M, NR)
Deakin University (M, NR)
Georgia Institute of Technology (M, NR)
National Technological University (M, NR)
Rochester Institute of Technology (B-M, SR)
University of Bradford (M-D, SR)
University of Denver (M, NR)
University of Idaho (M, NR)
University of Kent at Canterbury (M-D, SR)
University of London (M, NR)
University of Maryland (B-M, NR)
University of South Africa (M, NR)
University of Southern Queensland (B-M, NR)
See also Environmental Law
See also Environmental Studies
See also Public Health

Environmental Law
De Montfort University (M, NR)
University of Kent at Canterbury (M-D, SR)

Environmental Studies
Murdoch University (B-M, NR)
Prescott College (M, SR)
Skidmore College (B, SR)
Thomas Edison State College (B, NR)
University of Kent at Canterbury (M-D, SR)

University of London (M, NR)
University of Melbourne (M-D, NR)
University of Waterloo (B, NR)
Vermont College (B-M, SR)
See also Environmental Economics,
Engineering, and Management

Epidemiology
University of London (M, NR)

Ethics
Charles Sturt University (M-D, NR)
University of South Africa (B-M-D, NR)
See also Bioethics

Ethnomusicology
University of New England (B-M, NR)

European Studies
University of Bradford (M-D, NR)
University of Kent at Canterbury (M-D, SR)
University of Melbourne (M-D, NR)
University of New England (B-M, NR)

Evangelism
University of South Africa (B-M-D, NR)

Family Studies
Brigham Young University (B, SR)
Edith Cowan University (B, NR)
Laurentian University (B, NR)

Feminist Law
University of Kent at Canterbury (M, SR)

Film Studies
Burlington College (B, SR)
University of Kent at Canterbury (M-D, SR)
University of Melbourne (M-D, NR)

Finance
American College (M, SR)
Argosy University (M, SR)
Baker College (M, NR)
Charles Sturt University (M-D, NR)
City University (M, NR)
Excelsior College (B, NR)
Golden Gate University (M, NR)
Kansas State University (M, NR)
Nova Southeastern University (M, SR)
Thomas Edison State College (B, NR)
University of Leicester (M, NR)
University of London (B-M, NR)
University of Melbourne (M-D, NR)
University of New England (B-M, NR)
University of South Australia (B, NR)
University of Southern Queensland (B-M, NR)
See also Accounting
See also Taxation

Fire Science Service, Management, and Training
Charter Oak State College (B, NR)
Colorado State University (B, NR)
Eastern Oregon University (B, NR)
Empire State College (B, NR)
Thomas Edison State College (B, NR)
University of Maryland (B, NR)
Upper Iowa University (B, NR)

Food Industry and Restaurant Management
  See Food Science
  See Hospitality, Food Industry, and Restaurant
  Management

Food Law
  De Montfort University (M, NR)

Food Science
  Charles Sturt University (B-D, NR)
  Kansas State University (B, NR)
  University of Melbourne (M-D, NR)

Foreign Languages and Literature (General)
  Murdoch University (B, NR)
  Open University (B-M-D, NR)
  University of Bradford (M-D, NR)
  University of Melbourne (M-D, NR)
  University of South Africa (B-M-D, NR)
  University of Southern Queensland (B, NR)
  See also Applied Linguistics
  See also Comparative Literature
  See also [Language] Language and Literature
  (e.g., French Language and Literature)

Forensic Psychology
  See Criminology, Forensic Psychology, and
  Criminal Intelligence

Forestry
  Thomas Edison State College (B, NR)
  University of Melbourne (M-D, NR)

French Language and Literature
  Caldwell College (B, SR)
  Charter Oak State College (B, NR)
  Laurentian University (B, NR)
  Skidmore College (B, SR)
  University of London (B, NR)
  University of Melbourne (M-D, NR)
  University of New England (B-M, NR)
  University of South Africa (B-M-D, NR)
  University of Waterloo (B, NR)

Gender and Women's Studies
  Edith Cowan University (B, NR)
  Goddard College (B-M, SR)
  Laurentian University (B, NR)
  Murdoch University (B, NR)
  Skidmore College (B, SR)
  University of Bradford (M-D, NR)
  University of Kent at Canterbury (M-D, SR)
  University of Melbourne (M-D, NR)
  University of New England (B-M, NR)
  University of South Africa (B, NR)

General Studies
  Athabasca University (B, NR)
  Brigham Young University (B, SR)
  Capital University (B, NR)
  Charter Oak State College (B, NR)
  City University (B, NR)
  Columbia Union College (B, NR)
  Indiana University (B, NR)
  Murdoch University (B, NR)
  Murray State University (B, SR)
  Penn State University (B, NR)
  Texas Tech University (B, NR)
  University of Southern Queensland (B, NR)

Genetic Counseling
  Charles Sturt University (M, NR)

Genetics
  See Biology

Geographic Information Systems
  Charles Sturt University (B, NR)
  University of Denver (M, NR)
  University of Southern Queensland (B-M, NR)

Geography
  Charter Oak State College (B, NR)
  University of London (B-M, NR)
  University of New England (B-M, NR)
  University of South Africa (B-M-D, NR)
  University of Wales—Lampeter (M-D, NR)
  University of Waterloo (B, NR)

Geological Engineering
  University of Idaho (M, NR)

Geology
  Charter Oak State College (B, NR)
  Excelsior College (B, NR)
  Skidmore College (B, SR)

Geomatics
  See Geographic Information Systems

German Language and Literature
  Charter Oak State College (B, NR)
  Queens University (B, NR)
  Skidmore College (B, SR)
  University of Kent at Canterbury (M-D, SR)
  University of London (B, NR)
  University of New England (B-M, NR)
  University of South Africa (B-M-D, NR)

Gerontology
  Charles Sturt University (B-M, NR)
  Edith Cowan University (B, NR)
  Laurentian University (B, NR)
  Saint Mary-of-the-Woods College (B, SR)
  Thomas Edison State College (B, NR)

Gifted Education
  University of South Africa (B-M-D, NR)
  See also Special Education

Greek Language and Literature
  University of New England (B-M, NR)
  University of South Africa (B-M-D, NR)

Guidance Counseling
  Argosy University (M, SR)
  City University (M, NR)
  University of South Africa (M, NR)
  University of Southern Queensland (M, NR)

Health Care
  Argosy University (M, SR)
  Baker College (M, NR)
  California College for Health Sciences (B-M,
  NR)
  Edith Cowan University (B, NR)
  Empire State College (B, NR)
  Golden Gate University (M, NR)
  Open University (B-M-D, NR)
  Rochester Institute of Technology (M, SR)
  Saint Joseph's College (B-M, SR)
  Thomas Edison State College (B, NR)

University of London (M, NR)
University of South Africa (M, NR)
University of Southern Queensland (M, NR)
Walden University (D, SR)

Health Communication Systems
Stephens College (B, SR)
University of Southern Queensland (M, NR)

Health Education
University of South Africa (M, NR)

Health Psychology
University of Kent at Canterbury (M-D, SR)

Health Science
Athabasca University (M, NR)
Central Michigan University (B, NR)
Charles Sturt University (B-M-D, NR)
Deakin University (M-D, NR)
Edith Cowan University (M, NR)
George Washington University (B, NR)
Nova Southeastern University (M, SR)
Touro University International (B-M-D, NR)
University of Bradford (M-D, SR)
University of Kent at Canterbury (M-D, SR)
University of South Africa (B-M-D, NR)

Hebrew Bible
University of London (B, NR)
University of South Africa (B-M-D, NR)

Hebrew Language and Literature
University of South Africa (B-M-D, NR)

History
Brigham Young University (B, SR)
Caldwell College (B, SR)
California State University—Dominguez Hills (M, NR)
Charles Sturt University (M-D, NR)
Charter Oak State College (B, NR)
Excelsior College (B, NR)
Judson College (B, NR)
Murdoch University (B, NR)
Queens University (B, NR)
Saint Mary-of-the-Woods (B, SR)
Skidmore College (B, SR)
Southwestern Adventist University (B, SR)
Thomas Edison State College (B, NR)
Troy State University Montgomery (B, NR)
University of Kent at Canterbury (M-D, SR)
University of London (B, NR)
University of Maryland (B, NR)
University of New England (B-M-D, NR)
University of South Africa (B-M-D, NR)
University of Wales—Lampeter (M-D, NR)
University of Waterloo (B, NR)
Vermont College (B-M, SR)

Hospitality, Food Industry, and Restaurant Management
Charles Sturt University (B, NR)
University of London (M, NR)
See also Food Science

Human Development
See Developmental Psychology

Human Factors Psychology
University of Idaho (M, NR)

Human Resource Management
Argosy University (M, SR)
Baker College (B-M, NR)
Bellevue University (B, NR)
Charles Sturt University (M, NR)
Colorado State University (M, NR)
Saint Mary-of-the-Woods College (B, SR)
Thomas Edison State College (B, NR)
University of Illinois at Urbana-Champaign (M, NR)
University of Leicester (M, NR)
University of Louisville (M, NR)
University of Southern Queensland (B-M, NR)
Upper Iowa University (B, NR)

Human Science
Saybrook Graduate School (M-D, SR)

Human Services
Capella University (M-D, SR)
Charles Sturt University (B, NR)
Charter Oak State College (B, NR)
Empire State College (B, NR)
Prescott College (B, SR)
Saint Mary-of-the-Woods College (B, SR)
University of Alabama (B, SR)
Upper Iowa University (B, NR)
Walden University (D, SR)

Humanities
California State University—Dominguez Hills (M, NR)
City University (B, NR)
Laurentian University (M, SR)
Prescott College (M, SR)
Saint Mary-of-the-Woods College (B, SR)
Thomas Edison State College (B, NR)
University of Alabama (B, SR)
University of Maryland (B, NR)
Vermont College (B-M, SR)
See also Liberal Arts

Individualized Major
Antioch University (M, SR)
Burlington College (B, SR)
Capital University (B, NR)
Charter Oak State College (B, NR)
Eastern Illinois University (B, NR)
Empire State College (B, NR)
Goddard College (B-M, SR)
Governors State University (B, NR)
Judson College (B, NR)
Murray State University (B, SR)
National Technological University (M, NR)
Ohio University (B, NR)
Rensselaer Polytechnic Institute (M, NR)
Rochester Institute of Technology (M, SR)
Skidmore College (B, SR)
Stephens College (B, SR)
Southwestern Adventist University (B, SR)
Union Institute and University (B-D, SR)
University of Wisconsin—Superior (B, SR)
Vermont College (B-M, SR)

Western Illinois University (B, NR)
See also Interdisciplinary Studies

Indonesian Language and Literature
University of New England (B-M, NR)
University of Southern Queensland (B, NR)

Industrial Administration
See Industrial Management

Industrial Computing
University of Southern Queensland (B, NR)

Industrial Engineering
Auburn University (M, SR)
Colorado State University (M-D, NR)
Georgia Institute of Technology (M, NR)
University of Northern Iowa (B-M, NR)

Industrial Hygiene
Colorado State University (M, NR)
See also Occupational Health

Industrial Management
Baker College (M, NR)
Central Michigan University (B, NR)

Industrial Psychology
University of South Africa (B-M-D, NR)

Industrial Relations
See Labor Studies and Industrial Relations

Infectious Diseases
University of London (M, NR)

Information Science
See Library and Information Science

Information Technology and Information Technology Management
Capella University (B-M-D, SR)
Charles Sturt University (B, NR)
Charter Oak State College (B, NR)
City University (B, NR)
Golden Gate University (M, NR)
Jones International University (B, NR)
Murdoch University (M, NR)
Open University (B, NR)
Saint Mary-of-the-Woods College (B, SR)
Syracuse University (M, SR)
Touro University International (B-M, NR)
University of Denver (M, NR)
University of Maryland (M, NR)
University of Phoenix (B, NR)

Instructional Technology
See Educational Technology

Instrumentation
Excelsior College (B, NR)
University of Southern Queensland (B-M, NR)

Insurance and Insurance Law
Regis University (B, NR)
University of Leicester (M, NR)

Intellectual Property Law
University of South Africa (M, NR)

Intelligence Studies
Charles Sturt University (M, NR)
See also International Relations

Interdisciplinary Studies
Athabasca University (M, NR)
Edith Cowan University (D, NR)
Empire State College (B, NR)
Kansas State University (B, NR)
Ohio University (B, NR)
University of Alabama (B, SR)
Vermont College (B-M, SR)
See also General Studies
See also Humanities
See also Liberal Studies

International Business
Argosy University (M, SR)
Baker College (M, NR)
Caldwell College (B, SR)
Charles Sturt University (M, NR)
National Technological University (M, NR)
Thomas Edison State College (B, NR)
University of London (M, NR)
University of Maryland (M, NR)
University of New England (M, NR)
University of Phoenix (M, NR)
University of Southern Queensland (M, NR)
University of Texas (M, SR)

International Communication
University of South Africa (B-M-D, NR)

International Law
De Montfort University (M, NR)
Deakin University (M, NR)
Regent University (M, SR)
University of Leicester (M, NR)
University of South Africa (M, NR)

International Relations
Capital University (B, NR)
Deakin University (B-M, NR)
Murdoch University (B, NR)
Salve Regina University (M, SR)
Southwestern Adventist University (B, SR)
University of Kent at Canterbury (M-D, SR)
University of London (B, NR)
University of South Africa (B-M-D, NR)
University of Southern Queensland (B, NR)
University of Wales—Lampeter (M, NR)
See also Conflict Resolution and Peace Studies
See also Intelligence Studies

Investment Law
Deakin University (M, NR)

Islamic Studies
University of New England (M, NR)
University of South Africa (B, NR)
University of Wales—Lampeter (M-D, NR)

Italian Language and Literature
University of Kent at Canterbury (M-D, SR)
University of London (B, NR)
University of New England (B-M, NR)
University of South Africa (B-M-D, NR)

Japanese Language and Literature
University of New England (B-M, NR)

Jewish Studies
University of London (B, NR)
University of South Africa (B-M-D, NR)

Journalism
Charles Sturt University (M, NR)
Deakin University (B, NR)
Regent University (M, NR)
Saint Mary-of-the-Woods College (B, SR)
Southwestern Adventist University (B, SR)
Thomas Edison State College (B, NR)
University of Southern Queensland (B, NR)

Kinesiology
University of Texas (M, NR)
See also Physical Education

Labor Studies and Industrial Relations
Charles Sturt University (M, NR)
Empire State College (B-M, NR)
Indiana University (B, NR)
Thomas Edison State College (B, NR)
University of Kent at Canterbury (M-D, SR)
University of Leicester (M, NR)

Language Education
Indiana University (M, NR)
Murdoch University (B, NR)

Latin American Studies
Skidmore College (B, SR)
University of London (B, NR)

Latin Language and Literature
University of New England (B-M, NR)
University of South Africa (B-M-D, NR)
See also Classics

Law
Charles Sturt University (M, NR)
De Montfort University (M, NR)
Laurentian University (B, NR)
Open University (B-M-D, NR)
Regent University (M, NR)
Stephens College (B, SR)
University of Kent at Canterbury (M-D, SR)
University of Leicester (M, NR)
University of London (B-M, NR)
University of New England (B-M-D, NR)
University of South Africa (B-M-D, NR)
University of Southern Queensland (M, NR)
See also Agriculture Law
See also Business Law
See also Criminal Justice and Law Enforcement
See also Criminal Law
See also Environmental Law
See also Feminist Law
See also Food Law
See also Insurance and Insurance Law
See also Intellectual Property Law
See also International Law
See also Investment Law
See also Legal Psychology
See also Philosophy of Law

See also Taxation
See also Trade Law

Law Enforcement
See Criminal Justice and Law Enforcement

Leadership
Antioch University (D, SR)
Argosy University (D, SR)
Baker College (M, NR)
Bellevue University (B-M, NR)
City University (M, NR)
Goddard College (B-M, SR)
Penn State University (B, NR)
Regent University (M-D, NR)
University of South Africa (M-D, NR)
University of Southern Queensland (M-D, NR)
Upper Iowa University (M, NR)
See also Educational Leadership and
    Administration
See also Management

Legal Psychology
University of Leicester (M, NR)

Leisure Studies
Charles Sturt University (B, NR)
Edith Cowan University (M, NR)

Liberal Arts
Excelsior College (A-B, NR)
Prescott College (B, SR)
Syracuse University (A-B, SR)
Vermont College (B, SR)

Liberal Studies
Charter Oak State College (B, NR)
Eastern Oregon University (B, NR)
Empire State College (M, SR)
Excelsior College (M, NR)
Laurentian University (B, NR)
Saint Joseph's College (B, SR)
Salve Regina University (B, SR)
Skidmore College (M, SR)
Syracuse University (B, SR)
Thomas Edison State College (B, NR)
University of Denver (M, NR)
University of Iowa (B, NR)
University of Northern Iowa (B, NR)
University of Oklahoma (B-M, SR)
Vermont College (B-M, SR)

Library and Information Science
Charles Sturt University (M-D, NR)
Edith Cowan University (M, NR)
Nova Southeastern University (M-D, SR)
Syracuse University (M, SR)
University of Illinois at Urbana-Champaign
    (M, SR)
University of Northern Iowa (M, NR)
University of South Africa (B-M-D, NR)

Linguistics
Edith Cowan University (M, NR)
University of New England (B-M-D, NR)
University of South Africa (B-M-D, NR)
See also Applied Linguistics

Literacy Education
City University (M, NR)
Edith Cowan University (M-D, NR)
Indiana University (M, NR)
University of Texas (M, NR)

Literary Theory
University of South Africa (B-M-D, NR)
See also Comparative Literature

Logistics, Decision Sciences, and Operations Management
Charles Sturt University (M, NR)
Thomas Edison State College (B, NR)
University of Southern Queensland (B, NR)
Walden University (D, SR)
See also Project Management

Management
Argosy University (B, SR)
Bellevue University (B, NR)
Brigham Young University (B, SR)
Caldwell College (B, SR)
Capital University (B, NR)
Charles Sturt University (B-M-D, NR)
City University (B-M, NR)
Colorado State University (M, NR)
Edith Cowan University (B, NR)
Empire State College (B, NR)
Excelsior College (B, NR)
Fielding Graduate Institute (M, SR)
Northwood University (B, SR)
Prescott College (B, SR)
Regent University (M, SR)
Regis University (B, NR)
Rensselaer Polytechnic Institute (M, NR)
Salve Regina University (M, SR)
Southwestern Adventist University (B, SR)
Thomas Edison State College (M, SR)
University of Alabama (B, SR)
University of Bradford (M-D, NR)
University of Kent at Canterbury (M-D, SR)
University of London (B-M, NR)
University of Maryland (B-M, NR)
University of Phoenix (B, NR)
University of South Africa (B-M-D, NR)
University of South Australia (D, NR)
University of Southern Queensland (B-M, NR)
Upper Iowa University (B, NR)
Vermont College (B-M, SR)
Walden University (D, SR)
See also Business Administration

Management Information Systems
Bellevue University (B, NR)
Deakin University (M, NR)
ISIM University (M, NR)
Judson College (B, NR)
Nova Southeastern University (M, SR)
University of London (B, NR)
University of Maryland (B-M, NR)
See also Business Information Systems
See also Technology Management

Manufacturing and Manufacturing Engineering
Excelsior College (B, NR)
National Technological University (M, NR)
Rensselaer Polytechnic Institute (M, NR)
Thomas Edison State College (B, NR)
University of South Australia (M, NR)
Washington State University (B, NR)

Manufacturing Management
University of South Australia (M, NR)

Marketing
Argosy University (M, SR)
Baker College (M, NR)
Caldwell College (B, SR)
Charles Sturt University (B-M, NR)
City University (B-M, NR)
Deakin University (M, NR)
Edith Cowan University (B, NR)
Excelsior College (B, NR)
Golden Gate University (M, NR)
Northwood University (B, SR)
Nova Southeastern University (M, SR)
Saint Mary-of-the-Woods College (B, SR)
Syracuse University (M, SR)
Thomas Edison State College (A-B, NR)
University of Leicester (M, NR)
University of New England (M, NR)
University of Southern Queensland (B-M, NR)
Upper Iowa University (B, NR)

Mass Communication and Media Studies
Fielding Graduate Institute (D, SR)
Southwestern Adventist University (B, SR)
University of Bradford (M-D, NR)
University of Leicester (M, NR)
University of Southern Queensland (B-M, NR)
See also Communication

Materials Engineering
Auburn University (M, SR)
Columbia University (M, NR)
National Technological University (M, NR)
Thomas Edison State College (B, NR)
University of London (M, NR)

Mathematics
Charles Sturt University (B, NR)
Charter Oak State College (B, NR)
Excelsior College (B, NR)
Murdoch University (B, NR)
Open University (B-M-D, NR)
Saint Mary-of-the-Woods College (B, SR)
Skidmore College (B, SR)
Southwestern Adventist College (B, SR)
Thomas Edison State College (B, NR)
University of Bradford (M-D, NR)
University of Kent at Canterbury (M-D, SR)
University of London (B, NR)
University of New England (B-M-D, NR)
University of South Africa (B-M-D, NR)
University of Southern Queensland (B, NR)

Mathematics Education
Edith Cowan University (M-D, NR)
University of Idaho (M, NR)
University of Northern Iowa (M, NR)
University of South Africa (M, NR)

Mechanical Engineering
    Auburn University (M, SR)
    Colorado State University (M-D, NR)
    Columbia University (M-S, NR)
    Georgia Institute of Technology (M, NR)
    National Technological University (M, NR)
    Rensselaer Polytechnic Institute (M, NR)
    Rochester Institute of Technology (B, SR)
    Thomas Edison State College (B, NR)
    University of Bradford (M-D, NR)
    University of Idaho (M, NR)
    University of Illinois at Urbana-Champaign
        (M, NR)
    University of Southern Queensland (B-M, NR)

Media Arts
    See Mass Communication and Media Studies

Medical Ethics
    See Bioethics

Medical Imaging
    Charles Sturt University (B-M, NR)
    Clarkson College (B, NR)
    See also Radiology

Medieval Studies
    University of Kent at Canterbury (M-D, SR)
    University of Waterloo (B, NR)

Mental Health
    Argosy University (M, SR)
    Charles Sturt University (B, NR)
    Thomas Edison State College (B, NR)
    University of Kent at Canterbury (M-D, SR)
    University of South Africa (M, NR)

Metallurgical Engineering
    Murdoch University (B, NR)
    University of Idaho (M, NR)

Microbiology and Molecular Biology
    University of Kent at Canterbury (M-D, SR)
    University of New England (B-M, NR)

Microelectronics
    Rensselaer Polytechnic Institute (M, NR)

Midwifery
    University of Southern Queensland (M, NR)

Mining
    University of Idaho (M, NR)
    University of Southern Queensland (B, NR)

Ministry
    Charles Sturt University (M, NR)
    Saint Joseph's College (M, SR)
    Saint Mary-of-the-Woods College (M, SR)
    See also Divinity
    See also Evangelism
    See also Pastoral Counseling
    See also Religious Education

Molecular Biology
    See Microbiology and Molecular Biology

Moral Theology
    University of South Africa (B-M-D, NR)

Museum Studies
    University of Leicester (M, NR)

Music
    California State University—Dominguez Hills
        (M, NR)
    Excelsior College (B, NR)
    Judson College (B, NR)
    Skidmore College (B, SR)
    University of New England (B-M-D, NR)
    University of South Africa (B-M-D, NR)
    Vermont College (B-M, SR)

Music Education
    Edith Cowan University (M-D, NR)
    Judson College (B, NR)
    University of Northern Iowa (M, NR)

Music Technology
    Indiana University (M, NR)

Music Theory and History
    Charter Oak State College (B, NR)

New Testament Studies
    University of London (B, NR)
    University of South Africa (B-M-D, NR)

Nonprofit Management
    Regis University (M, NR)
    Saint Mary-of-the-Woods College (B, SR)
    See also Organizational Management

Nuclear Engineering
    Excelsior College (B, NR)
    Thomas Edison State College (B, NR)

Nursing
    Athabasca University (B, NR)
    California State University—Dominguez Hills
        (B-M, NR)
    Capital University (B, NR)
    Charles Sturt University (B, NR)
    Clarkson College (B-M, SR)
    Deakin University (M-D, NR)
    Eastern Oregon University (B, SR)
    Edith Cowan University (B-M-D, NR)
    Excelsior College (A-B-M, NR)
    Indiana University (M, NR)
    Laurentian University (B, NR)
    Murray State University (M, SR)
    Saint Joseph's College (B-M, SR)
    Salve Regina University (B, SR)
    Syracuse University (M, SR)
    Thomas Edison State College (B, NR)
    University of Phoenix (B-M, NR)
    University of South Africa (M, NR)
    University of South Australia (B, NR)
    University of Southern Queensland (B-M, NR)

Nutrition
    Central Michigan University (M, NR)
    Deakin University (M-D, NR)
    Thomas Edison State College (B, NR)

Occupational Health
    Edith Cowan University (M-D, NR)
    Nova Southeastern University (M-D, SR)
    University of London (M, NR)
    University of Southern Queensland (M, NR)
    See also Industrial Hygiene

Occupational Psychology
University of South Africa (B-M-D, NR)

Occupational Safety
Edith Cowan University (M-D, NR)
University of Southern Queensland (M, NR)
See also Industrial Hygiene
See also Occupational Health

Occupational Training and Development
University of Louisville (B, NR)

Old Testament
See Hebrew Bible

Oncology
University of Bradford (M-D, NR)

Open and Distance Education
See Distance Education

Optical Engineering
Excelsior College (B, NR)
National Technological University (M, NR)

Organizational Development
Fielding Graduate Institute (M-D, SR)
Saybrook Graduate School (M-D, SR)
University of Leicester (M, NR)

Organizational Management
Charter Oak State College (B, NR)
Regent University (M, NR)
Skidmore College (B, SR)
Thomas Edison State College (B, NR)
University of Phoenix (M, NR)
See also Management
See also Nonprofit Management

Organizational Psychology
Kansas State University (M, NR)
University of London (M, NR)

Orthodontics and Prosthodontics
University of London (M, NR)

Palliative Care
Edith Cowan University (M, NR)

Paralegal Studies
Saint Mary-of-the-Woods College (B, SR)
University of Maryland (B, NR)

Pareschatology
University of Wales—Lampeter (M, NR)

Pastoral Counseling
Argosy University (D, SR)
University of South Africa (M-D, NR)

Peace Studies
See Conflict Resolution and Peace Studies

Penology
University of South Africa (B-M-D, NR)

Petroleum Engineering
Texas Tech University (M, NR)

Pharmacy
De Montfort University (M, NR)
University of Bradford (M-D, NR)
University of South Australia (B, NR)
Washington State University (D, SR)

Philosophy
California State University—Dominguez Hills
(M, NR)
Capital University (B, NR)
Charter Oak State College (B, NR)
Eastern Oregon University (B, NR)
Excelsior College (B, NR)
Murdoch University (B, NR)
Saint Mary-of-the-Woods College (B, SR)
Skidmore College (B, SR)
Stephens College (B, SR)
Thomas Edison State College (B, NR)
University of Kent at Canterbury (M-D, SR)
University of London (B, NR)
University of New England (B, NR)
University of South Africa (B-M-D, NR)
University of Wales—Lampeter (M-D, NR)
University of Waterloo (B, NR)

Philosophy of Education
University of South Africa (M-D, NR)

Philosophy of Law
University of Kent at Canterbury (M-D, SR)
University of South Africa (M, NR)

Physical Education
Eastern Oregon University (B, NR)
Edith Cowan University (M-D, NR)
University of Texas (M, NR)

Physical Therapy
Indiana University (M, NR)
Nova Southeastern University (M-D, SR)

Physics
Charter Oak State College (B, NR)
Excelsior College (B, NR)
Georgia Institute of Technology (M, NR)
Murdoch University (B, NR)
Skidmore College (B, SR)
Thomas Edison State College (B, NR)
University of Kent at Canterbury (M-D, SR)
University of South Africa (B-M-D, NR)

Political Science, Public Policy, and Social Policy
Caldwell College (B, SR)
Capital University (B, SR)
Charles Sturt University (B-M-D, NR)
Charter Oak State College (B, NR)
Eastern Oregon University (B, NR)
Empire State College (B, NR)
Excelsior College (B, NR)
Murdoch University (B, NR)
Queens University (B, NR)
Regent University (M, SR)
Skidmore College (B, SR)
Thomas Edison State College (B, NR)
Troy State University Montgomery (B, NR)
University of Kent at Canterbury (M-D, SR)
University of London (B, NR)
University of New England (B-M-D, NR)
University of South Africa (B-M-D, NR)
University of Wales—Lampeter (M-D, NR)

Polymer Science and Engineering
De Montfort University (M, NR)

Portuguese Language and Literature
University of South Africa (B-M-D, NR)

Practical Theology
Regent University (M, SR)
Saint Mary-of-the-Woods College (M, SR)
University of South Africa (B-M-D, NR)

Preprimary Education
Charles Sturt University (B, NR)
Edith Cowan University (M-D, NR)
Nova Southeastern University (B, SR)
Saint Mary-of-the-Woods College (B, SR)
University of South Africa (B, NR)
University of South Australia (B, NR)

Primary Education
Charles Sturt University (B, NR)
Judson College (B, NR)
Murdoch University (B-M, NR)
Nova Southeastern University (B, SR)
Saint Mary-of-the-Woods College (B, SR)
Southwestern Adventist University (B, SR)
University of Leicester (M, NR)
University of Northern Iowa (B, NR)
University of South Africa (B, NR)

Professional Studies
See Applied and Professional Studies

Project Management
Capella University (B, NR)
City University (M, NR)
George Washington University (M, SR)
Henley Management College (M, NR)
ISIM University (M, NR)
National Technological University (M, NR)
University of Bradford (M-D, NR)
University of South Africa (M, NR)
University of South Australia (M, NR)
University of Southern Queensland (M, NR)

Psychology and Behavioral Science
Brigham Young University (B, SR)
Burlington College (B, SR)
Caldwell College (B, SR)
California State University—Dominguez Hills (M, NR)
Capella University (M-D, SR)
Capital University (B, SR)
Charles Sturt University (B-M-D, NR)
Charter Oak State College (B, NR)
City University (M, NR)
Columbia Union College (B, NR)
Edith Cowan University (B, NR)
Excelsior College (B, NR)
Judson College (B, NR)
Kansas State University (M, NR)
Laurentian University (B, NR)
Prescott College (M, SR)
Queens University (B, NR)
Saint Mary-of-the-Woods College (B, SR)
Saybrook Graduate School (M-D, SR)
Skidmore College (B, SR)
Southwestern Adventist University (B, SR)
Stephens College (B, SR)
Thomas Edison State College (B, NR)

Troy State University Montgomery (B, NR)
University of Idaho (M, NR)
University of Kent at Canterbury (M-D, SR)
University of Leicester (M, NR)
University of Maryland (B, NR)
University of New England (B, NR)
University of South Africa (B-M-D, NR)
University of Southern Queensland (B, NR)
University of Waterloo (B, NR)
Vermont College (B-M, SR)
Walden University (M-D, SR)
See also Clinical Psychology
See also Counseling

Public Administration
California State University—Dominguez Hills (M, NR)
Central Michigan University (B-M, NR)
City University (M, NR)
Golden Gate University (B-M, NR)
Regent University (M, SR)
Thomas Edison State College (B, NR)
University of London (M, NR)
University of Louisville (M, NR)
University of South Africa (B-M-D, NR)
Upper Iowa University (B, NR)

Public Health
California College for Health Sciences (M, NR)
Charles Sturt University (B, NR)
Edith Cowan University (M, NR)
Murdoch University (M, NR)
University of London (M, NR)

Public Order
University of Leicester (M, NR)
See also Criminal Justice and Law Enforcement

Public Relations
Capital University (B, NR)
Deakin University (B, NR)
University of Northern Iowa (M, NR)
University of Southern Queensland (B-M, NR)

Quality Assurance and Engineering
California State University—Dominguez Hills (B-M, NR)
Rensselaer Polytechnic Institute (M, NR)

Radiology
Georgia Institute of Technology (M, NR)
Thomas Edison State College (B, NR)
University of London (M, NR)
See also Medical Imaging

Real Estate
Thomas Edison State College (B, NR)

Religion and International Relations
University of Wales—Lampeter (M, NR)

Religious Education
Edith Cowan University (M-D, NR)
Judson College (B, NR)
Regent University (M, SR)

Religious Studies
Caldwell College (B, SR)
Capital University (B, SR)
Charter Oak State College (B, NR)
Columbia Union College (B, NR)
Judson College (B, NR)
Laurentian University (B, NR)
Skidmore College (B, SR)
Southwestern Adventist University (B, SR)
Thomas Edison State College (B, NR)
University of Kent at Canterbury (M-D, SR)
University of New England (B-M-D, NR)
University of South Africa (B-M-D, NR)
University of Wales—Lampeter (M-D, NR)
University of Waterloo (B, NR)

Respiratory Care
California College for Health Sciences (B, NR)
Charles Sturt University (M, NR)
Columbia Union College (B, NR)

Risk Management
Regis University (B, NR)
University of Leicester (M, NR)

Robotics
Excelsior College (B, NR)
University of Southern Queensland (B-M, NR)

Rural Development
Charles Sturt University (M, NR)
University of London (M, NR)
University of New England (B, NR)
University of South Africa (B, NR)
See also Development Studies and Sustainable
   Agriculture

Rural Health
University of Southern Queensland (M, NR)

Russian Language and Literature
University of South Africa (B-M-D, NR)

Science Education
Edith Cowan University (M-D, NR)
Nova Southeastern University (B, SR)
University of South Africa (M, NR)

Secondary Education
Judson College (B, NR)
Murdoch University (M, NR)
Nova Southeastern University (B, SR)
Southwestern Adventist University (B, SR)
University of South Africa (B, NR)

Security Management
University of Leicester (M, NR)

Semitic Languages and Literature
University of Melbourne (M-D, NR)
University of South Africa (B-M-D, NR)

Sexuality
Laurentian University (Cert., NR)

Social Sciences
Caldwell College (B, SR)
Charles Sturt University (B-M, NR)
City University (B, NR)
Edith Cowan University (M, NR)
Kansas State University (B, NR)

Open University (B-M-D, NR)
Southwestern Adventist University (B, SR)
Syracuse University (M, SR)
Troy State University Montgomery (B, SR)
University of Alabama (B, SR)
University of Bradford (M, SR)
University of Maryland (B, NR)
University of New England (B, NR)
University of South Africa (B-M-D, NR)
University of South Australia (M, NR)
Upper Iowa University (B, NR)
Washington State University (B, NR)

Social Work
Capital University (B, SR)
Charles Sturt University (B-M-D, NR)
Laurentian University (B, NR)
University of Kent at Canterbury (M-D, SR)
University of South Africa (B-M-D, NR)

Sociolinguistics
University of South Africa (M, NR)

Sociology
Caldwell College (B, SR)
Capital University (B, SR)
Charter Oak State College (B, NR)
Edith Cowan University (B, NR)
Excelsior College (B, NR)
Laurentian University (B, NR)
Murdoch University (B, NR)
Skidmore College (B, SR)
Thomas Edison State College (B, NR)
University of Kent at Canterbury (M-D, SR)
University of Leicester (M, NR)
University of London (B, NR)
University of New England (B-M, NR)
University of South Africa (B-M-D, NR)
University of Waterloo (B, NR)

Software Engineering
Kansas State University (M, NR)
Murdoch University (B-M, NR)
National Technological University (M, NR)
Rochester Institute of Technology (M, SR)
Texas Tech University (M, NR)
University of Maryland (M, NR)
University of Southern Queensland (B, NR)

Spanish Language and Literature
Caldwell College (B, SR)
Charter Oak State College (B, NR)
Skidmore College (B, SR)
University of Kent at Canterbury (M-D, SR)
University of London (B, NR)
University of South Africa (B-M-D, NR)
See also Catalan Language and Literature
See also Latin American Studies

Special Education
Charles Sturt University (M, NR)
Edith Cowan University (B-M-D, NR)
Nova Southeastern University (B, SR)
Saint Mary-of-the-Woods College (B, SR)
University of Louisville (M, NR)
University of Northern Iowa (M, NR)
University of South Africa (B-M-D, NR)
University of Southern Queensland (M, NR)

Spirituality
University of South Africa (M-D, NR)

Sport, Sport Sociology, and Sport Management
Edith Cowan University (M, NR)
University of Leicester (M, NR)

Statistics
Colorado State University (M, NR)
Murdoch University (B, NR)
Rochester Institute of Technology (M, SR)
University of Kent at Canterbury (M-D, SR)
University of London (B, NR)
University of New England (M, NR)
University of South Africa (B-M-D, NR)
University of Southern Queensland (B, NR)

Surveying
Thomas Edison State College (B, NR)
University of Southern Queensland (B, NR)

Systematic Theology
University of South Africa (B-M-D, NR)

Systems Engineering
Colorado State University (M-D, SR)
National Technological University (M, NR)
Rensselaer Polytechnic Institute (M, NR)
University of Southern Queensland (B-M, NR)

Systems Management
National Technological University (M, NR)
Texas Tech University (M, NR)
University of Maryland (M, NR

Taxation
Golden Gate University (M, NR)
Regent University (M, NR)
University of South Africa (M, NR)

Teaching
Charles Sturt University (B, NR)
Edith Cowan University (B-M-D, NR)
University of Maryland (M, NR)
University of South Africa (B-M-D, NR)
University of Southern Queensland (M, NR)
See also Education

Teaching English as a Second or Foreign Language
Deakin University (M, NR)
University of Southern Queensland (M, NR)
University of Texas (M, NR)

Technical Writing
Texas Tech University (M, NR)
See also Writing

Technology Management
Colorado State University (M, NR)
National Technological University (M, NR)
University of Maryland (M, NR)
University of Phoenix (M, NR)
University of Southern Queensland (B, NR)
University of Waterloo (M, NR)
See also Engineering Management
See also Information Technology and Information Technology Management
See also Systems Management

Telecommunications and Telecommunications Management
See Information Technology and Information Technology Management

Thanatology
University of Wales—Lampeter (M, NR)

Theater Studies
See Drama and Theater Studies

Theology and Theological Studies
Charles Sturt University (B-M, NR)
Columbia Union College (B, NR)
Murdoch University (B, NR)
Regent University (M, SR)
Saint Mary-of-the-Woods College (B-M, SR)
University of Kent at Canterbury (M-D, SR)
University of South Africa (B-M-D, NR)
University of Wales—Lampeter (M-D, NR)

Therapeutic Recreation
Indiana University (M, NR)
Nova Southeastern University (M-D, SR)
See also Leisure Studies

Trade Law
Deakin University (M, NR)

Transpersonal Studies
Burlington College (B, SR)
Naropa University (M, SR)

Transportation Management
Thomas Edison State College (B, NR)
University of South Africa (B, NR)

Urban Ministry
University of South Africa (M-D, NR)

Veterinary Science
Charles Sturt University (B, NR)
Kansas State University (B, NR)
Murdoch University (M, NR)
University of London (M, NR)

Women's Studies
See Gender and Women's Studies

Writing
Antioch University (M, SR)
Brigham Young University (B, SR)
Burlington College (B, SR)
Goddard College (M, SR)
Naropa University (M, SR)
Saint Mary-of-the-Woods College (B, SR)
Vermont College (B-M, SR)

Xhosa Language and Literature
University of South Africa (B-M-D, NR)

Youth Studies and Youth Work
Edith Cowan University (B, NR)
Nova Southeastern University (M-D, SR)

Zoology
University of New England (M, NR)

Zulu Language and Literature
University of South Africa (B-M-D, NR)

Index

More books on distance learning and alternative education from Degree.net and Ten Speed Press

Bears' Guide to the Best Computer Degrees by Distance Learning
by John Bear, Ph.D., and Mariah Bear, M.A.

It's a tough job market for the high-tech elite, but companies everywhere still need software designers, database programmers, Web site builders, network administrators, and IT professionals. *Best Computer Degrees* maps the most direct route to those top dollar salaries, showing you how to earn a fully accredited undergraduate or graduate high-tech degree without setting foot on a college campus.
$14.95 (Can $23.95) ISBN 1-58008-221-1

Bears' Guide to the Best MBAs by Distance Learning
by John Bear, Ph.D., and Mariah Bear, M.A.

Fast-growing companies pay top dollar for the business savvy of MBA holders. But who wants to carve out the two years and fork over the $60,000 it typically takes to get one? In this book, John and Mariah show you how to earn a fully accredited and widely respected MBA in as little as a year and for under $10,000—and you can do it while remaining fully employed.
$17.95 (Can $27.95) ISBN 1-58008-220-3

Bears' Guide to Earning Degrees by Distance Learning, 15th Edition
by John Bear, Ph.D., and Mariah Bear, M.A.

For almost thirty years, this book has been the most comprehensive, opinionated, and respected guide to the often baffling world of nontraditional education. And father-daughter team John and Mariah Bear—widely regarded as the leading experts in the field—have made this 15th edition bigger and better than ever.
$19.95 (Can $48.00) ISBN 1-58008-431-1

Cool Colleges
by Donald Asher

This unprecedented guide to the "coolest" colleges profiles 40 of the most innovative and unusual schools in the country. From studying on a cattle ranch to spending winters snowed in with classmates on a mountain in Vermont, Cool Colleges is the place for students to find education opportunities as unorthodox as they are.
$19.95 (Can $30.95) ISBN 1-58008-150-9

Available at your local bookstore, on our Web site at *www.degree.net*, or direct from the publisher.

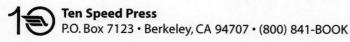
Ten Speed Press
P.O. Box 7123 • Berkeley, CA 94707 • (800) 841-BOOK